101 Jeep
Performance Projects

By James J. Weber

motorbooks

Dedication

Dedicated to the memory of my mother, Juliette Weber,
who taught me how to love, live, and succeed.

First published in 2009 by Motorbooks, an imprint of MBI Publishing Company, 400 First Avenue North, Suite 300, Minneapolis, MN 55401 USA

Motorbooks titles are also available at discounts in bulk quantity for industrial or sales-promotional use. For details write to Special Sales Manager at MBI Publishing Company, 400 First Avenue North, Suite 300, Minneapolis, MN 55401 USA.

To find out more about our books, visit us online at www.motorbooks.com.

ISBN-13: 978-0-7603-3164-4

Editor: Peter Schletty
Design Manager: Jon Simpson
Designer: Tina R. Johnson

Printed in China

About the author

James Weber is a longtime automotive journalist. He's been a contributing editor to *SPLASH!, 4 Wheel Drive & Sport Utility,* and *OFF-ROAD* magazines, and he has written articles for *TRUCKIN', Diesel Power,* and *Side x Side* magazines. Additionally, he has also been involved with automotive industry public relations for companies like Toyo Tires, AP Designs USA, and the Market Connection. He lives in San Diego, California.

Contents

Acknowledgments

Writing this book has reinforced many things that I value in my life: a strong work ethic; the importance of loving what you do for a living; and, most of all, the importance of family and friendship. Without these three things, this book could not have been written.

Having a strong work ethic is something I attribute to my mother, Juliette Weber, who taught me that if you want something in this world you have to pursue it relentlessly, because nothing is gained by those who do not show the desire, will, or initiative to have what they are searching for. Sadly, she succumbed to a long-term illness during the writing of this book and was unable to see the finished product, but I'm sure she is somewhere reading and enjoying it.

Second, the importance of loving what you do. If I did not have a true passion for my profession as a writer, photographer, and off-road enthusiast, I could not have put so much of my time, energy, and passion into this work.

Third, the importance of family and friends, without whom this book could not have been finished. To my family,

Violet Weber, Jean Weber, Traci Bonfiglio, Jason Bonfiglio, Tina Bonfiglio, Joe Bonfiglio, and Isaac Freestone, I thank you for the support and freedom that you afforded me while undergoing this project. To my friends, I thank you for being there when called upon and for the continued dedication, support, and friendship that you provide to me each and every day. Most notably, Dave and Sharon Wever, Mel and Lisa Wade, Dan Hewitt, Alex and Traci Paul, Spencer Stewart, Jerry and Sharon Wroblewski, Ted and Terri Bumgardner, Terry and Lynn McClanahan, Lauren Roll, Jay Jones, Phil Howell, and Sloane Stinson. Without all of your assistance, support, and words of encouragement this work could not have been accomplished. I am truly blessed to have such good family and friends in my life. To my editor, Peter Schletty, my thanks for all of your assistance and support. To the vendors who provided the various products used in some of the projects, without you this book truly could not have been made.

I hope you have as much fun reading the book as I had in creating it. Enjoy!

Introduction

Thank you for purchasing *101 Jeep Performance Projects*. I look forward to exploring each project with you. Ever since I can remember I have always been fascinated by the Jeep brand and the mystique that it possesses within the automotive community. From helping our G.I.s win World War II to traversing a 22-mile stretch of a trail in the High Sierras known as the Rubicon, Jeeps have always been at the forefront of whatever it is that they are doing. To help keep them one step ahead, this book has been created to familiarize you with the wide variety of performance projects available for this namesake.

One of this book's primary objectives is to provide you with a sampling of the tremendous amount of aftermarket products that are available for your Jeep that will increase the performance of your rig, both on and off the road. I personally chose the products featured for each project, based on their quality, technical attributes, and durability. Each project has been designed to provide a brief overview of the product and the reason for its necessity, followed by a step-by-step installation of the product so that you may see how they are installed, what tools are required to complete the task, and the level of difficulty involved.

While many of you will utilize this book as a reference or resource guide to whatever project you are working on, it should not be used as a replacement to mechanical experience. Some projects can be accomplished at home, in your garage or on your driveway, while some others will require a shop and highly skilled technicians; engine conversions and some drivetrain modifications come to mind. I encourage you to find a reputable off-road shop or fabricator, well versed in the Jeep brands, with whom you can build a relationship. Whether you do your own work or you have them do it for you, at least you will have added one additional resource to your tool belt. Much like any other motorsport, off-road driving and Jeep building require the same level of sharing, discussion, and combined expertise as any highly successful race team. Remember, no one can do it alone and have true success.

With this said, I hope you enjoy the book, I thank you for your interest in it, and hopefully I'll be seeing you out on the trails!

James J. Weber

How to Use This Book

The success of any project that you undertake with your Jeep will be largely dependent upon both your preparation and knowledge of the part or parts that you are about to purchase and install. In numerous cases, the so-called "domino effect" is present—altering, adding, or upgrading one component affects another. As an example, upgrading the suspension system of your Jeep would require larger tires and wheels, which in turn requires that the gear ratios of both axles are upgraded to match the new size of the tires, so that the vehicle's performance is unchanged from its stock performance. By considering the logical progression of related parts in advance, much time, effort, and cost can be saved by reducing the amount of work that must be performed once rather than two or three times.

In following with the preparation and knowledge of your project, we have included an informational box at the beginning of each project to serve as a quick reference. This guide will assist you in choosing a project that fits within your time constraints, mechanical knowledge, budget, tool inventory, etc.

The following components have been included:

 Time: This guide will orient you to the actual time the project takes to complete, including set up, installation, and cleanup. As everyone knows, sometimes the part that the manufacturer claimed could be installed in one hour actually takes three or four. So consider these times a ballpark average.

 Tools: Depending upon your inventory of tools, this may be a deciding factor between performing the job yourself or having your local off-road shop take care of it. This component will identify what tools are required.

 Talent: The talent component will measure for you the mechanical knowledge and skills the project requires. The mechanical abilities have been grouped as follows:

 1 Wrench: This is a project that a novice or first-timer could accomplish.

 2 Wrenches: This is a project that a novice or first-timer could accomplish with the assistance of someone who has mechanical experience.

 3 Wrenches: This is a project for someone who possesses mechanical skills and has the fundamental knowledge to work on their vehicle with some level of understanding of how a suspension system operates, what the key components of a transmission and engine are, as well as their respective functions. This individual will also have additional resources with slightly more experience, should they require it.

 4 Wrenches: This is a project for a professional who is certified as a mechanic or fabricator and who completes these tasks every day as a key component of his or her job. Typically, this level of mechanical proficiency is that of a dealership mechanic or off-road shop installer.

 Applicable Years: In some instances, the project may only be applicable to specific Jeep models, configurations, and model years.

 Tab: Another factor in deciding whether to embark on the project is cost, typically referring to the overall cost of the parts. In some cases, the costs for installation will be shown as a separate amount.

 Parts Required: Here we will address any parts needed to complete the installation according to the manufacturer's instructions and additional parts that might be required, such as additional sealants, gaskets, wire connectors, etc., that have not been included in the project parts.

 Tip: Professionals who install these parts every day on the job share these bits of information to help you with a quicker or better installation.

 Performance Gain: Essentially, this will tell you the benefits you should see—in performance, fuel economy, or aesthetics. This measurement touches on your reason for performing the project in the first place.

 Complementary Project: This information box addresses the "domino effect" mentioned above, as well as some other related projects. As an example, you might choose to install wheel locks on a new set of bead lock wheels.

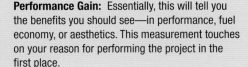

Tools and Safety

SAFETY

There should be no higher priority when performing work on a vehicle than safety. Regardless of whether the work is being performed by you, a close friend, relative, or mechanic, each of us has a moral duty to be concerned with each other's safety. With this said, the following items at a minimum should be considered when working on your Jeep.

Hand Protection

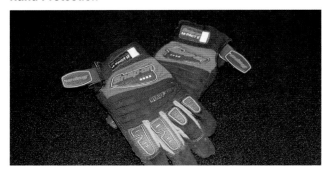

Look around at professional mechanics, and you will see that they are wearing work gloves as a normal course of business practice. Aside from keeping your hands clean, gloves are an essential part in keeping your hand and fingers from being cut, burned, and possibly removed from your body when working with power tools and other hazardous implements, such as razors, welders, torches, etc. While there are numerous types of gloves, some of the more popular ones are constructed from leather, cloth, and multifabric textiles.

Eye Protection

All it takes is one shard of metal or dirt to cut your cornea, and suddenly you're a believer in wearing eye protection. Most of us are so eager to start our projects, that we sometimes put our own safety aside. The primary reason for wearing eye protection is to stop debris from getting into your eyes, but they are also good for absorbing the impact from a falling nut, bolt, or component being worked on. Safety goggles are available in a wide variety of styles and lens colors. Some of

the most popular pairs are made to resemble normal glasses, while others stretch the imagination to the point of having built-in light-emitting diode (LED) lights on them. Just remember, you only have one set of eyes.

Jacks, Hoists, and Other Lifting Devices

Why work hard when you can work smart? Wrenching on your Jeep is no time to prove that you are the strongest of the group. Lifting devices such as jacks, jack stands, axle stands, and hoists are made to save your back, arms, and legs from the pain often encountered when trying to lift an engine, axle, or transmission that could weigh over 300 pounds. Not to mention that any one of these lifting devices could save your life.

Extra Set of Hands

Even with the writing of this book, an extra set of hands was required. This should be the rule when working on your Jeep, especially if your project involves swapping heavy parts such as axles, transfer cases, engines, or transmissions. In the event that you become trapped under the vehicle or need medical aid, someone will be there to get help. Keep in mind too that with two people on the job, it typically gets done in half the time.

TOOLS

When I bought my first Jeep the question was asked of me, "What did you buy first, the Jeep or the tools?" Not knowing the importance or humor associated with this question at the time, I answered "the Jeep." Many years and Jeeps later, however, the tools are still being purchased. Having a set of tools is paramount to owning a Jeep that is capable of going anywhere, anytime. Even when on the trail and away from the garage, a small toolbox should be kept in your Jeep for repairs in the field. Also, keep in mind that the old adage "the right tool for the right job" does apply when wrenching on a Jeep. Using the wrong tool for a project can sometimes cause an otherwise fixable part to become unfixable. But we won't go there; no use in bringing up the past.

Open-Ended Wrenches

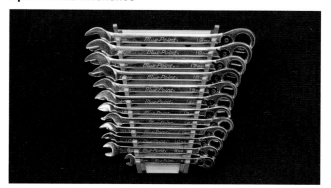

When it is impossible to gain access to a nut or bolt due to space constraints and tight tolerances, an open-ended wrench set is the answer. While available in numerous sizes and offsets, the most popular sizes that a Jeep owner will need will range between 3/4 inch and 5/16 inch or the metric equivalent.

Torque Wrench

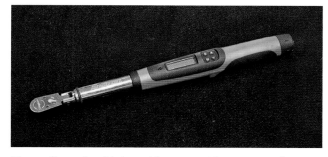

No toolbox should be without a wide variety of torque wrenches. Given some of the technological advances in tools, they are available with digital read-outs and sensors that alert you when the desired torque has been achieved. These wrenches are especially useful when working on key components of a drivetrain, axle, wheel, or suspension. In each of these categories, numerous bolts are specified to be tightened to a certain torque.

Socket Set

A socket set and ratchets will be among your most important tools. They have a wide variety of uses and applications, and they are called for in numerous projects throughout this book. Depending upon the style, size, and depth of the nut or bolt, chances are there is a socket available for it. In addition to those for the customary hexagonal-head bolts and nuts, there are Allen head sockets, star-head sockets, and torx head sockets, each of which can be used with a common ratchet and extensions. The most popular size socket sets to have for a Jeep are between 3/4 inch and 1/4 inch or the metric equivalent.

Pliers

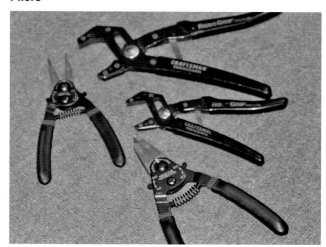

Pliers are a lot like a socket set in that they are a staple when working on a Jeep, not to mention that there is such a wide variety to choose from. Some of the most common types are general multipurpose pliers that will work for a wide variety of applications and are available in a variety of sizes. Depending on which projects you plan on tackling, it may be a good idea to have a couple of sizes. Needle-nose pliers are useful for those hard-to-reach spot; specialty pliers such as bent nose, extended shaft, side cutters, and channel-locks should also be considered to round out the group.

Screwdrivers

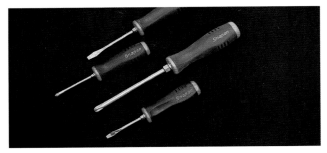

If you were to look in my toolbox, you would see that I have more screwdrivers than any other type of tool in it. Screwdrivers come in a variety of sizes and shapes. The type of screw being used and its location will dictate which one to use. A good sampling of screwdrivers will consist of large, medium, and small sizes to fit both standard and Phillips screws. A few specialty screwdrivers should also be kept on hand. These would include self-locking and magnetic tip drivers that retain the screw until it is threaded onto the nut, especially useful for tight spaces.

Nut Drivers

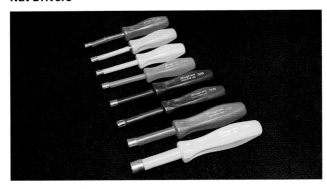

Many of today's fasteners and dashboard nuts can be removed or installed with a nut driver. A cross between a socket and a screwdriver, a nut driver is primarily used where the fasteners do not require any amount of defined torque. Nut drivers range in sizes and shaft lengths; the sizes most likely to be used on a Jeep will range between $3/16$ inch and $9/16$ inch or the metric equivalent.

Hex Keys, Allen Head, and Torx Head Wrenches

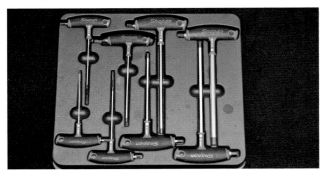

Hex head, Allen head, and torx head wrenches are most commonly used for trim pieces or mechanical pieces that require a great deal of torque but cannot afford the space for a socket or open-ended wrench to be used. These are specialty tools that come in a variety of sized and configurations.

Hammers and Mallets

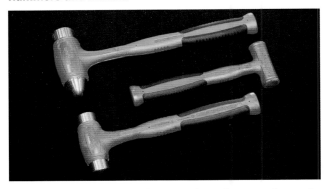

Who would have thought that something that is used to strike an object could be configured in so many different ways? Hammers and mallets are among the most commonly used tools in the automotive industry, due to their great power to persuade any object to move whenever the mechanic wishes. While there are many specialized hammers for various uses in the automotive repair industry, one of the most common and most often needed is the common ball-peen metal hammer. A variation has a pointed end that packs a tremendous amount of force in a focused area. The dead blow hammer has a head that is filled with pellets of different weights; when applied to a fender or damaged suspension component, it delivers a forceful blunt impact. A mallet is used when it's necessary to protect the surface. Typically, these items are made from either plastic or a composite material. It's good to have a sampling of these items in your toolbox.

Measuring Tools

Items such a tape measures, calipers, gauges, and rulers are a necessity when measuring components for fabrication or sizing. A 12-inch ruler is good to have on hand for small projects, while a larger tape measure may be needed when measuring tire or vehicle height.

Trim Tools

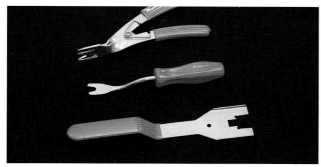

Depending upon the type of Jeep you own, there are undoubtedly interior panels or headliners that require custom tools for removal. Retainer clips and grommets that require special tools are most commonly found on door panels, dash pieces, and headliners and their trim. These tools are available in either plastic or metal; deciding which to use depends on the placement of the panel, the degree of difficulty to remove it, and what it is made of. With harder plastic pieces, metal tools can be used, while plastic tools are for panels that are prone to tearing or denting.

Mirrors

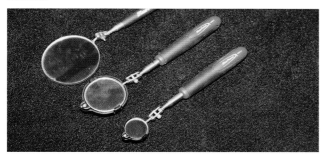

Mirrors are useful tools for the simple fact that they allow you to see somewhere you otherwise couldn't, which makes getting to a fastener or bolt that much easier. Mirrors are available in a wide variety of configurations, with moveable heads that rotate and swivel. Chances are that if you need to see something on your vehicle, there's a mirror that can show it to you.

Air Tools

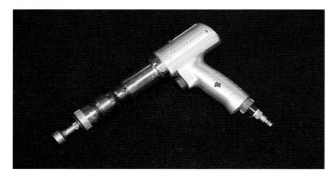

Among the staples in any serious garage, air tools are a fast and efficient way of getting a project completed in a timely manner with minimal fatigue to the mechanic. Some of the compressed air tools used on a Jeep include an impact gun, ratchet, air hammer, and cutting tool.

Cordless Tools

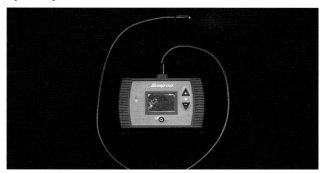

Cordless tools such as impact guns and screwdrivers are also a staple among mechanics for their proven ability to ease fatigue and perform the job fast. Available in a variety of sizes and configurations, these tools are powered by either nickel cadmium batteries or lithium ion batteries. Their charges vary depending upon the voltage of each machine. Some of the more powerful units are 24 volts, which allows them to have more torque and operate for a longer period of time. A typical cordless drill is 18 volts, and it will do just fine at drilling metal parts or securing trim pieces.

Specialty Tools

Your capacity and collection of specialty tools is often dictated by your trade specialty. For instance, a mechanic who works primarily on brake systems will have a better collection of specialty brake tools than someone who works on suspensions all day. Some of these specialty tools include brake line tubing sizers, cameras for inspecting the internal portions of engines, and special hooks for working in confined spaces. Other specialty tools include a welder, torch, air compressor, tap and die set, pop rivet gun, and a parts washer. It is a good idea to have a select group of specialty tools that match your interests and mechanical ability and your vehicle.

SECTION 1
GENERAL MAINTENANCE

Keeping your vehicle running and in top operating condition will allow your road trips and off-highway adventures to be that much more enjoyable, since the chances of your Jeep breaking down will be greatly reduced. In this chapter we review some projects that address general maintenance, as well as some things that should be inspected on a regular basis.

PROJECT 1
Trailhead Checklist

 Time: 1/2 Hour

 Tools: None

 Talent:

 Applicable Years: All

Tab: None

Parts Required: None

 Tip: After completing your off-road driving, the same checklist items should be performed prior to heading home to make sure the ride home is as safe as the trail ride.

 Performance Gain: Maintenance

 Complementary Project: Inspection of the drivetrain

For the majority of us, just the mere thought of being able to partake in a full day of off-road driving is enough to make us not be able to sleep the night before. However, when you awake in the morning and finally get to your trail destination, a few moments should be taken to do a quick review and inspection of your Jeep prior to hitting the terra firma.

During this review and inspection, the under hood components of your rig should be checked first. Items such as the oil level, fuel level (always start the trail on a full tank), belts, and other fluids should be checked for the proper levels and viscosity. (If your oil or fluid smells burnt or is excessively dirty, it should be replaced prior to your next outing.) Following these items, the underbody of your rig should be inspected for items such as secure brake lines, unbroken and solid suspension components, driveshaft, and any missing or loose bolts. A quick glance of the exterior of your rig may include checking the CB antenna, winch operation, and any extraction points. Check your CB radio and make sure the tire pressure is appropriate for the conditions you will be traveling in. You'll also want to ensure your lockers and four-wheel-drive system are operational.

While it may seem like there are a multitude of items to review and inspect, keep in mind it is better to know the condition of your rig going into the trail than to find out on it, when it may be too late. Listed below is a quick checklist that has been prepared by avid off-roader and trail leader Ted Bumgardner that will assist you with your review and inspection.

A general overview of the engine compartment should be performed to determine if there are any leaks from fluids, etc. Also, the general cleanliness of the engine will help its performance greatly, as dirt or other debris could inhibit its cooling capacity. *Photo courtesy of Terry Bumgardner*

The battery terminals should be inspected to ensure that they are secured onto the posts. If they become loose, power to key components, such as lights and winches, may be compromised. *Photo courtesy of Terry Bumgardner*

TRAILHEAD CHECKLIST

By Ted Bumgardner

The following list only takes a few minutes, but could make the difference between a great trip and a miserable one.

Under Hood Check

Check essential fluids
- Fuel level
- Engine oil
- Transmission fluid
- Radiator water
- Windshield washer fluid

Belts
- Hoses
- Battery cable and connection
- General visual observations

Under Jeep Check
- Make sure suspension components are not loose
- Check brake lines
- Look for any fluid leaks
- Look for any missing or loose bolts and nuts
- Check air lines or electrical connections for lockers
- General visual observations

Exterior Check
- Check winch function
- High lift secure
- Hood latches secure
- CB or short-wave antenna secure
- D-rings secure
- All racks, gas and water cans, and other accessories secure
- General visual observations

Check air-up air source.
- Air down to level appropriate for trail conditions
- Disconnect sway bar
- Check that all cargo is secure
- Radio check
- Engage and disengage low range
- Engage and disengage air or electric lockers
- Inspect any air compressor lines

3

Key fluids of the vehicle should be checked for proper levels. These fluids include coolant, engine oil, brake fluid, and power steering fluid. *Photo courtesy of Terry Bumgardner*

4

A simple hands-on inspection of key suspension components will tell what the general condition of the suspension is prior to the trail ride. *Photo courtesy of Terry Bumgardner*

5

Any apertures such as Hi-Lift jacks, etc. should be checked to be sure they are secured in their mounting locations. *Photo courtesy of Terry Bumgardner*

6

Hood latches on certain Jeep models should be inspected for proper closure and tightness. All too often hood restraints are either left unsecured or they break, which can cause damage to the fenders and hood. *Photo courtesy of Terry Bumgardner*

7

The CB antenna should be inspected for any breaks on the shaft and for tightness on its mount. If possible, the CB antenna cable should be inspected for any damage or wear as well. *Photo courtesy of Terry Bumgardner*

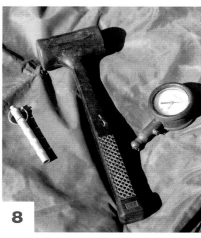

8

A few tools that can add to the thoroughness of the inspection and review of the vehicle before it hits the trail. *Photo courtesy of Terry Bumgardner*

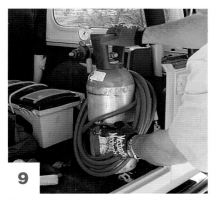

9

Cargo items are not exempt from being inspected to ensure they do not become missiles inside the cab when rock gardens are traversed. In this photo, the air bottle used to refill the tires at the end of the day is being inspected. *Photo courtesy of Terry Bumgardner*

10

The air pressure should be adjusted to meet the demands of your intended terrain. Typically, rocks and sandy conditions warrant between 10 and 15 psi per wheel. *Photo courtesy of Terry Bumgardner*

11

A CB check should be performed for proper operation. During this time, a strong, noise-free channel should be selected by everyone in your group. *Photo courtesy of Terry Bumgardner*

12

The winch should be inspected for proper operation and the winch line for any kinks, frays, or other damage that could compromise its ability to extract a stranded vehicle. *Photo courtesy of Terry Bumgardner*

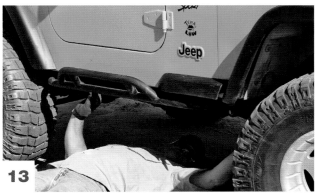

13

Crawling under your rig is one of the most effective ways to inspect the drivetrain and suspension components prior to your trail run. *Photo courtesy of Terry Bumgardner*

PROJECT 2
General Vehicle Maintenance

 Time: 1/2 Hour

 Tools: Flashlight

 Talent:

Applicable Years: All

Tab: $20

 Parts Required: Air cleaner, miscellaneous fluids

 Tip: None

 Performance Gain: Increases longevity and reliability of your vehicle

 Complementary Project: Drivetrain inspection

Maintaining a vehicle is often one of the most overlooked and underestimated items of importance. While relied upon heavily for work and pleasure, a vehicle needs to be maintained periodically to keep it functional and reliable. For the vast majority of vehicles, a maintenance schedule has been established to keep it in tiptop operating condition and on the road for many miles. These services are generally at 15,000; 30,000; 50,000; and 75,000 miles. Typically air cleaners and fluids are checked and replaced as needed, tires are rotated, brakes are inspected, and other maintenance duties are performed during these scheduled services.

Between these scheduled services, the engine and drivetrain should be inspected for proper fluid levels, any signs of leaks, and proper operation.

1 Some of the more common fluids found on a Jeep include motor oil, transmission fluid, brake fluid, parts cleaner, lubricant, and gear oil.

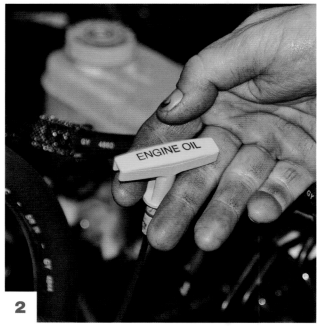

2 On the majority of new Jeeps, the key areas that should be accessed for inspection by the vehicle owner are identified with yellow markings. Here the dipstick for the motor oil is being inspected.

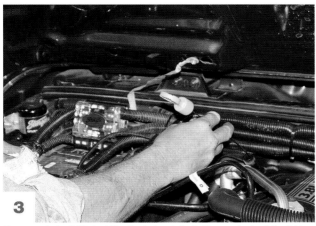

3

The transmission fluid should be checked periodically. To properly check the fluid, the vehicle should be parked on a level surface and the motor should be running.

4

The power steering reservoir has the acceptable levels of fluid embossed on its side. If the fluid level is low in the reservoir, fluid should be added.

5

When inspecting and adding brake fluid to the reservoir, it is important to make sure that the fluid strainer is in place. This will prevent any unwanted particles from being integrated into the brake lines.

6

The vehicle coolant should be inspected at the coolant reservoir. This reservoir will have two levels identified on the side of it; one for when the vehicle is hot and another for when the vehicle is cold.

7

Many of today's Jeeps utilize serpentine belts that run through and around the various pulleys on the engine. Given their constant use, the inner ribs of the belt may become frayed or cracked. If during your inspection there are visible cracks either on the inside or outside of the belt, it should be replaced immediately.

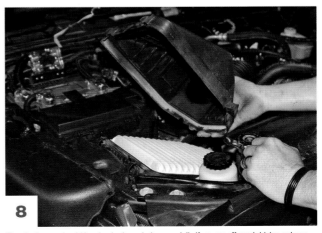

8

The air cleaner should be checked regularly, especially if you go off-road driving, where the air cleaner is exposed to more dirt and debris than with street driving.

PROJECT 3
Drivetrain Inspection

 Time: 1/2 Hour

 Tools: Flashlight

 Talent:

 Applicable Years: All

Tab: None

 Parts Required: None

 Tip: None

 Performance Gain: Increases longevity and reliability of your vehicle

 Complementary Project: General vechicle inspection

One of the most susceptible areas on your Jeep is the underbody. Depending on where you drive, a wide variety of components are exposed to the elements, especially your drivetrain items. Items such as driveshafts, axles, control arms, skid plates, and steering components can become loose, dented, or damaged without your knowledge until it's too late. As a preventative exercise, your drivetrain should be inspected at a minimum when you begin and conclude any off-highway driving. The reason for this is that anything identified as a concern can be assessed and dealt with; another reason is so you are not stranded, either on the trail or on your way home, because of a component that has been compromised.

When inspecting your drivetrain, your checklist should include axle U-joints, driveshafts, driveshaft U-joints, control arms, wheels, bushings, tie rods, ball joints, steering stabilizer brackets, and shocks, along with any other items you wish to include.

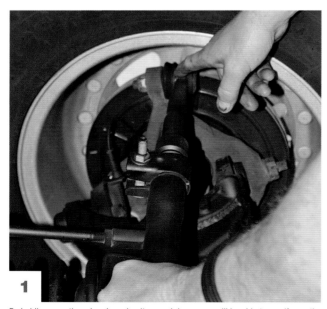

1

By holding your tie rod and moving it up and down, you will be able to see if your tie rod bushings are worn or performing properly. They should be tight, but not to the point where the tie rod bar has no resistance.

2

Bushings are another item that can become worn and cause the components that they are supporting to become loose and worn prematurely. In this photo, a track bar bushing is being inspected.

3 Control arms should be inspected for any excess wear and tear. In the event an arm is bent or cracked, it should be replaced immediately.

4 Driveshafts can become damaged and dented quite easily, given their position in relation to the axles and transfer case. In the event a driveshaft is dented or compromised, a vibration will be transferred to the wheels as a telltale sign that something is not right.

5 In this photo, a steering stabilizer was inspected and damage was found. It was replaced so that the steering system was not compromised.

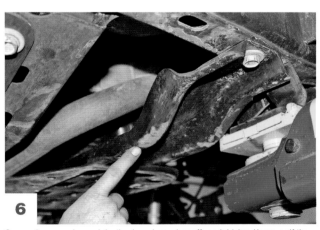

6 Some minor scraping and denting is a given when off-road driving. However, if the damage is severe enough to bend or compromise the integrity of crossbraces or suspension component mounts, they should be investigated and repaired.

7 The axle U-joints should be inspected for damage, debris, or excessive wear. This is easily accomplished by turning the wheels in the opposite direction to that of the U-joint that is being inspected.

8 The ball joints should also be inspected for movement. This is achieved by moving the tire vertically in and out. If there is an excessive amount of movement, there's a good chance that the bearings need replacing.

PROJECT 4
Bulb Replacement

 Time: 1/2 Hour

 Tools: Hand tools

 Talent:

 Applicable Years: All

Tab: $10

 Parts Required: Light bulb

 Tip: None

 Performance Gain: Safety

 Complementary Project: LED bulb upgrade

From a safety standpoint, the last thing you want is a burned-out bulb. Depending on the driving conditions, rough and bumpy roads, or the strength of the filament, a bulb can be easily burned out. When replacing a bulb, in addition to the actual bulb replacement, the fuse box should also be checked for any loose connections or blown fuses that may have caused the failure. Sometimes the bulb may be a sign of a larger issue. While it is sometimes difficult to know just when or why a light has burned out, a vehicle's lighting system should be checked periodically.

Given the wide variety of bulb styles, wattages, and mounting options, it is always a good idea to write the bulb style or model down so that the same unit is replaced.

1

During a routine inspection a burned-out stoplight was detected. It is important to note that a bulb filament may become damaged by the rough and bumpy roads often found when off-road driving. To access the bulb, the taillight assembly must be removed.

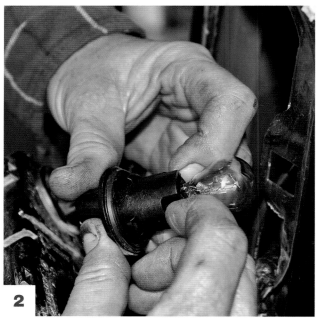

2

Once the bulb is identified, the housing should be unlocked to gain access to the bulb. Depending upon the bulb type, it may require some finesse and a gentle hand to release the retaining clips that are holding it in place.

3

Special care should be taken when reinstalling the new bulb. Upon its installation, any fingerprints should be wiped from the glass, as the oil on your fingers may cause the bulb to burn out quicker from the additional heat generated by the oil on the glass.

4

The bulb assembly is reinserted into the taillight housing with special attention being placed on the alignment of the locking cams to the housing.

5

With the cams aligned to the housing, the bulb assembly is twisted to lock it into place.

7

6

In this photo, the correct direction for locking and unlocking the bulb assembly is imprinted onto the taillight housing to be used for reference.

Once the taillight housing has been reassembled, the light is tested for proper operation and illumination.

PROJECT 5
General Lubrication

  Time: ½ Hour

 Tools: Grease gun

 Talent:

Applicable Years: All

Tab: $2

 Parts Required: Grease

 Tip: Do not overfill the zerk fittings

 Performance Gain: Increased longevity and reliability of your components

 Complementary Project: General vehicle inspection

Lubrication of key vehicle components is one of the most important things that a vehicle owner can do for his or her Jeep. While oil changes and other fluid changes could be considered a type of lubrication, some of the more overlooked items pertain to suspension, steering, and drivetrain components. While many of today's newer Jeeps contain self-sealed bearings and bushings, which require no external lubrication, some of the older versions of Jeeps do require the occasional lube job. In addition to the older Jeep models, there is an exception for the newer models in that if a suspension system has been installed, a good majority of the suspension components have fittings that allow the component to be greased. The majority of grease fittings are zerk fittings. When a grease gun is applied to a zerk fitting, a spring loaded ball is pushed down to allow the grease to enter the port. For our purposes, we have inspected the underbody of our project vehicle to highlight some of the components that should be greased once a month.

1

The front axle tube seals contain a built-in zerk fitting that is greaseable. Keeping these seals greased allows the bushing to rest tightly around the axle. Keeping things sealed as well helps keep any related noise quelled.

2

The driveshaft tubes contain zerk fittings that assist the driveshaft in moving in and out while under difficult driving conditions such as off-highway driving.

3

Our Superlift adjustable lower control arms have built-in zerk fittings to keep the arms fluid while driving off-road and being articulated.

4

Bushings such as this track bar bushing should also be lubricated to help keep them from being dried out and making excessive amounts of noise.

5

The universal joints on the driveshaft require lubrication to keep them moving freely and with ease. Zerk fittings are placed in strategic locations where wear is most prevalent.

PROJECT 6
Perform an Oil Change

 Time: 1/2 Hour

 Tools: Open-ended wrench, oil filter wrench

 Talent:

 Applicable Years: All

Tab: $30

 Parts Required: Motor oil, oil filter

 Tip: Prior to loosening the oil pan drain bolt, the oil cap on the valve cover should be removed to allow the oil to flow faster from the oil pan.

 Performance Gain: Maintenance

 Complementary Project: Transfer case fluid change

Changing your engine's oil and filter is one of the best insurance policies you can have to ensure that your engine will continue running for a long period of time. A quick review of your Jeep's owner's manual will give the intervals for an oil change. However, a good rule of thumb is to change oil and filter every 3,000 to 5,000 miles. The weight of your motor oil will be determined by your specific engine, as every engine requires a different weight. The choice to use synthetic or regular oil is purely up to your discretion when not designated in your owner's manual. If you do choose to use a synthetic formula, keep in mind that the oil change intervals should remain the same.

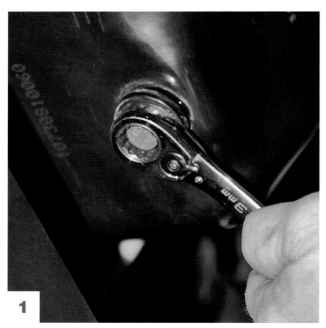

1

To begin the oil change, use an open-ended wrench and loosen the drain plug from the oil pan. Since the plug is relatively short, the wrench should be used to loosen it. Once loosened, the plug should be removed from the oil pan by hand. This will minimize chances of it being lost or dropped into the oil catch bucket.

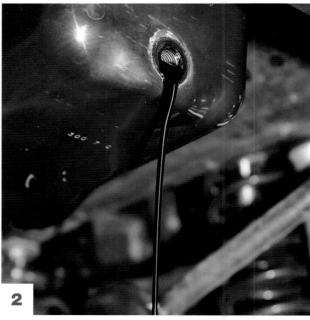

2

With the drain plug removed from the pan, the oil will begin draining. To help speed the draining, the oil filler cap at the top of the engine is removed, which alleviates the vacuum effect, and the oil flows faster.

3

When the oil has completely drained from the oil pan, the oil filter is removed. Care should be taken when removing it, as it will be filled with oil, especially if it mounts to the side of the engine.

4

The new K&N oil filter gasket has a small amount of new oil applied to it. This will assist the gasket in forming a tight seal against the oil filter bracket.

5

The new oil filter and drain plug should be reinstalled prior to the engine being filled with oil.

6

The size and type of engine your Jeep is outfitted with will determine the engine oil weight and quantities. For our application on our '08 Jeep Wrangler JK, a total of six quarts of 5W-20 synthetic oil was installed.

7

Once the oil has been installed, the motor is started for a few moments and then shut off. After sitting for another moment, the oil level is checked to ensure that an adequate amount of oil was installed.

PROJECT 7
Perform a Gear Oil Change

Time: 1 Hour

Tools: Socket set, plastic dead blow hammer

Talent: 🔧🔧

Applicable Years: All

Tab: $40

Parts Required: Gear oil, room temperature vulcanizing (RTV) silicone (black)

Tip: Prior to loosening the differential cover, make certain that there is a catch bucket for the gear oil in place under the differential.

Performance Gain: Increases longevity and reliability of your gears

Complementary Project: Transfer case fluid change

Some of the hardest-working and under-pressure components of your Jeep are the differentials. Always in motion, these units generate a tremendous amount of heat, and they work under grueling conditions. For these reasons, their fluid should be replaced often. While not the easiest of fluids to change, given their place on the vehicle, performing this exchange regularly will help minimize the chance of metal shavings generated from normal wear of the gears damaging your differential. Depending on the make and model of Jeep that you own, the fluid weight and viscosity will be different for each vehicle. Some important things to keep in mind are that in some cases an additive for rear ends equipped with electronic differentials may be necessary. Depending on the model of axle, there may be a built-in drain plug at the bottom of the differential which would circumvent the need to remove the differential housing.

1 Prior to removing the differential cover bolts to prepare for the oil change, inspect the bottom of the differential housing and look for a drain plug. If it has one, the differential cover will not need to be removed and the plug would be the only item that needs to be removed.

2 Once it has been determined that the cover must be removed to drain the oil, the cover bolts are removed and the differential cover is struck with a plastic dead blow hammer to loosen and break the silicone gasket seal.

3

With the silicone gasket seal broken, the gear oil flows freely from the differential. It is important to have a catch bucket that is large enough and wide enough.

4

Prior to cleaning the gasket material from the differential housing and the cover, the gears should be inspected for any damage or excessive wear. Also, the wear pattern on the ring gear teeth should be examined for a consistent center-wearing pattern.

5

The differential cover is reinstalled onto the differential housing, but not before a new RTV silicone gasket is applied to both the cover and housing. Special care is taken to avoid covering the mounting bolt holes with the silicone.

6

Prior to filling the differential with oil, the newly applied covers should be allowed to sit for 30 minutes to let the gasket material set up. A typical differential will require two quarts to be full. The oil used will more than likely be a synthetic formula, for added longevity and performance.

7

With the fluid in place, the filler plug is reinstalled and torqued to the manufacturer's specifications.

PROJECT 8
Perform a Transfer Case Fluid Change

 Time: 1 Hour

 Tools: Socket set

 Talent:

 Applicable Years: All

 Tab: $50

 Parts Required: Transmission fluid, oil catch bucket

 Tip: Prior to loosening the transfer case drain plug, remove the fill plug for better drainage.

 Performance Gain: Increases longevity and reliability of your transfer case

 Complementary Project: Oil change

The heart of any four-wheel-drive vehicle, especially a Jeep, is its transfer case. Used to distribute the power from the rear driveshaft to the front driveshaft as well, this is one component that definitely earns its keep. To make sure that the transfer case functions when called upon, the fluid needs to be replaced at regular service intervals. Depending upon what the specific service intervals are for each Jeep, the typical rule of thumb should be every 15,000 miles, if the unit is used off-road often. The fluid of choice is automatic transmission fluid, which will be defined in each vehicle's owner's manual. While a relatively easy task to perform, special care should be taken when removing and reinstalling the drain and fill plugs into the case housing. Sometimes there is a possibility that the threads may become cross-threaded or destroyed, which will cause larger and more expensive problems than just replacing fluid.

1

Prior to removing the transfer case drain plug, the filler plug is removed to expedite the drainage of the transfer case fluid.

2

Using an Allen head socket, the transfer case drain plug is removed. The plug removal should begin with the Allen head socket and finish with the plug being removed by hand, to prevent it from falling into the oil drain bucket or becoming lost.

3

Allow the fluid to drain completely before reinstalling the drain plug.

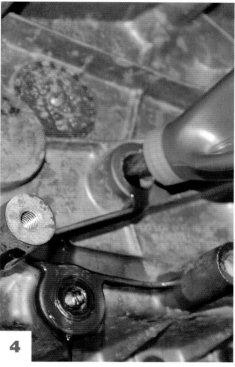

4

Given the high performance of today's vehicles, Jeeps included, the transfer case should be filled with a synthetic formula, which provides better lubrication to the internals of the component.

5

Upon filling the transfer case with the new fluid, the fill plug is reinstalled.

SECTION 2
ENGINE

The heart of any Jeep is its engine and related components. Depending upon the type of Jeep you have and the use of it, chances are that there either has been or will be some engine modifications performed to it, whether it's a new exhaust system or reprogramming the computer. In this chapter we review some projects that address potential engine performance upgrades that could add some significant horsepower.

PROJECT 9
Install an Electronic Fuel Injection (EFI) Conversion System

 Time: 9 Hours

 Tools: Hand tools, socket set, screwdrivers, hose cutter, cable ties

 **Talent:** ★★★★★

 Applicable Years: 1972–1991 Jeep 258-cid (4.2-liter) engines

 Tab: $1,200

 Parts Required: EFI kit

 Tip: To be fully emission legal, your Jeep must have a properly functioning catalytic converter, exhaust gas recirculation (EGR) valve, canister and purge system, positive crankcase ventilation (PCV) valve, and a vehicle speed sensor incorporated into the speedometer drive cable that is able to transmit the vehicle's speed information to the ECM.

 Performance Gain: Converts your old carbureted Jeep into a modern-day EFI-equipped model with more horsepower and performance

 Complementary Project: None

If you've ever tried off-road driving in a vehicle equipped with a carburetor, then you know it's no easy feat, especially if the vehicle keeps rocking from side to side as it drives over rocks and other obstacles. Between the sputtering, loss of power, and overall poor performance of the engine, due to the carburetor not being delivered a consistent amount of fuel or by not having a level amount of fuel in the float, converting from a carbureted system to an electronic fuel injection system just makes sense. While there are numerous conversions kits on the market that allow this swap, we chose the Howell Engine Developments, Inc., JP-1 EFI kit to be installed on a CJ-Series Jeep that was equipped with a carbureted setup. Since the installation requires someone with vast technical knowledge and mechanical skills, who is familiar with these conversions, we called on John Miroux of All Four-Wheel Drive in Corona, California, to perform the install.

The Howell Jeep EFI kit uses a new General Motors throttle body fuel injection unit from the 4.3-liter V-6 engine to replace your existing Jeep carburetor. It is fitted to the stock Jeep intake manifold with an adapter supplied in the kit, and controlled by a GM vehicle electronic control module (ECM) using a coolant sensor, manifold absolute pressure (MAP)

sensor, and heated oxygen sensor for input information. These components allow your Jeep to operate at the correct air/fuel ratio for minimum emissions, best power, and good fuel economy. This kit provides improved starting, both hot and cold, and immediate drive-away without lengthy warmups. Off-road maneuverability is greatly improved by eliminating troublesome stalls from flooding or fuel starvation.

In addition to the above improvements, the throttle body injection (TBI) kit simplifies the under hood area by removing many of the vacuum hoses and vacuum-controlled emission devices required with the OEM carburetor. These are no longer required, due to the advanced engine control system. In addition, you enhance durability through the use of genuine GM late-model components, developed and thoroughly tested by GM as OEM parts on the 4.3-liter V-6 engine.

With the JP-1 EFI kit, your Jeep will meet all Environmental Protection Agency (EPA) guidelines and California Air Resources Board (CARB) requirements up through model year 1991 by qualifying for CARB EO (Executive Order) D-452. This makes it legal for distribution and installation in all 50 states.

1 The Howell JP-1 EFI conversion kit contains everything needed to perform the conversion, from the air cleaner to the ECM. The increase in performance both on and off the trail is night and day.

2 Once the carburetor is removed, the manifold will be exposed to items that can fall into it, which could potentially cause a bigger issue than just replacing the fuel system. To minimize this risk, the opening has been covered with masking tape.

3 Since the new EFI system relies upon the O2 sensor for much needed input, the previous version was replaced. From the looks of it, the factory unit looked as though it had been around the block a few times.

4 When installing the new coolant sensor, it is important to use thread sealant and to remove and reinstall the new part quickly to minimize coolant loss.

5 Included with the kit is a billet aluminum two-barrel carburetor adapter plate and gasket that fits onto the manifold. Using the factory mounting locations, the adapter plate is installed. When finished, a small amount of sealant should be applied to each of the bolt holes to minimize any air gaps between the gasket and throttle body fuel injection unit.

6 The Howell Jeep EFI kit uses a new General Motors throttle body fuel injection unit from the 4.3-liter V-6 engine to replace your existing Jeep carburetor. The fuel injectors are located in roughly the same place as the previous carburetor barrels would have been.

7

The fuel pump is an in-line design that will maintain the 12–15 psi operating pressure at all times.

8

The fuel filter attaches to the rear main fuel line with about 12 inches of flexible fuel line between the cut-off fuel line and the fuel filter. The fuel pump and filter are both attached to the passenger side inner frame rail of the Jeep. When installing these items, place them in an area that will be shielded from rock hits or other obstacles encountered when off-road driving.

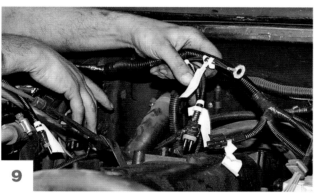

9

The new wiring harness features original equipment (OE)–style connectors that are weatherproof. Since the new loom will be communicating between the ECM and the TBI, it is stretched out and secured out of harm's way with each of the connectors being run to their point of contact. To communicate with the ECM, the wiring harness must penetrate the vehicle's firewall. The opening used was the same one as the factory loom.

10

Once routed through the firewall, the necessary connections are made to the TBI. When they are completed, any excess wire should be secured away from sources of heat or moving parts.

11

Tasked with relaying the information from the injector to the ECM are the fuel injector connections that are attached to the top of each fuel injector using OE-style hardware.

12

Once on the other side of the firewall, the new wiring harness is plugged into the Howell ECM, which is a derivative of a GM module and works perfectly with the GM-derived TBI unit. Wrapping up the install, the new Howell EFI controller was located in the glove box to help keep it protected from the elements.

PROJECT 10
Install a Ram-Air Intake System

 Time: 2 Hours

 Tools: Socket set, screwdrivers, needle-nose pliers

 Talent: ✦✦✦

 Applicable Years: 1997–2006 Jeep 4.0-liter engines

Tab: $300

 Parts Required: Ram-air kit

 Tip: Read the instruction manual prior to beginning the install and inventory the parts that have been included with the kit to confirm that all of the pieces are there.

 Performance Gain: Improved vehicle performance

 Complementary Project: Install an air filter

Breathing is an important function to being able to perform our daily tasks and duties; without doing it we would be dead. The same holds true for our vehicles as they go about performing the tasks that we ask of them. Keep in mind that while this is occurring, constant streams of fresh clean air are being filtered into the engine to keep it operating. In the event this air is restricted or stops altogether, the engine dies, just as we do if we had no air.

While the factory air intake system does the job, the Banks Ram-Air Intake System replaces the factory's flat panel filter with a large conical lifetime filter that provides maximum high-flow filtration. The Ram-Air's opening is over twice as big as a stock unit and without the 90-degree detours that choke airflow and kill power. The huge air inlet, enclosed housing, and much larger tubing work together to reduce the restrictions and dramatically improve airflow to the cylinders.

The results are impressive: Banks Ram-Air Intake more than doubles the factory intake's airflow, improving the Jeep's power and fuel economy. Additionally, the Ram-Air system has been designed to accommodate engine movement, which further helps prevent component damage and increase the service life of the components. Installing the new system is as simple as removing the factory air intake system and replacing it with the new Banks system. No modifications or cutting of the factory components is required.

1

The Banks Ram-Air Intake System replaces the factory's flat panel filter with a large conical lifetime filter that provides maximum high-flow filtration, which more than doubles the factory intake system's airflow.
Photo courtesy of Gale Banks Engineering

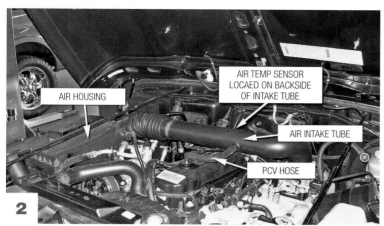

To begin the install, the intake air temperature (IAT) sensor located on the backside of the intake tube must be removed and set aside. The next component that should be disconnected is the PCV hose from the fitting on top of the valve cover. Following that part's removal, both air intake hose clamps should be loosened so that the air intake tube can be removed from the engine compartment along with the air intake filter. *Photo courtesy of Gale Banks Engineering*

Labels in image:
- AIR HOUSING
- AIR TEMP SENSOR LOCAED ON BACKSIDE OF INTAKE TUBE
- AIR INTAKE TUBE
- PCV HOSE

2

3

The next item to be removed is the air housing. This is performed by removing the three screws that hold it in place. It is important to keep all of the hardware, since some of it will be used for the reinstall. *Photo courtesy of Gale Banks Engineering*

4

Install the Banks Air housing into the engine compartment and align the screw holes to the fender panel. Depending upon the model year of Jeep, not all of the screw holes will be utilized. On some models, only two screw holes were utilized. Once installed, the new intake tube and hump hose are installed with the supplied hardware. *Photo courtesy of Gale Banks Engineering*

5

The supplied rubber IAT grommet is installed in the air intake tube to allow the IAT sensor to fit flush into the grommet on the air intake tube. If your specific Jeep does not utilize an IAT sensor, use the supplied grommet plug to cover the opening. The supplied PCV hose is installed back onto the valve cover on one end and onto the Banks short intake tube at the other. *Photo courtesy of Gale Banks Engineering*

6

After a quick check for tightness on all the connections, the new air filter is installed and the system is ready to produce added performance to the engine as well as double the airflow, which should make both the driver and engine much happier. *Photo courtesy of Gale Banks Engineering*

PROJECT 11
Install a Prefilter Snorkel

 Time: 1 Hour

 Tools: Pop-rivet tool, cut-off wheel, center punch, wax pencil, tape, 2-inch metal hole saw, drill, drill bit, socket set, silicone sealant

 Talent:

 Applicable Years: Jeep Wrangler JK (two-door and four-door models)

Tab: $350

 Parts Required: Snorkel and hardware

 Tip: Since the stock hood requires minor cutting, it is important to measure twice and cut once to ensure a tight fit around the snorkel and to avoid additional body and paint work.

 Performance Gain: Allows the engine to receive cleaner intake air

 Complementary Project: Installation of an aftermarket air cleaner

Clean, dry air is vital to any engine, and around town or on the highway a four-wheel-drive's stock air filter does an admirable job of protecting it from contamination. However, once that vehicle hits the trail, deep water crossing and plumes of thick bulldust can overwhelm its stock filter and literally destroy its engine. Experienced four-wheel-drive explorers have long known this, and they consider raising their engine's air intakes a vital step in creating greater protection. While offered for many Jeep models, we chose to install American Expedition Vehicles' (AEV) raised intake snorkel system for our Jeep Wrangler JK model. This easily installed product places the air intake point at roof level, which allows the engine and filter to breathe more safely from a location well above the deepest water crossings and densest dust.

AEV's JK snorkel can be had with either an air ram (scoop) or a cylindrical prefilter (bowl). Both snorkel tips will allow the engine to breathe equally well, but both have distinct advantages and disadvantages when compared to one other. The air ram is designed to draw in air and separate rainwater from the air charge. It is incredibly rugged and well suited to wooded terrain where impacts with trees and branches are likely. By comparison, the prefilter is designed to draw in air and separate both rain and dust from the air charge. Though the prefilter lacks the ruggedness of the air ram, it is well suited to dry desert terrain, where thick dust is likely. The prefilter is also cleanable and virtually reusable for the life of the snorkel.

The construction of the snorkel is derived from a high-strength cross-link polyethylene material to the exact fit of the JK body contours. Attaching the unit to the vehicle is as simple as removing the factory windshield boltholes and fender mounts and sliding the brackets into place. Best of all, there are no modifications required to the stock JK airbox inlet since the factory intake tube is removed and replaced with the snorkel. Minimal trimming of the stock hood is required. If the aftermarket AEV heat reduction hood is substituted, there are no required modifications. For installation purposes, AEV assisted with the installation, which was performed on a vehicle with a stock hood.

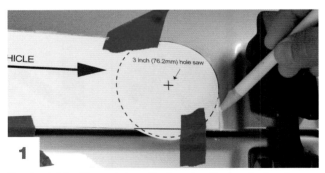

There is a definite difference between the size and quality of construction of the factory muffler compared with the Monster Muffler. In addition to its weight reduction, the smaller-sized muffler is not as prone to hitting obstacles when off-road driving as the factory unit was, which could be another reason for its replacement. Since the stock hood is being used, it is necessary to modify it to fit the snorkel. The first order of business is to cut out and place the supplied template onto the right side of the hood. Be sure to measure 1/2 inch (13mm) back from the hood latch indentation as shown on the template. Mark out the cut line on the exterior of the hood, using a wax pencil, and then center punch the center of the 2-inch (50.8mm) circle. *Photo courtesy of American Expedition Vehicles*

Next, temporarily prop the hood up approximately 4 to 6 inches (100–150mm) in order to cut the hood without damaging the fender or any of the under hood components. Cover and protect all glass, plastic, and painted parts from sparks and debris while performing this task. *Photo courtesy of American Expedition Vehicles*

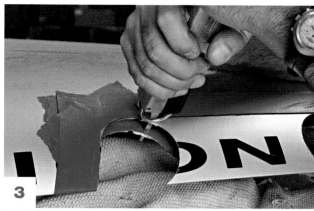

Use a pilot drill to drill both layers of the hood first, then use the 2-inch (50.8mm) hole saw to carefully cut through both layers of the hood. *Photo courtesy of American Expedition Vehicles*

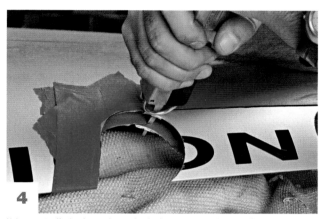

Using a cut-off wheel or reciprocating body saw, cut out the rest of the opening from the hood. *Photo courtesy of American Expedition Vehicles*

Mark the inside of the hood as shown. Draw the cut line approximately ¼ inch (6mm) lower than the bend of the hood as shown. This can easily be done by holding a marker in such a way that your finger can be used as a guide. Finish by marking the rest of the area to be removed. *Photo courtesy of American Expedition Vehicles*

Using the cut-off wheel, clearance the hood inner so that it clears the opening when viewed from the side. *Photo courtesy of American Expedition Vehicles*

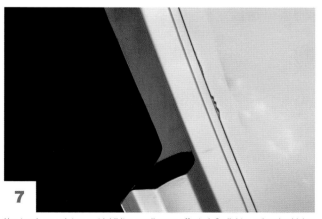

Use touch-up paint or rust inhibitor on all areas affected. On lighter-colored vehicles, you may want to "black out" the hood inner so that it is not as noticeable. Mask and paint as required. *Photo courtesy of American Expedition Vehicles*

8

Loosen the clamp on the engine intake hose. Separate the intake hose and crankcase breather hose (gas) from the airbox and remove the top of the airbox from the vehicle. *Photo courtesy of American Expedition Vehicles*

9

Install the mounting brackets to the snorkel. Center the mounts in the recessed areas in the snorkel and attach the brackets using the 1/4-inch bolts and washers. Do not tighten completely at this time—just enough to allow some movement for adjustment. *Photo courtesy of American Expedition Vehicles*

10

Remove the fender bolts and windshield bolts as shown to prepare the vehicle for mounting the snorkel. *Photo courtesy of American Expedition Vehicles*

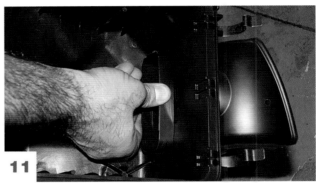

11

Remove the short factory snorkel by squeezing the part inside the airbox. Then install the new snorkel. It will be necessary to cut off the small locator on the factory airbox. Use black silicone to seal the snorkel-to-airbox joint and seal the holes in the bottom of the airbox and reinstall into the vehicle. *Photo courtesy of American Expedition Vehicles*

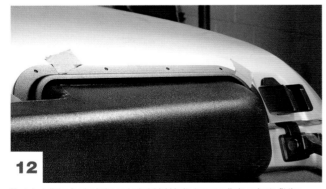

12

Next, install the fender bolts and windshield bolts temporarily in order to fit the snorkel for adjustment. Test fit the hood-to-snorkel clearance. The snorkel and hood should have roughly a 1/8-inch (3mm) gap surrounding the front and top of the snorkel. Adjust the brackets for the best fit and then tighten every bolt and bracket. Install the optional AEV Trim Ring. Place the AEV trim ring on the hood and adjust it so that the visual gap between the hood and the snorkel is even. Mark the location of the holes on the hood and drill to 1/8-inch. Paint the holes with touchup paint and install the AEV trim ring using the supplied stainless steel rivets. *Photo courtesy of American Expedition Vehicles*

13

Reinstall the filter, top of the airbox, and all hoses. Install the AEV air ram or prefilter. (Be sure to rotate the maintenance instruction label so that it is easily visible.) Tighten the supplied hose clamp. Adjust the AEV air ram or prefilter so that it sits straight and level when viewed from the front and side of the vehicle. *Photo courtesy of American Expedition Vehicles*

PROJECT 12
Install a Supercharger

 Time: 8 Hours

 Tools: Hand tools, screwdrivers, socket set, specialty tools, grinder, hose cutter, Teflon pipe sealant, pipe cutter, pliers

 Talent: ✦✦✦✦✦

 Applicable Years: Jeep Wrangler JK (two-door and four-door models)

Tab: $3,700

 Parts Required: Supercharger

 Tip: Before beginning installation, replace all spark plugs that are older than 1 year or 15,000 miles with original heat range plugs as specified by the manufacturer. Do not use platinum spark plugs unless they are original equipment. Change spark plugs every 20,000 miles.

 Performance Gain: Improved vehicle performance

 Complementary Project: Upgraded/ reprogrammed ECM

Let's face it. If you own a Jeep Wrangler TJ or JK model and add a considerable amount of off-road equipment to it, such as larger tires, a winch, heavier front and rear bumpers, etc., the rig can get heavy very quickly. While all of these items are necessities to conquering whatever trail is desired, the only problem may be having enough power to get there, given that the factory 3.8-liter V-6 and 4.0-liter I-6 engines can be somewhat taxed, thanks to the added weight. While there are numerous options available to increase the performance and power to the engines, the only options that can really make a significant increase in the horsepower numbers is one of two choices, either swap the engine for a Hemi V-8 or install a supercharger to the factory motor. Just as an FYI, the second option is much cheaper and provides almost as much horsepower as a 5.7-liter Hemi V-8.

Adventure Innovations is one company among many that manufacture supercharger systems for Jeep 4.0-liter and 3.8-liter engines. Consisting of a Vortech V2 SC trim centrifugal supercharger and a Unichip computer module, the typical performance gains are roughly a 35 to 40 percent increase in horsepower. Included with the system is a new high-performance inline fuel pump and Fuel Management Unit (FMU). All of the necessary components and hardware are included to make the installation as easy as it can be for someone with experience in installing superchargers and setting up the ECM and Fuel/Ignition Control Modules. While the parts look relatively simple to install, there is a greater amount of knowledge that goes into the install that cannot be seen by way of setup, integration, and overall mechanical ability requirements. This is one install that should be left to the professionals.

One of the vital components of the system is the heat exchanger, which is responsible for cooling the system. The provided self-tapping screws secure the assembly to the steel core support just in front of the radiator. *Photo courtesy of Adventure Innovations*

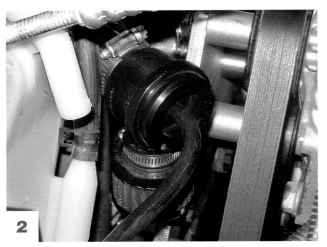

2

Using the supplied 1-inch rubber hose and two No. 16 hose clamps, the bypass valve is secured to the bung on the previously installed discharge tube. *Photo courtesy of Adventure Innovations*

3

An AEM fuel/ignition controller (F/IC) is installed as part of the system to aid in retarding ignition and to deliver accurate amounts of fuel without the need for an outdated fuel management unit (FMU) or "boost hiding" controllers. This system works parallel to the factory electronic control unit (ECU) by preventing tuning limitations due to the complex factory timing patterns. Rpm breakpoints are easily accessed with the F/IC's Windows-based tuning software. *Photo courtesy of Adventure Innovations*

4

The factory airbox is replaced with a larger and more efficient filter, which provides nearly double the amount of air into the engine, just what a supercharger requires to stay operational. *Photo courtesy of Adventure Innovations*

5

A 3.5-inch piece of flex duct is installed between the airbox flange and the cast inlet duct for air intake into the supercharger. It is secured in place by No. 52 hose clamps. *Photo courtesy of Adventure Innovations*

6

The completed installation looks as though it came from the factory with a supercharger installed. The 35 to 40 percent increase in horsepower from the Vortech-derived supercharger will make a JK Wrangler's horsepower output in the neighborhood of 275 horses, not bad from a V-6. *Photo courtesy of Adventure Innovations*

PROJECT 13
Install an AEV HEMI V-8 Builder Kit

 Time: 30 Hours

 Tools: Hand tools, socket set, open-ended wrenches, engine hoist, transmission jack

 Talent:

 Applicable Years: Jeep Wrangler JK (two-door and four-door models)

Tab: $20,000 (turn-key Hemi conversion)

 Parts Required: V-8 engine, AEV builder kit, miscellaneous parts

 Tip: Prior to performing the conversion, make sure that it is smog-legal in your state.

Performance Gain: It's a Hemi. Need we say more?

Complementary Project: Upgrade the factory ring and pinion gears and axles

Do you find yourself cringing as your 3.8-liter V-6 power plant hurtles to 5,000 rpm in a feeble attempt to pass another vehicle or make it up a hill, either on or off the road? Have you grown tired of your transmission constantly searching for a better gear? If so, the solution is one word, Hemi. Swapping the factory motor for either the 330-horsepower 5.7-liter Hemi V-8 with 375 lbs-ft of torque, or the larger 420-horsepower 6.1-liter V-8 with 420 lbs-ft of torque will definitely provide you with all of the power you need to move your Jeep JK with ease.

So once one has obtained the powertrain from a 2005–2008 Jeep Grand Cherokee or Jeep Commander, how does one go about installing it? One look under the hood of an American Expedition Vehicles–converted Jeep JK and you'll swear the engine must have been installed at the factory, thanks largely in part to the AEV HEMI V-8 Builder Kit that has every detail considered and provided for an effortless install for those do-it-yourself types. From a contoured custom coolant bottle, to the computer-tested, plug-and-play wiring harness, no detail has been overlooked. The end result is a clean, simple, and complete engine conversion kit that skips the headaches and quickly delivers you the best part of the build, the sound of a roaring Hemi!

1 AEV's conversion kit can be used with either the 5.7- or 6.1-liter Hemis. The end result is pure horsepower from start to stop. Best of all, though, are the impeccable manners that the JK has while in daily-driver mode and the stamina and performance to conquer anything off-road.

2 The engine mounts that are included in the kit use AEV's "No measuring" system, meaning that they line up directly to the existing holes in the frame with no modifications.

3

The massive powerplant's oil pan is nearly double that of the factory 3.8-liter V-6; we won't even go into the horsepower comparisons.

4

The custom AEV air filter shield has been designed to work in conjunction with a K&N air filter system and resides in the same location as the stock airbox.

5

The all-aluminum AEV radiator provides ample cooling for either the 5.7-liter or 6.1-liter applications and is an OE-style direct bolt-in part. The radiator also works with the vehicle's stock electric fan.

6

AEV's custom wiring harnesses use OE connecters and are computer-tested for proper function before shipping. This eliminates costly mistakes requiring harness removal and shipment back to the manufacturer. The kit utilizes the stock fusebox.

7

Included with the kit is an AEV computer that has been preprogrammed for the desired engine size and is ready for use, a true plug-and-play application.

8

The AEV programmer that is also included allows the vehicle identification number (VIN), several setup procedures, gear ratio, and tire size adjustments to be done without a visit to the local dealer.

9

AEV's custom steel battery tray holds either the stock battery or an Optima Group 31 battery and allows for proper valve-cover clearance.

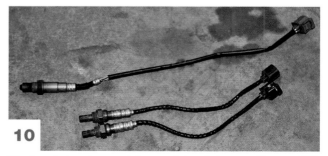

10

Other items that remain unseen but are equally important are new O2 sensors, CNC (computer numerical control)–bent fuel lines, CNC-bent two-piece power steering lines, CNC-bent three-piece air conditioning lines, a heavy-duty transmission cooler, and a Flowmaster exhaust system.

PROJECT 14
Install a Set of Bolt-on Headers

 Time: 4 Hours

 Tools: Socket set, open-ended wrenches, rags, screwdrivers, and pliers

 Talent:

Applicable Years: All 4.0-liter, 3.8-liter, and 2.5-liter Jeep engines

 Tab: $475

 Parts Required: Gale Banks Engineering Torque Tubes

 Tip: Disconnect the ground cables from the battery before beginning work. If the vehicle has more than one battery, be sure that the engine primary battery is disconnected. This is necessary for safety and to ease the installation on the passenger side.

 Performance Gain: Increased performance

 Complementary Project: Installation of an exhaust system

The exhaust system on a Jeep can be very influential when it comes to power and performance of the engine. Many times, the only item upgraded in an exhaust system is the muffler and accompanying tailpipes. Often the headers are left out for various reasons, perhaps because people feel they are not needed, since they do not have a high-performance race engine, or because they are unaware of just what headers do. Regardless of whether your engine is stock with no modifications to it or completely built to the hilt, a set of aftermarket performance headers will definitely make a difference to your powerplant. Essentially the first half of an exhaust system, headers are responsible for routing the spent gasses from the cylinders of the engine through to the muffler. They often require replacement because they become cracked from the heat at the casting seams. Their gaskets also become worn and begin to cause leaks between the cylinder head and the header's flange. Among the best replacement systems for Jeeps are the Gale Banks Engineering Torque Tubes. They are built of the highest-quality products and produce excellent performance for all 4.0-liter, 3.8-liter, and 2.5-liter Jeep engines. The Torque Tubes used for our install were on a 3.8-liter engine.

Banks Torque Tubes exhaust manifolds have been streamlined to optimize exhaust flow and engine efficiency. Since the stock manifold flanges don't align squarely with the ports, exhaust flow is restricted, robbing the engine of

performance. Torque Tubes feature thicker flanges that are machined dead flat and precisely fitted to the port pattern of each engine. The end result is a healthier, less bogged down exhaust note and better engine performance. Unlike the stock exhaust manifolds that are cast and then welded at the seam, the Banks Torque Tubes are built of heavy-gauge 400-series stainless steel to weather a lifetime of heat, stress, and abuse. The flanges, welded to the tube assemblies on both sides, will never crack or separate. The gaskets are made of SMI 900, a material that stands up to superhot temperatures without compromising.

A comparison between the factory headers and the new Torque Tube unit shows the subtle but meaningful differences between the two. Note the solid-piece flanges at the engine block point of connection, as opposed to the cutout pieces on the factory units; the solid one-piece exhaust tubes, as opposed to the cast factory units; and the overall shape of the new units versus the factory units. It all adds up to the additional power that is gained by installing a set on the Wrangler JK. *Photo courtesy of Gale Banks Engineering*

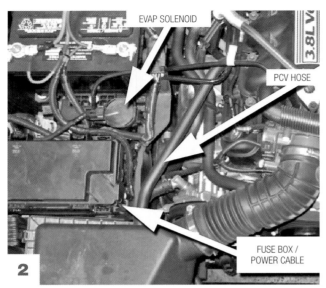

EVAP SOLENOID

PCV HOSE

FUSE BOX / POWER CABLE

2

With the vehicle raised, the battery is disconnected at both battery terminals, and the airbox cover intake tube hose clamp is loosened and removed. The PCV hose connected at the airbox is then removed along with the lower half of air filter box from the engine compartment. The evaporative emissions control system (EVAP) solenoid should also be removed along with any associated electrical connections. *Photo courtesy of Gale Banks Engineering*

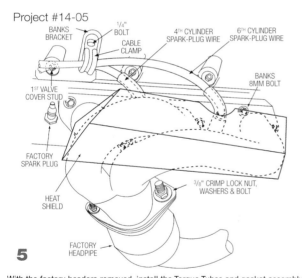

Project #14-05

BANKS BRACKET

1/4" BOLT

CABLE CLAMP

4TH CYLINDER SPARK-PLUG WIRE

6TH CYLINDER SPARK-PLUG WIRE

BANKS 8MM BOLT

1ST VALVE COVER STUD

FACTORY SPARK PLUG

3/8" CRIMP LOCK NUT, WASHERS & BOLT

HEAT SHIELD

FACTORY HEADPIPE

5

With the factory headers removed, install the Torque Tubes and gasket assembly to the cylinder head. The Torque Tubes are attached with the new hardware that has been included with the kit. Once both sides of the engine have had the Torque Tubes installed, the Y-pipe is secured to the Torque Tubes using the supplied bolts, washers, and crimp locknuts. *Photo courtesy of Gale Banks Engineering*

8

3

The fusebox is removed by simply pressing in on the release tabs located on the outer edge of the fusebox. Once the fusebox is removed, the bracket is also removed to provide additional space when removing and installing the tubes. *Photo courtesy of Gale Banks Engineering*

4

Since the path of travel is blocked by the steering knuckle U-joint, it must be removed, to be reinstalled upon completion of the job. A line should be drawn across the steering shaft, on the firewall side, marking its position, so that it can be realigned to its previous position when being reinstalled. *Photo courtesy of Gale Banks Engineering*

6

The plastic battery tray compartment is resecured to the vehicle along with the fuse compartment to the sheet metal brackets. The power cables are reconnected along with the other related components. Once this is completed, a hole must be drilled through the battery tray to relocate the heater hose brackets. *Photo courtesy of Gale Banks Engineering*

7

Using the supplied screw and locknut, the heater hose bracket has been relocated and the hoses have been repositioned away from the Torque Tubes. *Photo courtesy of Gale Banks Engineering*

When finished with the install, the included Banks Power sticker should be installed on both front fenders of the Jeep above the Wrangler sticker to show everyone what the rumble under the hood is all about. *Photo courtesy of Gale Banks Engineering*

PROJECT 15
Install a Bolt-on Exhaust System

 Time: 30 Hours

 Tools: Spray lubricant, socket set, pry bar, hand tools

Talent:

Applicable Years: All 4.0-liter and 3.8-liter Jeep engines

 Tab: $400

 Parts Required: Monster Exhaust System

 Tip: Do not begin to install or remove the factory exhaust system until the vehicle has had a chance to cool down, as exhaust components can be excessively hot.

 Performance Gain: Improved vehicle performance

 Complementary Project: Install aftermarket headers

A quick and inexpensive way to help get the most performance from your motor is to replace its exhaust system. Over the years, the system deteriorates, and the connections between the muffler and tubing rust and leak. Performance that used to be there diminishes, due to the internals of the muffler wearing out. Some telltale signs that your exhaust needs replacing are a sudden loss in low-end power, loud obnoxious noises from the rear of your vehicle, and the smell of exhaust fumes. No stranger to the requirements of Jeep owners, Gale Banks Engineering has created the Monster Exhaust system, which is a direct bolt-in replacement from the factory version.

Available for all Jeep 4.0-liter and 3.8-liter engines, the Monster Exhaust system is constructed entirely of heavy-gauge stainless steel and features a supersized, 2.5-inch tailpipe with a stainless tailpipe tip polished to a mirror finish. Banks' straight-through performance muffler is the industry's least restrictive, which means that it more than doubles the stock flow, not to mention that the size of the unit is smaller as well. Virtually eliminating back pressure from the catalytic converter back, this system should be on every Jeeper's performance upgrade list.

Installation is achieved easily by simply removing and unbolting the factory system and replacing it with the Monster Exhaust pieces. The Monster Exhaust components are connected using new stainless-steel 2.5-inch saddle clamps, which seal the fittings while still allowing some minor adjustments, either in or out of each other during the install.

1

The Monster Exhaust system is a complete bolt-on replacement kit that is available for all 4.0-liter and 3.8-liter Jeep engines. Included with the kit are a heavy-gauge stainless steel muffler, tubing, and a 2.5-inch tailpipe.
Photo courtesy of Gale Banks Engineering

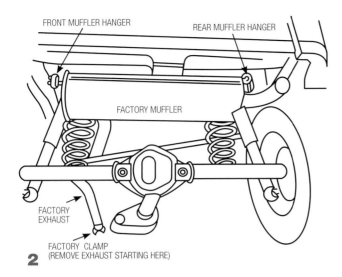

FRONT MUFFLER HANGER

REAR MUFFLER HANGER

FACTORY MUFFLER

FACTORY EXHAUST

FACTORY CLAMP (REMOVE EXHAUST STARTING HERE)

2

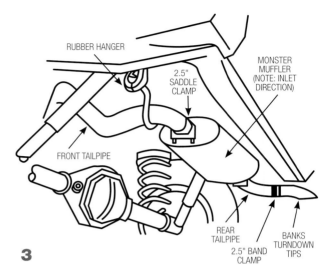

RUBBER HANGER

2.5" SADDLE CLAMP

MONSTER MUFFLER (NOTE: INLET DIRECTION)

FRONT TAILPIPE

REAR TAILPIPE

2.5" BAND CLAMP

BANKS TURNDOWN TIPS

3

To remove the rear muffler, the 2.5-inch factory clamp after the Y-pipe must be removed, which will then allow the muffler to be removed from the rubber hanger pins at the rear and front of the unit. Once the muffler is out of the way, the intermediate pipe assembly, the pipe between the catalytic converter and the muffler, can then be removed from the vehicle, making room for the new Monster Exhaust system. *Photo courtesy of Gale Banks Engineering*

With the entire factory exhaust removed, the new Banks system will install with ease. Place a 2.5-inch saddle clamp onto the inlet of the Banks front tailpipe. From the vehicle rear, route the tailpipe over the rear end. Install the tailpipe onto the intermediate pipe outlet. Insert the two hanger pins into the vehicle's rubber hangers and loosely tighten the 2.5-inch clamp. Following this, place another 2.5-inch saddle clamp onto the inlet of the Monster Muffler (the inlet of the muffler is labeled to avoid confusion) and install the Monster Muffler onto the front tailpipe. The muffler should be oriented in such a way that it is parallel to the cab and the Monster logo is visible once the exhaust is installed. Loosely tighten the 2.5-inch clamp. Using another 2.5-inch saddle clamp, install the rear tailpipe, which is supported by the hanger pin. *Photo courtesy of Gale Banks Engineering*

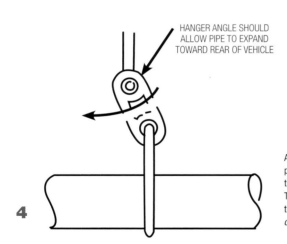

HANGER ANGLE SHOULD ALLOW PIPE TO EXPAND TOWARD REAR OF VEHICLE

4

Adjust each of the pipes to ensure that all of the hanger pins are parallel with the frame-mounted pins and that the rubber hangers are all positioned slightly forward. This allows the hangers to be properly positioned once the exhaust reaches operating temperature. *Photo courtesy of Gale Banks Engineering*

5

There is a definite difference between the size and quality of construction of the factory muffler compared with the Monster Muffler. In addition to its weight reduction, the smaller muffler is not as prone to hitting obstacles when off-road driving as the factory unit was, which could be another reason for its replacement. *Photo courtesy of Gale Banks Engineering*

6

Upon completion of the install, the new Monster Exhaust system will provide increased performance as well as a deep authoritative sound. *Photo courtesy of Gale Banks Engineering*

PROJECT 16
Install an Air Filter

  Time: 1/2 Hour

 Tools: None

 Talent:

Applicable Years: All

Tab: $18

  Parts Required: Air filter insert

 Tip: This can be performed while performing a routine inspection of other components.

 Performance Gain: Improved vehicle performance

Complementary Project: Vehicle inspection

Clean air is essential to the proper operation and longevity of your engine. The frequency with which the filter must be changed depends on where your Jeep is driven. If you are in dry, dusty conditions, your air filter will need to be changed more frequently than if you remained on the highway. Constructed in the form of an accordion, the filter fabric allows air to pass through it while debris remains embedded in the folds. While not difficult to install, the airbox lid is secured in place by four latches which must be unclipped for the top to be removed. To make the lid removal easier, the PCV hose that is attached to it is removed from the lid as well. Once off, the filter is lifted from its tray and a new unit is dropped in. The lid is reinstalled, and your engine is breathing clean once again.

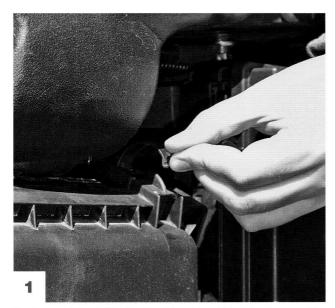

1 To gain access to the air filter, the airbox lid must be unlatched at each corner of the lid and lifted off the airbox and set aside.

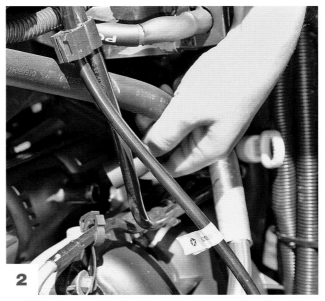

2 The PCV hose is removed from the airbox to allow the lid to be lifted off the airbox more easily.

3

The air filter is form-fitted to the interior dimensions of the airbox and has a rubber gasket built into it to help create a seal. It is easily lifted from the tray.

4

The filter shown here is only six months old, but after repeated trips to the desert, the dust and debris can be seen trapped inside the folds of the filter's fabric.

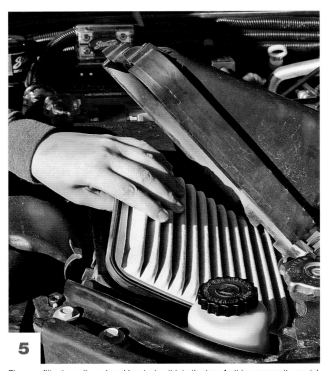

5

The new filter is easily replaced by placing it into the tray. As it is a new unit, special attention should be taken to ensure that it seats properly with an airtight seal formed at the edges.

6

When completed, the lid is reinstalled, the latches are resecured and the PCV hose is reattached so your engine can breathe and perform better.

PROJECT 17
Install Dual Batteries

 Time: 3½ Hours

 Tools: Socket set, crimper, hand tools

 Talent:

 Applicable Years: All models

 Tab: $700

Parts Required: Batteries, cables, solenoid, battery tray and brackets

 Tip: Prior to installation determine where the secondary battery is to be placed and verify the measurements of the battery cables for the appropriate lengths.

Performance Gain: Increase in on-demand power for auxiliary power items such as stereo systems, winches, and lights

 Complementary Project: Installation of a high-output alternator

The amount of electronics that are offered in today's marketplace for Jeeps is staggering. Everything from high-powered audio/video systems, global positioning system (GPS) units, winches, lights, refrigerators—if you can name it, it can be installed on your rig. Having all of these items and then some is great as long as your vehicle's charging system can sustain them. Install enough electronics or electrical-related items and suddenly the factory battery will not perform as required.

The factory battery system for many Jeeps has been designed to operate the original factory equipment, which consists of the starter motor, hazard lights, and a limited amount of car audio. When the loads of additional components are placed on the factory system, it becomes inadequate and a full system failure is inevitable. The solution is to install a dual battery system, which nearly doubles the reserve power your vehicle currently has and minimizes by half the possibility of a system failure. Once you have decided to install a dual battery setup, the next step is to select the type of batteries that will be used, as well as the type of isolator and the wiring configuration of the system.

BATTERY TYPES

Not all batteries are created equal, and when installing dual batteries, a deep-cycle type should be used, since it has high-cranking amps that hold up well to heavy starting loads and continual discharges. There are three types of lead-acid batteries: Flooded cell (wet cell), gel, and absorbed glass mat (AGM). A flooded cell (wet cell) battery utilizes older technology and a liquid (wet) battery uses acid. They require periodic maintenance and cleaning and are susceptible to damage caused from vibration. They are, however, a tried and true design and relatively inexpensive. A gel battery is one in which the battery acid is suspended in a silica-based gel, allowing the battery to be installed in virtually any position without the threat of leakage occurring and making them vibration-proof. The disadvantages with these types of batteries are the cost and their somewhat temperamental charging requirements. An AGM battery is sometimes referred to as a "dry cell" battery, which means that an electrolyte paste is absorbed into fine fiberglass mats to roughly 95 percent saturation and then sandwiched between the plates. The most popular type of AGM batteries are the "spiral cell" units, which resemble a six-pack. However, the more conventional box-type configuration has more cell volume, which translates to more reserve power. Given the nature of their construction, these batteries are the perfect choice for off-road driving since they withstand vibration and have high reserve powers.

ISOLATORS

Every dual battery system contains an isolator, which refers to the device's ability to isolate the primary battery from the secondary battery when a charging current is not present. There are four types of isolators to choose from, each with its own advantages and disadvantages. The four types of isolators are manual switches, diodes, solenoids, and metal-oxide-semiconductor field effect transistors (MOSFETs). A manual switch is the easiest type of isolator to use, given that the operator can select between combining, isolating, or individually charging the batteries. The challenge to this type of isolator is that it requires manual interaction, which may or may not always be the best, especially if there are other distractions present. A diode isolator is similar to a one-way valve, in that it allows the current to flow in only one direction. One of these isolators resembles a heat sink with three metal lugs mounted atop it. The drawbacks to these units is that the higher the amperage, typically the larger the unit—important when space is at a premium. A solenoid isolator (or relay) consists of heavy-duty mechanical contacts similar to those used on winches, starters, etc. These units function when the charging voltage drops below a preset level and the device switches to isolate the batteries. When charging resumes and the voltage increases to a preset level, the device connects both batteries to the charging current. Economical, durable, and easily installed, these are the most common types of isolators found in systems. The drawback to them is that the contacts may become pitted, causing voltage drops or possible failure. A MOSFET isolator is a sold-state device that is able to switch power without any moving parts. They can be sensitive to voltage spikes and power surges.

Their benefit is that they are small in size and put out no heat, as do some of the other isolators.

WIRING CONFIGURATION

Configuring your dual battery setup can be done in two ways. One way is to use your primary (starting) battery to run all of your accessory loads, leaving the secondary battery to be used for reserve capacity; the second way is to run all of the accessory loads from the secondary battery and leave the primary (starting) battery for starting the vehicle and operating the factory components. While there is no good way or bad way to configure the system, it will ultimately be up to you to decide how to wire it, based on the amount of accessories and your level of comfort between the two methods.

For our installation we utilized a set of Stinger "dry cell" batteries and a solenoid type of isolator. Custom secondary battery brackets were fabricated, along with custom charging cables. Utilizing advanced battery technology, the Stinger batteries produce a staggering high-current capability, superior fast-recharge rate, and a true deep-cycle operation. These batteries allow for a complete discharge with no negative effects; which is exactly what is needed in order for the charging system to function properly with multiple items attached to it.

1 When the alternator is not running, any electrical auxiliary components that are turned on are functioning solely on battery power. Depending upon the age, capacity, and functionality of the system, this could drain the factory battery in a matter of minutes. It is quite possible even that it could cause a major malfunction in the system altogether.

2 For our purposes, we utilized the Stinger SP680 for our secondary battery, given its small footprint. For our primary battery, we used the Stinger SP1500d, which features an impressive amount of power and a five-second discharge of 1,500 amps, 825 cold cranking amps, and a reserve capacity of 120 minutes. Both units feature extremely fast recharge capabilities.

3 A solenoid isolator was used to connect both batteries together. The function of the solenoid isolator is such that when the charging voltage drops below a preset level, the device switches to isolate the batteries. When charging resumes and the voltage increases to a preset level, the device connects both batteries to the charging current. They are also economical, durable, and easy to install.

4 A custom-fabricated battery bracket was installed for the secondary battery to keep it in place during those off-road expeditions. The bracket is secure to the top of the inner fender well for a solid foundation.

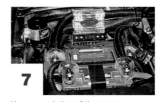

5 Once the batteries have been installed, the new charging cables are attached. Given the tight space constraints, the top terminals of both batteries were used; however, if the opportunity exists, the side terminals may be used as well.

6 The main cable from the alternator to the primary battery is resecured to the fuse block. When performing the install, this cable should be disconnected to avoid any potential hazards to either the installer or the vehicle's electrical components.

7 Upon completion of the system, your battery reserve capacity is theoretically doubled, and the chances of system failure have been cut in half.

PROJECT 18
Upgrade to a High-Output Alternator

 Time: 2 Hours

 Tools: Socket set, open-ended wrenches, screwdrivers, drill, drill bits, wire cutters

Talent:

 Applicable Years: All

 Tab: $900 to $1,200, based on vehicle model

 Parts Required: Alternator, cable ties, wire loom

 Tip: Make sure that the vehicle is off and disconnect the cables to the battery prior to beginning the upgrade.

 Performance Gain: Improves the performance of the charging and electrical system components

 Complementary Project: Installation of a dual battery setup

It is not out of the ordinary for a well-built and trail-capable Jeep to have numerous items installed on it. Items such as auxiliary lights, a winch, a high-power stereo system, various CB and VHF radios, a portable refrigerator, an on-board welder, and a host of other electrical gadgets all need a tremendous amount of power, and they take their toll on a vehicle's charging system. All too often the factory alternator on a Jeep is unable to supply these high demands, and the alternator fails. This causes uneven voltage to the system components, which in turn causes them to become damaged. To protect yourself and your electrical equipment, we suggest upgrading your factory alternator with a high-output version. In their factory forms, alternators only put out 60 to 70 amps, which is nothing when all of these components are installed. The typical high-output alternator puts out anywhere from 150 to 250 amps, proving to be more than enough power to handle all of these items without so much as a hiccup.

Known for their high-output units, Wrangler NW Power Products alternators are custom built to deliver a higher output at idle than factory units. Wrangler's alternators feature hand-wound stator windings using heavy-gauge wire and 200-degree Celsius slot insulation; precision balanced and aligned rotors; copper brushes with heavy-gauge wire leads; oversized bearings to handle extreme belt loads; and Grade 8 socket head bolts with Nordlock high-torque lock washers for mechanical stability. They also utilize 50-amp button diodes on aluminum heat sinks to enhance the alternator's cooling efficiencies. Given the tremendous amount of auxiliary equipment on our Jeep, we installed a 250-amp high-output unit that has performed flawlessly.

Upon our completion of the new alternator installation, we noticed a considerable increase in the brightness of our interior dome lights as well as our headlights, all proof that the high-output unit was just what we needed to get back in the thick of things.

1

The factory alternator is removed from the vehicle to make room for the new high-output model. A typical factory alternator generates between 60 and 70 amps, which pales in comparison to our 250-amp unit.

2

One of the benefits to installing a Wrangler NW Power Products alternator is that their units retain the factory cases and are completely rebuilt with all-new components from the ground up. By retaining the factory alternator case, the new unit bolts into the factory location with ease.

3

The factory serpentine belt can still be used. Here the belt tensioner is being relieved to allow the belt to be reinstalled onto the pulleys.

4

Given the increase in power output, higher-gauge cable is required. The new cable replaces the factory units to both the battery and the engine ground.

5

Included in the new power bale kit is a 250-amp circuit breaker that is placed inline between the battery and the alternator to prevent any overcharging, should the alternator fail.

6

Based upon the sheer thickness of the new power cable, a number of cable ties were needed to secure it to the firewall to keep it protected from moving parts of the engine as well as to shield it from heat.

7

The new alternator power cable has been attached to our dual battery setup, which solidifies the fact that our charging and electrical system is now up to par with all of the components that we have added to the vehicle.

8

The new alternator is installed and looks exactly as if it were a factory unit, with one exception; the pulley on the new unit is fabricated from a solid piece of billet aluminum and is smaller in diameter than the factory one. This is required, given the increase in power that is being produced.

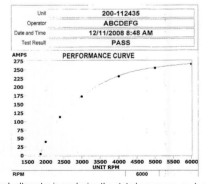

9

To verify that each alternator is producing the stated amperage, each of Wrangler's high-output alternators is bench tested prior to delivery. As you can see from our alternator's test sheet, it is producing an incredible 266 amps and has passed with flying colors.

PROJECT 19
Install an Aluminum Radiator

 Time: 3 Hours

 Tools: Socket set, hose clamp tool

 Talent:

 Applicable Years: All

Tab: $1,000

Parts Required: Hose clamps, hoses, radiator cap, mounting hardware, electrical connections, and antifreeze

 Tip: Prior to the installation, make sure the mounting foundation has been sized accordingly and that it is ready for the radiator to be mounted on.

 Performance Gain: Improved cooling and engine performance

 Complementary Project: Installation of braided stainless steel hoses and a new thermostat

Replacing your old radiator with a new aluminum version is one of the best items that you can spend your money on, and your engine will thank you. Over the years, the stock brass and copper units become degraded with clogged tubes, corroded fittings, and bent heat fins, which reduce the cooling properties of the unit. The occasional rock or tree limb penetrating the unit may also be another reason for replacing the unit. Rather than put good money into bad trying to get a stock unit repaired or reconditioned, spending the money on an aluminum version is definitely the way to go.

Right off the bat, an aluminum radiator will weigh less, increase performance, and provide a custom appearance to your engine bay. While there are numerous manufacturers of aluminum radiators, the units that PWR Performance Products build have been designed with off-road driving in mind. Knowing that a Jeep can sit idle for long periods while the rigs in front of it are traversing a trail, PWR builds radiators with dual Spal electric cooling fans installed on them from the factory, which provides an increase in the cooling capacity of the radiator. Considering the additional cooling fins, wider interior tube configurations, high-quality components, TIG welding, and 30 percent more efficiency than a stock unit, it's a no-brainer that every Jeep should have one.

1 Installing an aluminum radiator such as this unit from PWR Performance Products will increase your performance and decrease your engine's temperature. When your Jeep is stuck on a trail for a few hours and moving 3 miles per hour or less, this can be a big benefit.

2 Dual Spal electric fans, included on this unit can provide up to 2,500 cfm each of air movement.

3

Prior to installation, the core support of the vehicle must be measured to ensure that the new unit will fit and have plenty of clearance. The mounting plates must be in alignment with the mounting locations on the new radiator.

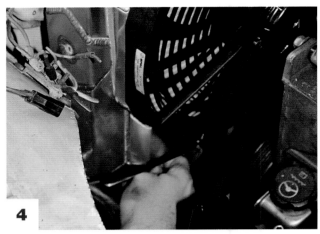

4

Once situated in place, the unit should be secured to the vehicle to measure for hose lengths and to connect the electric fan wiring.

5

The top and bottom hoses should be installed next. New hose clamps should be used to guarantee a tight fit.

6

A new cap and gasket should also be used, since chances are that the previous one will not be compatible with the new unit. Also, after time, the gaskets tend to dry out, which could cause the system to not be sealed completely.

7

A new overflow vent hose is also installed for the same reasons as the new radiator cap.

8

The new unit features a trick brass purge valve, which will assist in removing any excess air from the system. This will eliminate any chances of vapor lock in the system.

9

With the install complete, the heart of the cooling system looks good, and it will perform better than its predecessor, at almost half the weight.

PROJECT 20
Reprogram Electronic Control Unit (ECU) for Larger Tire Size

 Time: 1/2 Hour

 Tools: Personal computer, tire gauge, air hose, tape measure

 Talent:

 Applicable Years: All

 Tab: $225

 Parts Required: Programmer module

 Tip: Make sure the tires are inflated to the appropriate pressures, as the tire pressure affects the vehicle height.

 Performance Gain: Improves the performance of the engine and transmission by resetting the speedometer/odometer calibration and factory transmission shift points

 Complementary Project: Reprogram the ECU for added horsepower and torque

With the technical advancement of today's vehicle computer and operating systems, it is getting more difficult to alter a vehicle without affecting it. Take for instance the Jeep Wrangler JK model, with a minimal amount of suspension lift, 35-inch tires can be fitted on the vehicle. However, as soon as these larger tires are installed and hit the ground, the factory shift points and speedometer/odometer settings are miscalibrated. The same is true for when gear ratios are adjusted to compensate for the larger tires. To reestablish the factory settings to take into consideration the new tire size and gear ratio, the HyperMax Speedometer Calibrator has been created.

By connecting the tuner to your JK's OBDII diagnostic port, the factory settings are once again established but have taken the new add-ons into consideration. The programming is relatively easy and requires a personal computer and information on the height of the new tires and the gear ratio size. The end result is a definite change in performance for the better.

1 By reprogramming the ECM on the vehicle, the factory shift points of the transmission as well as the factory speedometer and odometer calibrations are reset, taking the new tire and gear ratio (if changed) into account.

2 A personal computer is required as part of the install, since the software used in the tuner is contained on the supplied CD-ROM. Insert the CD-ROM into your computer's disc drive and load the program.

3

Once the software is installed, the supplied USB cable must be connected to both the computer and the tuner, so it can be updated with the latest firmware available.

4

Prior to connecting the tuner to the vehicle's factory port, the tires should be measured to determine their height. Also, if it has changed, the new gear ratio should also be available.

5

The tuner is supplied with a cable that will connect it to the Jeep OBD II diagnostic port. Connect both devices and do not disturb the device. It will then instruct you to turn the ignition on.

6

Once connected and communicating with your vehicle's ECM, the tuner display will check to see if your vehicle has any diagnostic codes (DTCs) stored in the computer. If there are such codes, they will be displayed and you will be given the choice of clearing them. Have a pen and paper handy to write them down. If there are any codes found, you will have to clear then in order to proceed with the reprogramming.

7

As the programming continues, the display will walk you through the steps by asking questions that you will answer either yes or no by pushing the corresponding buttons on the tuner. It will also ask for the gear ratio and tire height to be input, once again using the corresponding buttons on the tuner.

8

After the tuner is completed with the reprogramming, you will be notified to disconnect the cable from the OBD II diagnostic port to complete the process.

PROJECT 21
Checking and Translating Diagnostic Trouble Codes (DTCs)

 Time: 1/2 Hour

 Tools: Pencil, paper

 Talent:

 Applicable Years: Jeep Wrangler JK (two-door and four-door models)

Tab: None

 Parts Required: Ignition key

 Tip: Have your pencil and paper ready so that you can transcribe the diagnostic codes.

 Performance Gain: Improved vehicle performance by correcting the DTCs

 Complementary Project: None

Computers rule the world, and we humans only operate them. From our offices to the vehicles we drive—yes, even our beloved Jeep—it seems as though behind every item is a computer operating system. We are occasionally reminded of their stature and power in our vehicles when driving our Jeep Wrangler JK and a malfunction indicator light (MIL) is illuminated on our dashboard, usually in the shape of an engine, with no rhyme or reason. When this light is seen, the mind begins to wonder just how many more minutes until the vehicle explodes. Often, after a quick trip to the dealership for either a reset or to correct the problem, the light vanishes. While definitely worth having as a feature for safety and vehicle maintenance, the only problem is that the light does not provide any specifics as to why it went on. That is often left for the mechanics to determine, once an hour or so has been spent at the dealership. If you're like us, we want to know the cause for it immediately. After a few top-secret luncheons with some Jeep technicians, we stumbled upon a method that anyone can use to retrieve the specific Diagnostic Trouble Codes (DTCs) that trigger the light. We also learned what each of the encrypted codes means.

Checking the DTCs can be used anytime, regardless of whether the MIL is illuminated. The first step is to enter the vehicle, insert the key in the ignition, and turn it to the ON position. This is as far as you should turn it; the engine should not be started at this time. Following this step, the key should be turned back and forth from the ON position to the OFF position three times with the key finishing at the ON position; the engine is still not to be started. If performed correctly, all of the dashboard lights will turn on and the indicator screen where the odometer is will display a series of dashes. If there are any DTCs logged into your computer's memory, they will be displayed at this time. If there are any, they should be transcribed so that they can be checked to determine what they are for. Shortly after they are displayed, the indicator screen will display the word DONE. If no codes are shown, the screen will go from the dashes to the word DONE immediately. Once the word DONE has been displayed, it is safe to turn the key to the OFF position and remove it from the ignition.

JEEP JK COMPUTER DIAGNOSTIC CODES

B1001—A/C SWITCH REQUEST INPUT CIRCUIT LOW (ATC and MTC)

B1002—A/C SWITCH REQUEST INPUT CIRCUIT HIGH (CCN)

B1016—REAR DEFROST SWITCH INPUT CIRCUIT LOW (CCN)

B1031—EVAPORATOR FIN TEMPERATURE SENSOR CIRCUIT LOW (MTC)

B1032—EVAPORATOR FIN TEMPERATURE SENSOR CIRCUIT HIGH (MTC)

B10C1—A/C SELECT SWITCH STUCK (CCN)

B10C2—REAR DEFROST SWITCH STUCK—CLUSTER

B123F—MENU SWITCH STUCK

B127A—COMPASS PERFORMANCE

B1288—TRIP/TOGGLE SWITCH PERFORMANCE

B1401—FRONT LEFT AUDIO SPEAKER OUTPUT CIRCUIT LOW

B1402—FRONT LEFT AUDIO SPEAKER OUTPUT CIRCUIT HIGH

B1403—FRONT LEFT AUDIO SPEAKER OUTPUT CIRCUIT OPEN

B1405—FRONT RIGHT AUDIO SPEAKER OUTPUT CIRCUIT LOW

B1406—FRONT RIGHT AUDIO SPEAKER OUTPUT CIRCUIT HIGH

B1407—FRONT RIGHT AUDIO SPEAKER OUTPUT CIRCUIT OPEN

B1409—REAR LEFT AUDIO SPEAKER OUTPUT CIRCUIT LOW

B140A—REAR LEFT AUDIO SPEAKER OUTPUT CIRCUIT HIGH

B140B—REAR LEFT AUDIO SPEAKER OUTPUT CIRCUIT OPEN

B140D—REAR RIGHT AUDIO SPEAKER OUTPUT CIRCUIT LOW

B140E—REAR RIGHT AUDIO SPEAKER OUTPUT CIRCUIT HIGH

B140F—REAR RIGHT AUDIO SPEAKER OUTPUT CIRCUIT OPEN

B1420—AUDIO CASSETTE ERROR/ INOPERABLE CASSETTE

B1421—AUDIO CD READ ERROR/INOPERABLE DISC

B1422—AUDIO DVD READ ERROR/ INOPERABLE DISC

B1423—VES DVD READ ERROR/INOPERABLE DISC

B1424—IMPROPER DVDWRONG REGION

B1429—RADIO DISPLAY HIGH TEMPERATURE

B142A—RADIO UNIT HIGH TEMPERATURE

B142C—VES VIDEO SCREEN DISCONNECTED

B142D—AUDIO ANTENNA NOT CONNECTED

B142E—GPS ANTENNA NOT CONNECTED

B142F—SATELLITE RADIO ANTENNA NOT CONNECTED

B1430—SATELLITE RADIO ANTENNA INTERNAL PERFORMANCE

B1460—CHANNEL 1 AUDIO SPEAKER OUTPUT CIRCUIT PERFORMANCE

B1461—CHANNEL 1 AUDIO SPEAKER OUTPUT CIRCUIT LOW

B1462—CHANNEL 1 AUDIO SPEAKER OUTPUT CIRCUIT HIGH

B1463—CHANNEL 1 AUDIO SPEAKER OUTPUT CIRCUIT OPEN

B1464—CHANNEL 1 AUDIO SPEAKER OUTPUT CIRCUIT SHORTED TOGETHER

B1465—CHANNEL 2 AUDIO SPEAKER OUTPUT CIRCUIT PERFORMANCE

B1466—CHANNEL 2 AUDIO SPEAKER OUTPUT CIRCUIT LOW

B1467—CHANNEL 2 AUDIO SPEAKER OUTPUT CIRCUIT HIGH

B1468—CHANNEL 2 AUDIO SPEAKER OUTPUT CIRCUIT OPEN

B1469—CHANNEL 2 AUDIO SPEAKER OUTPUT CIRCUIT SHORTED TOGETHER

B146A—CHANNEL 3 AUDIO SPEAKER OUTPUT CIRCUIT PERFORMANCE

B146B—CHANNEL 3 AUDIO SPEAKER OUTPUT CIRCUIT LOW

B146C—CHANNEL 3 AUDIO SPEAKER OUTPUT CIRCUIT HIGH

B146D—CHANNEL 3 AUDIO SPEAKER OUTPUT CIRCUIT OPEN

B146E—CHANNEL 3 AUDIO SPEAKER OUTPUT CIRCUIT SHORTED TOGETHER

B146F—CHANNEL 4 AUDIO SPEAKER OUTPUT CIRCUIT PERFORMANCE

B1470—CHANNEL 4 AUDIO SPEAKER OUTPUT CIRCUIT LOW

B1471—CHANNEL 4 AUDIO SPEAKER OUTPUT CIRCUIT HIGH

B1472—CHANNEL 4 AUDIO SPEAKER OUTPUT CIRCUIT OPEN

B1473—CHANNEL 4 AUDIO SPEAKER OUTPUT CIRCUIT SHORTED TOGETHER

B1474—CHANNEL 5 AUDIO SPEAKER OUTPUT CIRCUIT PERFORMANCE

B1475—CHANNEL 5 AUDIO SPEAKER OUTPUT CIRCUIT LOW

B1476—CHANNEL 5 AUDIO SPEAKER OUTPUT CIRCUIT HIGH

B1477—CHANNEL 5 AUDIO SPEAKER OUTPUT CIRCUIT OPEN

B1478—CHANNEL 5 AUDIO SPEAKER OUTPUT CIRCUIT SHORTED TOGETHER

B1479—CHANNEL 6 AUDIO SPEAKER OUTPUT CIRCUIT PERFORMANCE

B147A—CHANNEL 6 AUDIO SPEAKER OUTPUT CIRCUIT LOW

B147B—CHANNEL 6 AUDIO SPEAKER OUTPUT CIRCUIT HIGH

B147C—CHANNEL 6 AUDIO SPEAKER OUTPUT CIRCUIT OPEN

B147D—CHANNEL 6 AUDIO SPEAKER OUTPUT CIRCUIT SHORTED TOGETHER

B1613—PANEL ILLUMINATION CONTROL CIRCUIT LOW

B1615—PANEL ILLUMINATION CONTROL CIRCUIT OPEN

B161A—COURTESY/DOME LAMP CONTROL CIRCUIT

B161E—READING LAMP CONTROL CIRCUIT

B162B—LEFT LOW BEAM CONTROL CIRCUIT LOW

B162C—LT LOW BEAM CONTROL CKT HI

B162F—RIGHT LOW BEAM CONTROL CIRCUIT LOW

B1630—RIGHT LOW BEAM CONTROL CIRCUIT HIGH

B1633—LEFT HI BEAM CONTROL CIRCUIT LOW

B1634—LEFT HI BEAM CONTROL CIRCUIT HIGH

B1637—RIGHT HI BEAM CONTROL CIRCUIT LOW

B1638—RIGHT HI BEAM CONTROL CIRCUIT HIGH

B163B—FRONT LEFT TURN CONTROL CIRCUIT LOW

B163C—FRONT LEFT TURN CONTROL CIRCUIT HIGH

B163F—FRONT RIGHT TURN CONTROL CIRCUIT LOW

B1640—FRONT RIGHT TURN CONTROL CIRCUIT HIGH

B1643—REAR LEFT TURN CONTROL CIRCUIT LOW

B1644—REAR LEFT TURN CONTROL CIRCUIT HIGH

B1645—RIGHT STOP LAMP CONTROL CIRCUIT HIGH

B1647—REAR RIGHT TURN CONTROL CIRCUIT LOW

B1648—REAR RIGHT TURN CONTROL CIRCUIT HIGH

B1663—REAR FOG LAMP CONTROL CIRCUIT LOW

B1664—REAR FOG LAMP CONTROL CIRCUIT HIGH

B166B—LEFT TRAILER TOW LAMP CONTROL CIRCUIT LOW

B166C—LEFT TRAILER TOW LAMP CONTROL CIRCUIT HIGH

B166F—RIGHT TRAILER TOW LAMP CONTROL CIRCUIT LOW

B1670—RIGHT TRAILER TOW LAMP CONTROL CIRCUIT HIGH

B16B1—LEFT STOP LAMP CONTROL CIRCUIT HIGH

B16F8—FRONT LEFT FOG LAMP CONTROL CIRCUIT LOW

B16F9—FRONT LEFT FOG LAMP CONTROL CIRCUIT HIGH

B16FC—FRONT RIGHT FOG LAMP CONTROL CIRCUIT LOW

B16FD—FRONT RIGHT FOG LAMP CONTROL CIRCUIT HIGH

B17B8—LEFT STOP LAMP CONTROL CIRCUIT OVERCURRENT

B17B9—RIGHT STOP LAMP CONTROL CIRCUIT OVERCURRENT

B17BA—HEADLAMP LEVELING MOTOR CONTROL CIRCUIT OVERCURRENT

B17BF—LEFT SIDEMARKER LAMP CONTROL CIRCUIT OVERCURRENT

B17C4—RIGHT SIDEMARKER LAMP CONTROL CIRCUIT OVERCURRENT

B1801—DRIVER DOOR LOCK/UNLOCK SWITCH CIRCUIT LOW—CLUSTER

B1806—PASSENGER DOOR LOCK/UNLOCK SWITCH CIRCUIT LOW—TIPM

B1934—DRIVER DOOR LOCK/UNLOCK SWITCH CIRCUIT STUCK—CLUSTER

B1935—PASSENGER DOOR LOCK/UNLOCK SWITCH CIRCUIT STUCK—TIPM

B1A08—RKE FOB 1 PERFORMANCE

B1A09—RKE FOB 2 PERFORMANCE

B1A0A—RKE FOB 3 PERFORMANCE

B1A0B—RKE FOB 4 PERFORMANCE

B1A0C—RKE FOB 5 PERFORMANCE

B1A0D—RKE FOB 6 PERFORMANCE

B1A0E—RKE FOB 7 PERFORMANCE

B1A0F—RKE FOB 8 PERFORMANCE

B1A10—RKE FOB 1 BATTERY LOW

B1A11—RKE FOB 2 BATTERY LOW

B1A12—RKE FOB 3 BATTERY LOW

B1A13—RKE FOB 4 BATTERY LOW

B1A14—RKE FOB 5 BATTERY LOW

B1A15—RKE FOB 6 BATTERY LOW

B1A16—RKE FOB 7 BATTERY LOW

B1A17—RKE FOB 8 BATTERY LOW

B1A20—PRE_ARM TIMEOUT

B1A23—RKE RECEIVER PERFORMANCE

B1A24—KEY NOT PROGRAMMED

B1A25—INVALID KEY

B1A26—MAXIMUM NUMBER OF KEYS PROGRAMMED

B1A27—SKREEM PROGRAMMING PERFORMANCE

B1A28—ECM MISMATCH WITH SKIM

B1A29—SKIM BASESTATION MISMATCH

B1A3C—INTERNAL SIREN BATTERY

B1A3D—SIREN BATTERY/LOSS OF POWER SUPPLY

B1A3E—SIREN/ITM MISMATCH

B1A3F—ITM ARMING SEQUENCE PERFORMANCE

B1A48—INTRUSION SENSOR 1 INTERNAL

B1A5F—INTRUSION SENSOR 2 INTERNAL

B1A6D—INTRUSION SENSOR 3 INTERNAL

B1B00—DRIVER AIRBAG SQUIB 1 CIRCUIT LOW

B1B01—DRIVER AIRBAG SQUIB 1 CIRCUIT HIGH

B1B02—DRIVER AIRBAG SQUIB 1 CIRCUIT OPEN

B1B03—DRIVER AIRBAG SQUIB 1 CIRCUIT SHORTED TOGETHER

B1B04—DRIVER AIRBAG SQUIB 2 CIRCUIT LOW

B1B05—DRIVER AIRBAG SQUIB 2 CIRCUIT HIGH

B1B06—DRIVER AIRBAG SQUIB 2 CIRCUIT OPEN

B1B07—DRIVER AIRBAG SQUIB 2 CIRCUIT SHORTED TOGETHER

B1B08—PASSENGER AIRBAG SQUIB 1 CIRCUIT LOW

B1B09—PASSENGER AIRBAG SQUIB 1 CIRCUIT HIGH

B1B0A—PASSENGER AIRBAG SQUIB 1 CIRCUIT OPEN

B1B0B—PASSENGER AIRBAG SQUIB 1 CIRCUIT SHORTED TOGETHER

B1B0C—PASSENGER AIRBAG SQUIB 2 CIRCUIT LOW

B1B0D—PASSENGER AIRBAG SQUIB 2 CIRCUIT HIGH

B1B0E—PASSENGER AIRBAG SQUIB 2 CIRCUIT OPEN

B1B0F—PASSENGER AIRBAG SQUIB 2 CIRCUITS SHORTED TOGETHER

B1B54—1ST ROW PASSENGER SEAT BELT SENSOR CIRCUIT LOW

B1B55—1ST ROW PASSENGER SEAT BELT SENSOR CIRCUIT HIGH

B1B56—1ST ROW PASSENGER SEAT BELT SENSOR CIRCUIT OPEN

B1B70—UP_FRONT LEFT SATELLITE ACCELERATION SENSOR INTERNAL

B1B71—UP_FRONT RIGHT SATELLITE ACCELERATION SENSOR INTERNAL

B1B72—LEFT SIDE SATELLITE ACCELERATION SENSOR 1 INTERNAL

B1B75—RIGHT SIDE SATELLITE ACCELERATION SENSOR 1 INTERNAL

B1B78—PASSENGER SEAT WEIGHT SENSOR 3—LEFT FRONT PERFORMANCE

B1B79—PASSENGER SEAT WEIGHT SENSOR 3—LEFT FRONT INPUT CIRCUIT LOW

B1B7A—PASSENGER SEAT WEIGHT SENSOR 3—LEFT FRONT INPUT CIRCUIT HIGH

B1B7D—PASSENGER SEAT WEIGHT SENSOR 2—RIGHT FRONT PERFORMANCE

B1B7E—PASSENGER SEAT WEIGHT SENSOR 2—RIGHT FRONT INPUT CIRCUIT LOW

B1B7F—PASSENGER SEAT WEIGHT SENSOR 2—RIGHT FRONT INPUT CIRCUIT HIGH

B1B82—PASSENGER SEAT WEIGHT SENSOR 4—LEFT REAR PERFORMANCE

B1B83—PASSENGER SEAT WEIGHT SENSOR 4—LEFT REAR INPUT CIRCUIT LOW

B1B84—PASSENGER SEAT WEIGHT SENSOR 4—LEFT REAR INPUT CIRCUIT HIGH

B1B87—PASSENGER SEAT WEIGHT SENSOR 1—RIGHT REAR PERFORMANCE

B1B88—PASSENGER SEAT WEIGHT SENSOR 1—RIGHT REAR INPUT CIRCUIT LOW

B1B89—PASSENGER SEAT WEIGHT SENSOR 1—RIGHT REAR INPUT CIRCUIT HIGH

B1B8D—DRIVER SEAT TRACK POSITION SENSOR CIRCUIT LOW

B1B8E—DRIVER SEAT TRACK POSITION SENSOR CIRCUIT HIGH

B1B8F—DRIVER SEAT TRACK POSITION SENSOR CIRCUIT OPEN

B1B93—PASSENGER SEAT TRACK POSITION SENSOR CIRCUIT LOW

B1B94—PASSENGER SEAT TRACK POSITION SENSOR CIRCUIT HIGH

B1B95—PASSENGER SEAT TRACK POSITION SENSOR CIRCUIT OPEN

B1BA5—AIRBAG SQUIB CONFIGURATION MISMATCH

B1BA6—OCCUPANT CLASSIFICATION UNDETERMINED

B1BA7—OCCUPANT CLASSIFICATION SYSTEM VERIFICATION REQUIRED

B1BA8—OCM SYSTEM OUT OF CALIBRATION/NOT CALIBRATED

B1BAA—OCCUPANT CLASSIFICATION MODULE CONFIGURATION MISMATCH

B1BBA—PASSENGER SEAT WEIGHT SENSOR SUPPLY CIRCUIT

B1BBB—PASSENGER SEAT WEIGHT SENSOR INPUTS SHORTED TOGETHER

B1BBC—OCS NEGATIVE SYSTEM WEIGHT

B1BBD—OCM CURRENT CONFIGURATION TABLE UNPROGRAMMED

B1BC7—DEPLOYMENT DATA RECORD FULL

B1C27—LEFT SIDE SEAT THORAX SQUIB 1 LOW

B1C28—LEFT SIDE SEAT THORAX SQUIB 1 HIGH

B1C29—LEFT SIDE SEAT THORAX SQUIB 1 OPEN

B1C2A—LEFT SIDE SEAT THORAX SQUIB 1 SHORTED TOGETHER

B1C2B—RIGHT SIDE SEAT THORAX SQUIB 1 LOW

B1C2C—RIGHT SIDE SEAT THORAX SQUIB 1 HIGH

B1C2D—RIGHT SIDE SEAT THORAX SQUIB 1 OPEN

B1C2E—RIGHT SIDE SEAT THORAX SQUIB 1 SHORTED TOGETHER

B1C38—1ST ROW DRIVER RETRACTOR PRETENSIONER CIRCUIT LOW

B1C39—1ST ROW DRIVER RETRACTOR PRETENSIONER CIRCUIT HIGH

B1C3A—1ST ROW DRIVER RETRACTOR PRETENSIONER CIRCUIT OPEN

B1C3B—1ST ROW DRIVER RETRACTOR PRETENSIONER CIRCUIT SHORTED TOGETHER

B1C47—1ST ROW PASSENGER RETRACTOR PRETENSIONER CIRCUIT LOW

B1C48—1ST ROW PASSENGER RETRACTOR PRETENSIONER CIRCUIT HIGH

B1C49—1ST ROW PASSENGER RETRACTOR PRETENSIONER CIRCUIT OPEN

B1C4A—1ST ROW PASSENGER RETRACTOR PRETENSIONER CIRCUIT SHORTED TOGETHER

B2101—IGNITION RUN/START INPUT CIRCUIT LOW

B2101—IGNITION RUN/START INPUT CIRCUIT LOW

B2102—IGNITION RUN/START INPUT CIRCUIT HIGH

B2102—IGNITION RUN/START INPUT CIRCUIT HIGH

B210A—SYSTEM VOLTAGE LOW (WCM)

B210B—SYSTEM VOLTAGE HIGH (WCM)

B210D—BATTERY VOLTAGE LOW (WCM)

B210D—BATTERY VOLTAGE LOW

B210E—BATTERY VOLTAGE HIGH (WCM)

B212C—IGNITION RUN/START INPUT CIRCUIT OPEN

B212D—IGNITION RUN ONLY INPUT CIRCUIT OPEN

B2142—IGNITION OFF DRAW (IOD) FUSE NOT PRESENT

B219A—IGNITION UNLOCK RUN/START CONTROL CIRCUIT OVERCURRENT

B219F—IGNITION OFF DRAW (IOD) FUSE BLOWN

B2201—CALIBRATION MISMATCH

B2204—ECU CONFIGURATION MISMATCH

B2205—ORIGINAL VIN MISSING/MISMATCH

B2206—CURRENT VIN MISSING / MISMATCH

B2207—OCCUPANT RESTRAINT CONTROLLER INTERNAL 1

B2208—OCCUPANT RESTRAINT CONTROLLER INTERNAL 2

B2209—OCCUPANT RESTRAINT CONTROLLER INTERNAL 3

B220A—OCCUPANT RESTRAINT CONTROLLER INTERNAL 4

B220B—OCCUPANT RESTRAINT CONTROLLER FIRING STORED ENERGY

B220C—OCCUPANT RESTRAINT CONTROLLER ACCELEROMETER 1 INTERNAL

B220D—OCCUPANT RESTRAINT CONTROLLER ACCELEROMETER 2 INTERNAL

B2212—OCCUPANT CLASSIFICATION MODULE INTERNAL

B2222—SATELLITE RADIO RECEIVER INTERNAL

B2224—SKREEM INTERNAL

B2229—SKREEM INTERNAL—SKIM IMMOBILIZER

B222A—VEHICLE LINE MISMATCH

B222C—VEHICLE CONFIGURATION NOT PROGRAMMED

B223B—VEHICLE CONFIGURATION MISMATCH

B223C—INTRUSION TRANSCEIVER MODULE INTERNAL

B223D—OCCUPANT CLASSIFICATION MODULE DTC PRESENT

B2254—COLUMN LOCK MODULE INTERNAL

B2304—WIPER PARK SWITCH INPUT CIRCUIT LOW

B2305—WIPER PARK SWITCH INPUT CIRCUIT HIGH

B230D—REAR WIPER PARK SWITCH INPUT CIRCUIT LOW (STUCK LOW)

B230E—REAR WIPER PARK SWITCH INPUT CIRCUIT HIGH (STUCK HIGH)

B2323—HEADLAMP WASHER MOTOR CONTROL CIRCUIT LOW

B2324—HEADLAMP WASHER MOTOR CONTROL CIRCUIT HIGH

B2339—HORN SWITCH STUCK

C0077—LOW TIRE PRESSURE

C1404—TRANSFER CASE RANGE POSITION SENSOR CIRCUIT LOW (TIPM)

C1405—TRANSFER CASE RANGE POSITION SENSOR CIRCUIT HIGH (TIPM)

C1417—FRONT DIFFERENTIAL CONTROL CIRCUIT LOW

C1418—FRONT DIFFERENTIAL CONTROL CIRCUIT HIGH

C141D—REAR DIFFERENTIAL CONTROL CIRCUIT LOW

C141E—REAR DIFFERENTIAL CONTROL CIRCUIT HIGH

C1501—TIRE PRESSURE SENSOR 1 INTERNAL

C1502—TIRE PRESSURE SENSOR 2 INTERNAL

C1503—TIRE PRESSURE SENSOR 3 INTERNAL

C1504—TIRE PRESSURE SENSOR 4 INTERNAL

C2100—BATTERY VOLTAGE LOW

C2101—BATTERY VOLTAGE HIGH

C2207—OFF ROAD ECU INTERNAL

P0016—CRANKSHAFT/CAMSHAFT TIMING MISALIGNMENT

P0031—O2 SENSOR 1/1 HEATER CIRCUIT LOW

P0032—O2 SENSOR 1/1 HEATER CIRCUIT HIGH

P0037—O2 SENSOR 1/2 HEATER CIRCUIT LOW

P0038—O2 SENSOR 1/2 HEATER CIRCUIT HIGH

P0051—O2 SENSOR 2/1 HEATER CIRCUIT LOW

P0052—O2 SENSOR 2/1 HEATER CIRCUIT HIGH

P0057—O2 SENSOR 2/2 HEATER CIRCUIT LOW

P0058—O2 SENSOR 2/2 HEATER CIRCUIT HIGH

P0071—AMBIENT AIR TEMPERATURE SENSOR PERFORMANCE

P0072—AMBIENT AIR TEMPERATURE SENSOR CIRCUIT LOW

P0073—AMBIENT AIR TEMPERATURE SENSOR CIRCUIT HIGH

P0107—MANIFOLD ABSOLUTE PRESSURE SENSOR CIRCUIT LOW

P0108—MANIFOLD ABSOLUTE PRESSURE SENSOR CIRCUIT HIGH

P0111—INTAKE AIR TEMPERATURE SENSOR RATIONALITY

P0112—INTAKE AIR TEMPERATURE SENSOR CIRCUIT LOW

P0113—INTAKE AIR TEMPERATURE SENSOR CIRCUIT HIGH

P0116—ENGINE COOLANT TEMPERATURE SENSOR PERFORMANCE

P0117—ENGINE COOLANT TEMPERATURE SENSOR CIRCUIT LOW

P0118—ENGINE COOLANT TEMPERATURE SENSOR CIRCUIT HIGH

P0121—THROTTLE POSITION SENSOR 1 PERFORMANCE

P0122—TPS/APPS CIRCUIT LOW

P0122—THROTTLE POSITION SENSOR 1 CIRCUIT LOW

P0123—TPS/APP CIRCUIT HIGH

P0123—THROTTLE POSITION SENSOR 1 CIRCUIT HIGH

P0124—TPS/APP INTERMITTENT

P0125—INSUFFICIENT COOLANT TEMPERATURE FOR CLOSED_LOOP FUEL CONTROL

P0128—THERMOSTAT RATIONALITY

P0129—BAROMETRIC PRESSURE OUT_OF_RANGE LOW

P0131—O2 SENSOR 1/1 CIRCUIT LOW

P0132—O2 SENSOR 1/1 CIRCUIT HIGH

P0133—O2 SENSOR 1/1 SLOW RESPONSE

P0135—O2 SENSOR 1/1 HEATER PERFORMANCE

P0137—O2 SENSOR 1/2 CIRCUIT LOW

P0138—O2 SENSOR 1/2 CIRCUIT HIGH

P0139—O2 SENSOR 1/2 SLOW RESPONSE

P013A—O2 SENSOR 1/2 SLOW RESPONSE—RICH TO LEAN

P013C—O2 SENSOR 2/2 SLOW RESPONSE—RICH TO LEAN

P0141—O2 SENSOR 1/2 HEATER PERFORMANCE

P0151—O2 SENSOR 2/1 CIRCUIT LOW

P0152—O2 SENSOR 2/1 CIRCUIT HIGH

P0153—O2 SENSOR 2/1 SLOW RESPONSE

P0155—O2 SENSOR 2/1 HEATER PERFORMANCE

P0157—O2 SENSOR 2/2 CIRCUIT LOW

P0158—O2 SENSOR 2/2 CIRCUIT HIGH

P0159—O2 SENSOR 2/2 SLOW RESPONSE

P0161—O2 SENSOR 2/2 HEATER PERFORMANCE

P0171—FUEL SYSTEM 1/1 LEAN

P0172—FUEL SYSTEM 1/1 RICH

P0174—FUEL SYSTEM 2/1 LEAN

P0175—FUEL SYSTEM 2/1 RICH

P0201—FUEL INJECTOR 1 CIRCUIT

P0202—FUEL INJECTOR 2 CIRCUIT

P0203—FUEL INJECTOR 3 CIRCUIT

P0204—FUEL INJECTOR 4 CIRCUIT

P0205—FUEL INJECTOR 5 CIRCUIT

P0206—FUEL INJECTOR 6 CIRCUIT

P0218—HIGH TEMPERATURE OPERATION ACTIVATED

P0221—THROTTLE POSITION SENSOR 2 PERFORMANCE

P0222—THROTTLE POSITION SENSOR 2 CIRCUIT LOW

P0223—THROTTLE POSITION SENSOR 2 CIRCUIT HIGH

P0300—MULTIPLE CYLINDER MISFIRE

P0301—CYLINDER 1 MISFIRE

P0302—CYLINDER 2 MISFIRE

P0303—CYLINDER 3 MISFIRE

P0304—CYLINDER 4 MISFIRE

P0305—CYLINDER 5 MISFIRE

P0306—CYLINDER 6 MISFIRE

P0315—NO CRANK SENSOR LEARNED

P0325—KNOCK SENSOR 1 CIRCUIT

P0335—CRANKSHAFT POSITION SENSOR CIRCUIT

P0339—CRANKSHAFT POSITION SENSOR INTERMITTENT

P0340—CAMSHAFT POSITION SENSOR CIRCUIT

P0344—CAMSHAFT POSITION SENSOR INTERMITTENT

P0401—EGR SYSTEM PERFORMANCE

P0403—EGR SOLENOID CIRCUIT

P0404—EGR POSITION SENSOR RATIONALITY OPEN

P0405—EGR POSITION SENSOR CIRCUIT LOW

P0406—EGR POSITION SENSOR CIRCUIT HIGH

P0420—CATALYST EFFICIENCY (BANK 1)

P0430—CATALYST EFFICIENCY (BANK 2)

P0440—GENERAL EVAP SYSTEM FAILURE

P0441—EVAP PURGE SYSTEM PERFORMANCE

P0443—EVAP PURGE SOLENOID CIRCUIT

P0452—EVAP PRESSURE SWITCH STUCK CLOSED

P0455—EVAP PURGE SYSTEM LARGE LEAK

P0456—EVAP PURGE SYSTEM SMALL LEAK

P0457—LOOSE FUEL CAP

P0461—FUEL LEVEL SENSOR 1 PERFORMANCE

P0462—FUEL LEVEL SENSOR 1 CIRCUIT LOW

P0463—FUEL LEVEL SENSOR 1 CIRCUIT HIGH

P0480—COOLING FAN 1 CONTROL CIRCUIT

P0481—COOLING FAN 2 CONTROL CIRCUIT

P0501—VEHICLE SPEED SENSOR 1 PERFORMANCE

P0503—VEHICLE SPEED SENSOR 1 ERRATIC

P0506—IDLE SPEED PERFORMANCE LOWER THAN EXPECTED

P0507—IDLE SPEED PERFORMANCE HIGHER THAN EXPECTED

P050B—COLD START IGNITION TIMING PERFORMANCE

P050D—COLD START ROUGH IDLE

P0513—INVALID SKIM KEY

P0522—ENGINE OIL PRESSURE TOO LOW

P0532—A/C PRESSURE SENSOR CIRCUIT LOW

P0533—A/C PRESSURE SENSOR CIRCUIT HIGH

P0562—BATTERY VOLTAGE LOW

P0563—BATTERY VOLTAGE HIGH

P0571—BRAKE SWITCH 1 PERFORMANCE

P0572—BRAKE SWITCH 1 STUCK ON

P0573—BRAKE SWITCH 1 STUCK OFF

P0579—SPEED CONTROL SWITCH 1 PERFORMANCE

P0580—SPEED CONTROL SWITCH 1 CIRCUIT LOW

P0581—SPEED CONTROL SWITCH 1 CIRCUIT HIGH

P0585—SPEED CONTROL SWITCH 1/2 CORRELATION

P0591—SPEED CONTROL SWITCH 2 PERFORMANCE

P0592—SPEED CONTROL SWITCH 2 CIRCUIT LOW

P0593—SPEED CONTROL SWITCH 2 CIRCUIT HIGH

P0600—SERIAL COMMUNICATION LINK

P0601—INTERNAL MEMORY CHECKSUM INVALID

P0602—CONTROL MODULE PROGRAMMING ERROR/NOT PROGRAMMED

P0604—INTERNAL CONTROL MODULE RAM

P0605—INTERNAL CONTROL MODULE ROM

P0606—INTERNAL ECM PROCESSOR

P060B—ETC A/D GROUND PERFORMANCE

P060D—ETC LEVEL 2 APP PERFORMANCE

P060E—ETC LEVEL 2 TPS PERFORMANCE

P060F—ETC LEVEL 2 ECT PERFORMANCE

P0613—INTERNAL TRANSMISSION PROCESSOR

P061A—ETC LEVEL 2 TORQUE PERFORMANCE

P061C—ETC LEVEL 2 RPM PERFORMANCE

P0622—GENERATOR FIELD CONTROL CIRCUIT

P0627—FUEL PUMP CONTROL CIRCUIT

P062C—ETC LEVEL 2 MPH PERFORMANCE

P0630—VIN NOT PROGRAMMED IN PCM

P0632—ODOMETER NOT PROGRAMMED IN PCM

P0633—SKIM SECRET KEY NOT STORED IN PCM

P063A—GENERATOR VOLTAGE SENSE CIRCUIT

P0642—SENSOR REFERENCE VOLTAGE 1 CIRCUIT LOW

P0643—SENSOR REFERENCE VOLTAGE 1 CIRCUIT HIGH

P0645—A/C CLUTCH CONTROL CIRCUIT

P0652—SENSOR REFERENCE VOLTAGE 2 CIRCUIT LOW

P0653—SENSOR REFERENCE VOLTAGE 2 CIRCUIT HIGH

P0685—AUTO SHUTDOWN CONTROL CIRCUIT

P0688—AUTO SHUTDOWN SENSE CIRCUIT LOW

P0691—COOLING FAN 1 CONTROL CIRCUIT LOW

P0692—COOLING FAN 1 CONTROL CIRCUIT HIGH

P0693—COOLING FAN 2 CONTROL CIRCUIT LOW

P0694—COOLING FAN 2 CONTROL CIRCUIT HIGH

P0700—TRANSMISSION CONTROL SYSTEM (MIL REQUEST)

P0703—BRAKE SWITCH 2 PERFORMANCE

P0706—TRANSMISSION RANGE SENSOR RATIONALITY

P0711—TRANSMISSION TEMPERATURE SENSOR PERFORMANCE

P0712—TRANSMISSION TEMPERATURE SENSOR LOW

P0713—TRANSMISSION TEMPERATURE SENSOR HIGH

P0714—TRANSMISSION TEMPERATURE SENSOR INTERMITTENT

P0716—INPUT SPEED SENSOR 1 CIRCUIT PERFORMANCE

P0721—OUTPUT SPEED SENSOR CIRCUIT PERFORMANCE

P0726—ENGINE SPEED INPUT CIRCUIT RANGE/PERFORMANCE

P0731—GEAR RATIO ERROR IN 1ST

P0732—GEAR RATIO ERROR IN 2ND

P0733—GEAR RATIO ERROR IN 3RD

P0734—GEAR RATIO ERROR IN 4TH

P0736—GEAR RATIO ERROR IN REVERSE

P0740—TCC OUT OF RANGE

P0750—LR SOLENOID CIRCUIT

P0755—2/4 SOLENOID CIRCUIT

P0760—OD SOLENOID CIRCUIT

P0765—UD SOLENOID CIRCUIT

P0841—LR PRESSURE SWITCH RATIONALITY

P0845—2/4 HYDRAULIC PRESSURE TEST

P0846—2/4 PRESSURE SWITCH RATIONALITY

P0850—PARK/NEUTRAL SWITCH PERFORMANCE

P0853—OVERDRIVE/TOW SWITCH INPUT CIRCUIT STUCK

P0868—LINE PRESSURE LOW

P0869—LINE PRESSURE HIGH

P0870—OD HYDRAULIC PRESSURE TEST

P0871—OD PRESSURE SWITCH RATIONALITY

P0882—TCM POWER INPUT LOW

P0883—TCM POWER INPUT HIGH

P0884—POWER UP AT SPEED

P0888—TRANSMISSION RELAY ALWAYS OFF

P0890—SWITCHED BATTERY

P0891—TRANSMISSION RELAY ALWAYS ON

P0897—TRANSMISSION FLUID DETERIORATED

P0933—LINE PRESSURE SENSOR CIRCUIT PERFORMANCE

P0934—LINE PRESSURE SENSOR CIRCUIT LOW

P0935—LINE PRESSURE SENSOR CIRCUIT HIGH

P0944—LOSS OF HYDRAULIC PUMP PRIME

P0992—2/4/OD HYDRAULIC PRESSURE TEST

P1115—GENERAL TEMPERATURE RATIONALITY

P1128—CLOSED LOOP FUELING NOT ACHIEVED—BANK 1

P1129—CLOSED LOOP FUELING NOT ACHIEVED—BANK 2

P1273—A/C CLUTCH CONTROL CIRCUIT 2 HIGH (TIPM)

P1275—A/C CLUTCH CONTROL CIRCUIT 2 OVERCURRENT (TIPM)

P128B—TCM POWER CONTROL CIRCUIT 2 LOW—TIPM

P128C—TCM POWER CONTROL CIRCUIT 2 HIGH—TIPM

P128D—TCM POWER CONTROL CIRCUIT 2 OPEN—TIPM

P128E—TCM POWER CONTROL CIRCUIT 2 OVERCURRENT—TIPM

P129C—INVERTER CONTROL CIRCUIT HIGH (TIPM)

P129E—INVERTER CONTROL CIRCUIT OVERCURRENT (TIPM)

P1404—EGR POSITION SENSOR RATIONALITY CLOSED

P1501—VEHICLE SPEED SENSOR 1/2 CORRELATION—DRIVE WHEELS

P1502—VEHICLE SPEED SENSOR 1/2 CORRELATION—NON DRIVE WHEELS

P1572—BRAKE PEDAL STUCK ON

P1573—BRAKE PEDAL STUCK OFF

P1593—SPEED CONTROL SWITCH 1/2 STUCK

P1602—PCM NOT PROGRAMMED

P1607—PCM INTERNAL SHUTDOWN TIMER RATIONALITY TOO SLOW

P1618—SENSOR REFERENCE VOLTAGE 1 CIRCUIT ERRATIC

P1628—SENSOR REFERENCE VOLTAGE 2 CIRCUIT ERRATIC

P1684—BATTERY WAS DISCONNECTED

P1696—EEPROM MEMORY WRITE DENIED/ INVALID

P1697—EMR (SRI) MILEAGE NOT STORED

P1713—RESTRICTED MANUAL VALVE IN T2 RANGE

P1745—TRANSMISSION LINE PRESSURE TOO HIGH FOR TOO LONG

P1775—SOLENOID SWITCH VALVE LATCHED IN TCC POSITION

P1776—SOLENOID SWITCH VALVE LATCHED IN LR POSITION

P1790—FAULT IMMEDIATELY AFTER SHIFT

P1794—SPEED SENSOR GROUND ERROR

P1797—MANUAL SHIFT OVERHEAT

P1897—LEVEL 1 RPM BUS UNLOCK

P2072—ELECTRONIC THROTTLE CONTROL SYSTEM—ICE BLOCKAGE

P2096—DOWNSTREAM FUEL TRIM SYSTEM 1 LEAN

P2097—DOWNSTREAM FUEL TRIM SYSTEM 1 RICH

P2098—DOWNSTREAM FUEL TRIM SYSTEM 2 LEAN

P2099—DOWNSTREAM FUEL TRIM SYSTEM 2 RICH

P2100—ELECTRONIC THROTTLE CONTROL MOTOR CIRCUIT

P2101—ELECTRONIC THROTTLE CONTROL MOTOR PERFORMANCE

P2107—ELECTRONIC THROTTLE CONTROL MODULE PROCESSOR

P2110—ELECTRONIC THROTTLE CONTROL—FORCED LIMITED RPM

P2111—ELECTRONIC THROTTLE CONTROL—UNABLE TO CLOSE

P2112—ELECTRONIC THROTTLE CONTROL—UNABLE TO OPEN

P2115—ACCELERATOR PEDAL POSITION SENSOR 1 MINIMUM STOP PERFORMANCE

P2116—ACCELERATOR PEDAL POSITION SENSOR 2 MINIMUM STOP PERFORMANCE

P2118—ELECTRONIC THROTTLE CONTROL MOTOR CURRENT PERFORMANCE

P2122—ACCELERATOR PEDAL POSITION SENSOR 1 CIRCUIT LOW

P2123—ACCELERATOR PEDAL POSITION SENSOR 1 CIRCUIT HIGH

P2127—ACCELERATOR PEDAL POSITION SENSOR 2 CIRCUIT LOW

P2128—ACCELERATOR PEDAL POSITION SENSOR 2 CIRCUIT HIGH

P2135—THROTTLE POSITION SENSOR 1/2 CORRELATION

P2138—ACCELERATOR PEDAL POSITION SENSOR 1/2 CORRELATION

P2161—VEHICLE SPEED SENSOR 2 ERRATIC

P2166—ACCELERATOR PEDAL POSITION SENSOR 1 MAXIMUM STOP PERFORMANCE

P2167—ACCELERATOR PEDAL POSITION SENSOR 2 MAXIMUM STOP PERFORMANCE

P2172—HIGH AIRFLOW/VACUUM LEAK DETECTED (INSTANTANEOUS ACCUMULATION)

P2173—HIGH AIRFLOW/VACUUM LEAK DETECTED (SLOW ACCUMULATION)

P2174—LOW AIRFLOW/RESTRICTION DETECTED (INSTANTANEOUS ACCUMULATION)

P2175—LOW AIRFLOW/RESTRICTION DETECTED (SLOW ACCUMULATION)

P2181—COOLING SYSTEM PERFORMANCE

P2271—O2 SENSOR 1/2 SIGNAL STUCK RICH

P2273—O2 SENSOR 2/2 SIGNAL STUCK RICH

P2299—BRAKE PEDAL POSITION/ ACCELERATOR PEDAL POSITION INCOMPATIBLE

P2302—IGNITION COIL 1 SECONDARY CIRCUIT_ INSUFFICIENT IONIZATION

P2305—IGNITION COIL 2 SECONDARY CIRCUIT_ INSUFFICIENT IONIZATION

P2308—IGNITION COIL 3 SECONDARY CIRCUIT_ INSUFFICIENT IONIZATION

P2503—CHARGING SYSTEM OUTPUT LOW

P2504—CHARGING SYSTEM OUTPUT HIGH

P2610—PCM INTERNAL SHUTDOWN TIMER RATIONALITY TOO FAST

U0001—CAN C BUS CIRCUIT

U0002—CAN C BUS OFF PERFORMANCE

U0010—CAN INTERIOR BUS

U0011—CAN INTERIOR BUS OFF PERFORMANCE

U0019—CAN INTERIOR BUS(+)/(_) CIRCUIT

U0020—CAN INTERIOR BUS OFF PERFORMANCE

U0100—LOST COMMUNICATION WITH ECM/ PCM

U0101—LOST COMMUNICATION WITH TCM

U0114—LOST COMMUNICATION WITH FINAL DRIVE MODULE

U0121—LOST COMMUNICATION WITH ANTI_LOCK BRAKE SYSTEM (ABS) CONTROL MODULE

U0126—LOST COMMUNICATION WITH SAS— CAN C (STEERING ANGLE SENSOR)

U0141—LOST COMMUNICATION WITH FRONT CONTROL MODULE (TIPM)

U0146—LOST COMMUNICATION WITH CENTRAL GATEWAY

U0151—LOST COMMUNICATION WITH OCCUPANT RESTRAINT CONTROLLER (ORC)

U0154—LOST COMMUNICATION WITH OCCUPANT CLASSIFICATION MODULE

U0155—LOST COMMUNICATION WITH CLUSTER/CCN

U0161—LOST COMMUNICATION WITH COMPASS MODULE

U0164—LOST COMMUNICATION WITH HVAC CONTROL MODULE

U0167—LOST COMMUNICATION WITH INTRUSION TRANSCEIVER CONTROL MODULE

U0168—LOST COMMUNICATION WITH VEHICLE SECURITY CONTROL MODULE (SKREEM/WCM)

U0170— LOST COMMUNICATION W/ UP_FRONT LEFT SATELLITE ACCELERATION SENSOR

U0171—LOST COMMUNICATION W/UP_ FRONT RIGHT SATELLITE ACCELERATION SENSOR

U0172—LOST COMMUNICATION W/LEFT SIDE SATELLITE ACCELERATION SENSOR 1

U0175—COMMUNICATION W/RIGHT SIDE SATELLITE ACCELERATION SENSOR 1

U0184—LOST COMMUNICATION WITH RADIO

U0186—LOST COMMUNICATION WITH AUDIO AMPLIFIER

U0193—LOST COMMUNICATION WITH TRAFFIC INFORMATION RECEIVER MODULE

U0195—LOST COMMUNICATION WITH SDARS

U0197—LOST COMMUNICATION WITH HANDS FREE PHONE MODULE

U0199—LOST COMMUNICATION WITH DRIVERS DOOR MODULE

U0200—LOST COMMUNICATION WITH PASSENGER DOOR MODULE

U0415—IMPLAUSIBLE DATA RECEIVED FROM ABS

U0447—IMPLAUSIBLE DATA RECEIVED FROM CENTRAL

U1008—LIN 1 BUS

U110A—LOST COMMUNICATION WITH SCM

U110C—LOST FUEL LEVEL MESSAGE

U110D—LOST COMMUNICATION WITH SECURITY SIREN

U110E—LOST AMBIENT TEMPERATURE MESSAGE

U110F—LOST FUEL VOLUME MESSAGE

U1110—LOST VEHICLE SPEED MESSAGE

U1113—LOST A/C PRESSURE MESSAGE

U1120—LOST WHEEL DISTANCE MESSAGE

U113B—LOST COMMUNICATION WITH SWITCH BANK MODULE

U1149—LOST COMMUNICATION WITH MULTIFUNCTION

U1159—LOST COMMUNICATION WITH ASBS

U1169—LOST COMMUNICATION WITH INTRUSION SENSOR 1

U1170—LOST COMMUNICATION WITH INTRUSION SENSOR 2

U1179—LOST COMMUNICATION WITH INTRUSION SENSOR 3

U1403—IMPLAUSIBLE FUEL LEVEL SIGNAL RECEIVED

U1411—IMPLAUSIBLE FUEL VOLUME SIGNAL RECEIVED

U1412—IMPLAUSIBLE VEHICLE SPEED SIGNAL RECEIVED

U1414—IMPLAUSIBLE/MISSING ECU NETWORK CONFIGURATION DATA

U1415—IMPLAUSIBLE/MISSING VEHICLE CONFIGURATION DATA

U1416—IMPLAUSIBLE SECURITY SIREN SIGNAL RECEIVED

U1417—IMPLAUSIBLE LEFT WHEEL DISTANCE SIGNAL RECEIVED

U1418—IMPLAUSIBLE RIGHT WHEEL DISTANCE SIGNAL

U1419—IMPLAUSIBLE DATA RECEIVED FROM OCS SENSOR 3—LEFT FRONT

U141A—IMPLAUSIBLE DATA RECEIVED FROM OCS SENSOR 2—RIGHT FRONT

U141B—IMPLAUSIBLE DATA RECEIVED FROM OCS SENSOR 4—LEFT REAR

U141C—IMPLAUSIBLE DATA RECEIVED FROM OCS SENSOR 1—RIGHT REAR

Checking your JK's vehicle computer for any DTCs is easier than one would think. The first step is to enter the vehicle, insert the key in the ignition, and turn it to the ON position. This is as far as you should turn it; the engine should not be started at this time. Following this step, the key should be turned back and forth from the ON position to the OFF position three times, with the key finishing at the ON position; the engine is still not to be started.

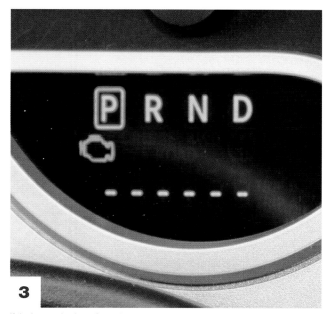

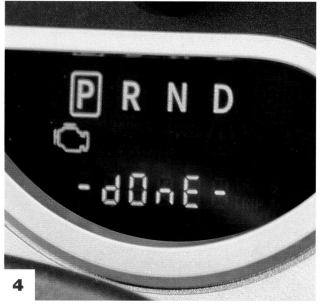

If the key turning is performed correctly, all of the dashboard lights will turn on, and the indicator screen where the odometer is will display a series of dashes. If there are any DTCs logged into your computer's memory, they will be displayed at this time. If there are any, they should be transcribed so that they can be checked to determine what they are for.

Shortly after they are displayed, the indicator screen will display the word "DONE." If no codes are shown, the screen will go from the dashes to the word "DONE" immediately. Once the word "DONE" has been displayed, it is safe to turn the key to the OFF position and remove it from the ignition.

PROJECT 22
Update an Engine Control Module

 Time: ½ Hour

 Tools: None

 Talent:

Applicable Years: Jeep Wrangler JK (two-door and four-door models)

Tab: $129

 Parts Required: ProCal module

 Tip: Be sure to read the instructions carefully before starting the upgrade, as the instructions may call for something specific to be done to the vehicle prior to reprogramming the ECM.

 Performance Gain: Increased vehicle performance

 Complementary Project: None

With the technical intricacies of today's Jeeps, nothing has been left untouched for the vehicle's ECM to control. Some of the specific settings that have been installed on Jeeps from the factory may change or become devoid of their intended purpose as soon as alterations are made to the vehicle. As an example, if a winch is installed on a newer Jeep and it is to be operated, the engine should idle at a few hundred more rpm for optimum performance; this is not something that the dealer or your mechanic can do.

To assist in resetting these settings, American Expedition Vehicles has released the ProCal module, which is an essential tool in reconfiguring your ECM to fit with your vehicle in its post alterations and additions stage. Currently available for Jeep Wrangler JK models only, this hand-held unit is a superpower. This low-cost unit is an effective way of making a variety of useful changes that are not offered by the dealership or any other type of vehicle reprogrammer. Topping the list is the ability to correct the speedometer and gear ratio when larger tires are installed. With the speedometer left uncorrected, there is a major degradation in the performance of the stability control (ESP), transmission shifting, and engine performance. The best part of the ProCal is that it isn't just for correcting the speedometer. The tire pressure monitoring system can now be recalibrated to better suit aftermarket tires without triggering the dash light. Further, the ProCal module makes it possible to activate daytime running lamps, use one-touch turn signals, increase engine idle speed for winching, clear engine codes, and even help align the vehicle perfectly for optimal ESP performance.

The ProCal module is equipped with a series of easy-to-use DIP switches. By reading the simple Quick Reference Guide included with the ProCal module, a user can quickly dial in a code for the desired recalibration. Once the DIP switches are set, simply plug the module into the vehicle's OBDII. The whole process can be completed in mere minutes; and it's just as easy to restore the vehicle back to its original settings with the ProCal.

For AEV HEMI Builders Kit customers, the ProCal module can also be used to program the vehicle's VIN into the new PCM Controller and to program the pedal calibration and tolerance levels.

1

The ProCal module allows the user to reprogram several factory parameters including tire size, gear ratio, one-touch lane change, daytime running lamps, low tire pressure indicator, smart bar indicator disable (after smart bar removal), and clear diagnostic trouble codes (DTCs). *Photo courtesy of American Expedition Vehicles*

2

The programmer is equipped with a series of easy-to-use DIP switches on the back of the unit that allow the setting to be either turned on or off depending upon the owner's specifications for each of them. *Photo courtesy of American Expedition Vehicles*

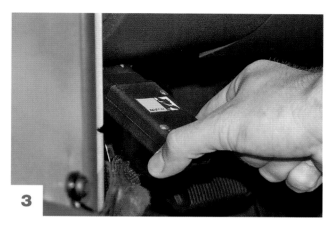

3

No cables, computer connections, or any other items are required for the programmer to function. Simply plug the module into the OBD port and leave it alone. *Photo courtesy of American Expedition Vehicles*

4

Once the ProCal module has completed its reprogramming, the unit alerts the owner that it is finished and can be removed from the port at that time. *Photo courtesy of American Expedition Vehicles*

5

With the speedometer left uncorrected, there is a major degradation in the performance of the stability control (ESP), transmission shifting, and engine performance. *Photo courtesy of American Expedition Vehicles*

6

The daytime running lamp (DRL) mode allows the user to activate, deactivate, or change the vehicle's daytime running lights with the flip of a switch. *Photo courtesy of American Expedition Vehicles*

7

The Extended Idle mode allows the user to set the vehicle's idle speed at a higher level than the stock level (up to 2,000 rpm). The newer engine systems found in the latest Jeeps idle at a lower speed than vehicles of previous generation. These lower idle speeds combined with an electronically sensitive vehicle network can create issues for power intensive tools such as winches and on-board welders.

SECTION 3
DRIVETRAIN

By a long shot Jeep's drivetrains have made Jeeps what they are today. From crossing rivers in World War II to conquering the Rubicon, their drivetrains have always been the soul of what they are. In this chapter we review projects that address some potential upgrades and improvements to the system, such as replacing differential covers, upgrading the steering system, and installing new ring and pinion gears, to name just a few.

PROJECT 23
Perform a Ring and Pinion Exchange

Time: 3½ Hours

Tools: Socket set, impact gun, torque wrench, puller, paint, micrometer

Talent:

Applicable Years: All models

Tab: $500 per axle

Parts Required: Gear set, gear oil, gasket

Tip: Have a professional perform this exchange. If you do decide to tackle this project though, make certain that you have all of the necessary tools, shims, and parts needed prior to tearing the unit down. Also, know how to properly set the backlash for the gears. If not set correctly, the gears could become damaged or not wear evenly.

Performance Gain: Correct gearing for the tire size

Complementary Project: Installation of upgraded axles

A capable off-road vehicle is typically viewed as consisting of two things—large tires and a raised suspension; however, that is very often the least of the components that qualifies a rig as being truly off-road ready. Like many other things in this world, the tires and suspension height are only the only items that people see, but in order for these components to function, there is a laundry list of components that must be installed to make the vehicle truly perform as it should off-road. One of the most important of these components is the ring and pinion gears that are housed in the front and rear axles.

Their sole function is to transfer and distribute power from the engine to the tires through the axles. Typically, the size of the gear ratio, which is what the ring and pinion set produces, are matched to the tire size. Consequently, any changes in tire size will affect the performance of the vehicle, often through a loss of power and performance. A vehicle equipped with 40-inch tall tires will perform completely differently from the same vehicle that has 31-inch tires. Add into the equation the added weight of not only the tires, but any accessories that have been added and the same amount of torque that was previously needed has been increased as well, which is also what the ring and pinion gears establish.

Choosing the correct gear ratio is often a matter of personal preference. As an example, on our project vehicle, we increased the size of the tires from a 31-inch to a 35-inch. With this swap, the stock ring and pinion gears made the vehicle sluggish and extremely slow, even at highway speeds, which took forever and a day to reach. Upon deciding to swap the gear set, we had two options, a 4.88 ratio or a 5.33 ratio. While both gear sets would put our vehicle's performance back to stock, at speed the higher ratio would have our rpm running higher than we would have liked. We chose the 4.88s, which would put our Jeep pretty close to its stock settings as far as torque and rpm went.

Performing the swap between gear sets is not an easy task and should be handled by a professional. Given the number of specialized tools and other components required, the skill and knowledge required to set them correctly is something that only working with them on a daily basis can give you. For our installation, we utilized a set of 4.88 Superior gears on our 2008 Jeep JK Rubicon with a Dana 44 axle. In following our own advice, we called upon Mel Wade of Off-Road Evolution to perform the exchange. He has numerous years of experience in building some of the finest Jeeps to ever hit a trail, and the exchange went without a hitch.

1

To begin the project, the vehicle should be placed on a lift and the differential cover removed to gain access to the stock ring and pinion gears.

2

When working on these components, cleanliness is especially important, since any debris that may enter the axle could remain and cause damage to the new components. For this reason, once the fluid has completed draining from the pumpkin, brake cleaner is sprayed on the internals to further sterilize the environment.

3

The rear axles were removed to allow the ring gear to be removed from the differential housing. Regardless of whether performing the ring and pinion swap on the front or rear axle, the axles must be removed.

4

Prior to loosening the carrier bolts, the case of the axle housing must be spread slightly to allow some leeway for the gears to be removed from the housing. Depending on the installer performing the work, some use spreaders such as the unit pictured, while others use pry bars, etc. The least intrusive method is to use a spreader assembly, as the chances of scarring or damaging the case is greatly diminished.

5

A trick of the trade: Prior to removing the carrier assembly, a small indentation is made to either the left or right side, which will allow the same side to be reinstalled, minimizing any chance for the parts to not fit correctly.

6

Once all of the carrier bolts have been loosened, the gears are removed from the housing. Special care should be taken when disconnecting the electrical wiring associated with the electric locking differentials.

7

The empty cavity of the housing is leaned once more, and the pinion gear is set to be removed.

8

Placed on a sturdy workbench, the stock ring gear is removed from the carrier using an impact wrench. Special care should be taken to avoid damaging the bearings and differential.

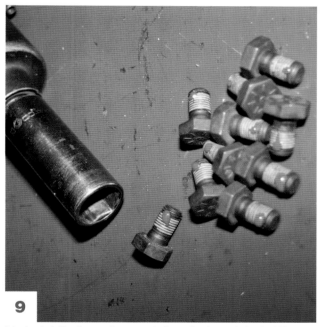

9

Prior to reinstalling the new ring gear onto the carrier, the new bolts should have a drop of thread sealant applied to them.

10

Once reinstalled, the new ring gear should be torqued per the manufacturer's specifications.

11

The pinion gear is placed in a press to have the pinion bearings removed from the stock unit. This is the best method to ensure that damage does not occur to any of the components.

12

Once the pinion gear has been reset into the housing, the carrier is installed and aligned with the pinion gear.

13

To measure the alignment of the ring and pinion gear, yellow paint is applied to the teeth of the ring gear to show the wear pattern, which will determine if more or fewer shims are required.

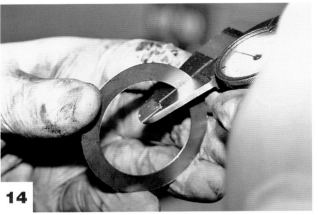

14

Shims such as this one are placed on the pinion shaft to help with the adjustment of the wear pattern and backlash.

15

The telltale sign that the wear pattern is set is determined by looking at the teeth on the ring gear. Notice how the point of contact is on the paint in the direct center of each tooth as well as the backlash. Typically, if the pinion gear is not set properly, the wear pattern is either at the top or the bottom of the tooth.

16

The backlash is measured with a specialized gauge. In the event that the backlash is not within the acceptable parameters, the carrier may need to be removed and reinstalled with shims either being added or subtracted until it is within the acceptable range. This can be the most time-consuming task of the entire install.

17

Once the correct settings have been determined, the carrier is reinstalled into the housing.

18

The axles are reinstalled as the final step of the exchange.

19

The last item to be installed is the differential cover. As we said earlier, by looking at it from the outside, there is no evidence that such a tedious and time-consuming effort just occurred that affects so much of the vehicle's performance.

PROJECT 24
Axle Upgrade

 Time: 2 Hours

 Tools: Cut-off wheel, press, impact gun, socket set

 Talent:

Applicable Years: All

Tab: $500 per axle

 Parts Required: Axles

 Tip: To save time, the axle upgrade may occur at the same time that the ring and pinion gears are being exchanged.

 Performance Gain: Drivetrain performance increase

 Complementary Project: Installation of ring and pinion gears

The stress that is applied to a drivetrain while off-road driving is tremendous, much more than a person would think. Typically the factory-issue axle shafts are rated for a fair amount of abuse, but as soon as larger tires and wheels are installed, the additional weight, combined with the forces required to four-wheel over rocks, etc. just becomes too much, and the shaft breaks. Another scenario that is often found on older Jeeps is that the bearings become worn and begin to leak, which causes the shafts to become exposed to the elements, water, dirt, and rust. Once they have become compromised, they are susceptible to breaking just as easily.

In the event that an axle shaft is broken, it will render the wheel for whatever side the shaft is broken at inoperable. While many people have no choice but to continue on, moving a rig with a snapped axle is never good for the inner workings of the axle, as other parts can become damaged by the turning shaft. To avoid having this occur to you and your rig, upgrading your axle shafts for stronger units is highly suggested. Superior Axle and Gear manufactures a number of replacement shafts for all makes and models of Jeep. Their Evolution Series shafts are fabricated from SAE4340 chromoly that has been induction hardened, CNC turned, and rotoflow spline rolled for toughness. Designed to absorb shock rather than break under it, the shafts have also had their profiles adjusted for additional on- and off-road performance.

The swap from the factory versions to the Superior units is achieved by removing the tires and brake assembly for the applicable axle and loosening the nuts on the retainer plate, which is responsible for holding the axle shaft in place inside the axle tube. Once completed, the factory shaft is removed and the new shaft is prepped for install. In order to remove the factory retainer plate from the axle, so it can be reinstalled on the new shaft, the factory bearing must be cut off. This bearing can be pressed off as well, but it is not worth the time and effort it takes to remove it from the shaft. Once the bearing has been removed, the retainer plate can be removed, as well as the ABS sensor gear; that piece too will go onto the new Superior units. Once the ABS gear and retainer plate have been placed onto the new shaft, the included bearing is pressed into place and the shaft can be reinstalled in the same manner as they were removed.

1

Superior Axle and Gear Evolution Series shafts are fabricated from SAE4340 chromoly that has been induction hardened, CNC-turned, and rotoflow spline rolled for toughness. They are available for many different makes and models of Jeeps and in multiple axle sizes. *Photo courtesy of Superior Axle and Gear*

2

Prior to beginning the project, the tires for the axle that is being replaced must be removed.

3

The brake assembly and retainer plate bolts are both removed to allow the shafts to slide out of the axle housing.

4

When removing the shaft from the axle tube, be sure not to scratch the inner surface of the tube with the shaft tip, as it could cause future damage. The same goes when installing the new shaft.

5

Once removed, the factory axle shaft must have the retainer plate and ABS gear removed from it.

6

As part of the replacement, the inner bearings are replaced as well. This is much easier if performing the swap in conjunction with a gear swap, as the pumpkin will be clear of parts, making access a cinch.

7

The ABS gear must be reinstalled onto the new shaft in order for the ABS system to continue functioning uninterrupted.

8

While the factory bearing can be pressed off to gain access to the retainer plate and ABS gear, the vast majority of mechanics find it faster and easier just to cut it off with a cut-off wheel.

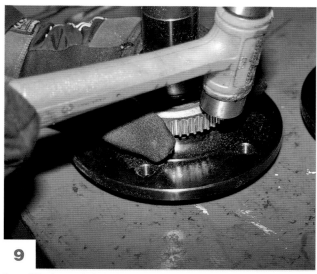

9

Once off the factory shaft, the ABS gear and then retainer plate are installed onto the new Superior shaft.

10

Ready to be installed, the new shafts will not only provide peace of mind when hardcore wheeling, but they will actually do the job and keep you from being stranded on a trail.

11

The brake assembly and wheels are reinstalled to complete the upgrade.

PROJECT 25
Convert to a Hydraulic Steering System

 Time: 4 Hours

 Tools: Open-ended wrenches, screwdrivers, bench vice, socket set, impact gun, pitman arm puller

 Talent: 🔧🔧🔧🔧

 Applicable Years: All

Tab: $1,700

 Parts Required: Steering fluid, hydraulic steering components

 Tip: Prior to cutting the hydraulic hoses, make sure you know their path of travel from the pump to the steering ram. Failure to know this could result in the hose being cut too short.

 Performance Gain: Improves the steering system's performance and reliability

 Complementary Project: None

Almost as important as your brake system is your steering system. If you have installed larger tires on your Jeep, it is almost inevitable that your steering system will suffer for it unless you do something about it. While they do not look that damaging, larger tires can wreak havoc on your steering pump and the related components. A typical factory steering pump on a Jeep cannot withstand the high temperatures that are generated by this extra work, which in turn makes it go into overdrive and burn up. One good way to know if your pump is headed down this road is if your steering fluid is a burnt brown color and when you turn the steering wheel, it just gets harder and harder.

The answer to this problem is to replace your factory steering system with a hydraulically assisted one. These systems contain a new hydraulic pump, steering gear, fluid reservoir, hydraulic steering rod, and all of the associated brackets and hoses required for the job. For years, Power Steering Components (PSC) has been building some of the most reliable and best performing hydraulic steering systems on the market. Their Extreme Duty Cylinder Assist kit has been designed specifically for Jeep Wranglers and is easily installed using minimal tools. With the addition of the new hydraulic steering pump and hydraulic steering rod, never again will you experience steering system fade or the inability to turn the wheel, which is a good thing when a tire is wedged between two rocks and the only way out is to steer yourself out.

1

In its stock configuration, the factory steering system is great with stock wheels and tires; however, as soon as you increase tire and wheel size, the chances of your steering pump and related steering system components failing increases as well, due to the added stresses and forces being applied to the factory system.

2

Depending upon the type of Jeep you have and the route that your hydraulic hoses take from the pump to the steering rod, the hoses will have to be made to fit each application. In this picture one of the hydraulic fittings is being installed onto the hose.

3

Making sure the fittings are installed correctly and are tight will minimize any leaks or failures that could result in the system being compromised, not to mention one huge and oily mess from the fluid.

4

The factory steering pump is easily replaced with the new PSC unit. One of the benefits of this system is that the pump is a direct replacement part, meaning that it installs in the factory mounting brackets.

5

When routing the hydraulic hoses from the steering pump to the steering rod, make sure they are placed away from any moving parts and heat sources.

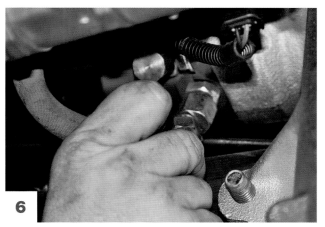

6

Once routed, the hydraulic hose fittings are secured onto the steering pump.

7

The fluid reservoir is easily mounted in an accessible space within the engine and is fabricated from billet aluminum to reduce weight and increase performance. The hardware is Grade 8 for durability and longevity.

8

Included with the system are new brackets and mounts for the hydraulic steering rod. The rod end fittings are Teflon lined for both quiet and smooth operation.

9

The hydraulic steering rod fittings and lines should be routed in such as way as to avoid being caught or pinched during operation.

10

With all of the system's components installed and all of the necessary hydraulic lines run, Royal Purple steering fluid is introduced into the system.

11

A breather hose fitting is integrated into the solid billet aluminum fluid reservoir cap.

12

The PSC hydraulic steering system provides a much-needed boost to the all-around performance of your Jeep, not to mention that it adds that no-nonsense approach in the appearance department.

PROJECT 26
Upgrade a Driveshaft

 Time: 1½ Hours

 Tools: Open-ended wrenches, impact gun, socket set

 Talent: ✎✎✎

 Applicable Years: All

Tab: $500

 Parts Required: Driveshaft, grease

 Tip: It is best to have the vehicle placed on a lift to perform the replacement of the driveshaft.

 Performance Gain: Minimizes driveline failure

 Complementary Project: Installation of upgraded axles

Many things are affected when a vehicle is lifted, especially a Jeep. Given their typically short wheelbases, any increase in height dramatically affects the steepness of the pinion angle, which in turn will cause the factory CV joints attached to the factory driveline to wear prematurely due to the lack of lubrication that the bearings are receiving. This premature wear is translated to the driver by vibrations from the factory driveshaft. This is especially noticeable on Jeeps that have been lifted three inches or higher, and especially on the two-door models. As a rule of thumb, the higher the suspension lift, the steeper the angle of the driveshaft becomes and the quicker the OE part fails.

Making a preemptive strike against this failure to our drivetrain, a set of J. E. Reel 1350-Series driveshafts for our 2008 Jeep Wrangler Rubicon two-door were installed. While considerably different from the factory CV versions,

the J. E. Reel units are built to the exact specifications of the vehicle and take into consideration whether the vehicle is lifted or not. If the vehicle is lifted, the height of the lift will be factored into the equation for an appropriately sized unit. The 1350 Series drivelines utilize flanges and yokes with U-bolts, as opposed to the CV joints on the factory versions. They also feature 1⅜-inch diameter slips compared to the 1¼-inch OE versions and have a 1-inch-longer stroke in slip joint. This type of setup allows for easy trail repairs should a component of the shaft break, and it makes for an easy installation at the garage.

Speaking of installation, it couldn't be any easier. Once the OE drivelines have been removed, OE flanges are removed from the transfer case and the rear axle. After this, the new flanges are installed, the flange nuts are tightened, and the new driveshaft is bolted into place.

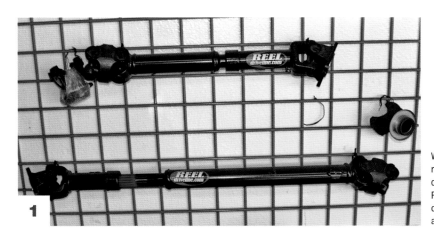

Whenever lifting a Jeep, the drivelines should be replaced with longer and more durable units to compensate for a steeper pinion angle. The J. E. Reel units also feature 1⅜-inch diameter slips compared to the 1¼-inch OE versions and have a 1-inch-longer stroke in the slip joint.

2

The OE CV joint is loosened from the rear differential flange. Note the factory CV joint that has a steep pinion angle caused by the installation of our 3-inch lift kit.

3

Once the driveline is removed from the Jeep, the flange nuts are loosened so that the new flanges and yokes can replace them.

4

The new flange will accommodate a 1350 Spicer joint and utilize U-bolts to keep the components in their place.

5

The new drivelines have been built with the additional amount of suspension lift on the vehicle being taken into consideration. Once the new flanges are installed, the driveline is lifted into place.

6

Through a series of bolts, lock washers, and nuts around the flange, the driveline is first attached to the transfer case so that gravity can assist with the remaining portions of the installation.

7

The new J. E. Reel driveline U-joints are secured to the new differential flange with great ease.

8

Looking right at home, the new drivelines have had their pinion angles inspected for any imperfections or angle concern.

9

Prior to starting the vehicle and moving it down the street, the driveline must be greased at key locations to prevent it from burning up.

PROJECT 27
Strengthen a Steering Sector Shaft

 Time: 2 Hours

 Tools: Drill, drill bits, impact gun, socket set

 Talent:

 Applicable Years: All

 Tab: $150

Parts Required: Steering sector shaft brace

 Tip: Inspect the steering box and shaft for any excessive wear, prior to the installation of the brace. If wear is identified, it should be corrected prior to the installation of this shaft.

 Performance Gain: Reduces the side loading on the steering shaft

 Complementary Project: Installation of a steering stabilizer

As with any part on your Jeep, as soon as you make one adjustment to one component, numerous others are affected. An example of this cause and effect is exhibited by the additional forces and stresses that are applied to the factory sector shaft on the steering box of all Jeep Wrangler JK models. The side loading is a direct response to larger wheels and tires being installed onto the vehicle as well as the addition of a dropped pitman arm, which is usually included with a suspension lift.

To alleviate the chances of the sector shaft shearing off, Off-Road Evolution has fabricated the Evo 1015 Sector Shaft brace system. An easy-to-install kit, the brace is a bolt-on application that requires two holes to be drilled, which double shears the factory sector shaft inside the steering box, thereby helping to alleviate the chances for side-loading issues. Best of all, the brace can be use with any suspension kit that has a drop track bar bracket on the side of the frame.

1

Sold as a complete bolt-on system, the necessary mounting hardware is included as well as the sector shaft brace bar, which features a Teflon-lined rod end, for durability and ease of operation.

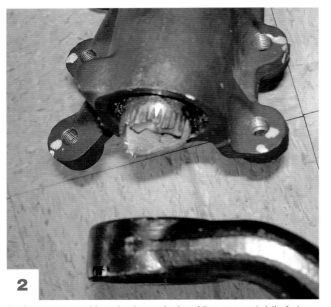

2

An all too common problem when larger wheels and tires are mounted, the factory steering sector shaft shears off with little way to repair it when in the field.

3

As part of the installation, two holes must be drilled through the frame to allow the brace to be mounted. Each side of the frame is saddled with a piece of the brace.

4

A steel tube spanning the width of the vehicle to the point of the dropped pitman arm is part of the brace and helps absorb and minimize any side loading forces.

5

The sector shaft brace attached to the dropped pitman arm with a Teflon-lined rod end that is adjustable and locked into adjustment with a locknut.

6

Upon completion of the install, one would be hard-pressed not to know that this was an added item, as the overall appearance of it resembles a factory part, especially given its black powder-coated finish and Grade 8 mounting bolts.

PROJECT 28
Install Axle Tube Seals

Time: 1½ Hours

Tools: Socket set, torque wrench, screwdriver, grease gun

Talent: ✎✎✎

Applicable Years: All Jeep models and years

Tab: $300 per axle

Parts Required: Axle tube seals, grease

Tip: When removing the front axle from the axle tube, take special care not to slide the end of the splines along the inner axle tube, as doing so could cause the splines to be damaged.

Performance Gain: Any time foreign materials or particles can be kept from key components of your drivetrain, it is a gain in system longevity and vehicle life

Complementary Project: Installation of new axles

Depending upon where your travels take you and your Jeep, the environments that your vehicle is subjected to will more than likely range from sand, rocks, silt, water, and mud or a good combination of all. With this said, a key component to keeping your vehicle running and performing properly in these conditions is to protect key elements of the system from intrusive elements such as debris and foreign materials. Among the most exposed components of any solid axle vehicle are the front axles and the area where they enter the axle tube to connect with the differentials. Placed directly in the line of fire for any terrain your vehicle is going through, the installation of axle tube seals is a much needed item in protecting your axles from damage by unwanted materials as well as keeping the axle fluids in place.

Superior Axle and Gear produces axle tube seals that utilize dual O-rings on the exterior of the unit to ensure a tight seal onto the shaft and a flexible seal that surrounds the axle. The flexible seal is fully serviceable, with an integrated zerk fitting that allows the inner seal to be greased, causing the seal to expand for a tighter fit and helping it perform as desired.

1 Fabricated from solid pieces of billet aluminum, these lightweight units from Superior Axle and Gear feature dual O-ring seals and a zerk grease fitting for serviceability to the integrated rubber boot.

2 Once the axles have been removed from the axle tubes, a liberal amount of grease should be applied to the inner portion of the axle tubes, which will allow the dual O-ring seals to slide right into place.

3

The axle tube seals are installed into the axle tube. The placement of the seal should have the zerk fitting on the collar facing backward to aid in the reduction of dirt buildup around the fitting.

4

Prior to replacing the axles, and aiding in threading the axle through the seal, a liberal amount of grease should be applied to the exterior portion of the seal. Applying the grease will also minimize any unwanted noises during the break-in period of the seal.

5

With the tube seals in place, the axles are reinstalled onto the spindle. Special care should be taken when reinserting the axle into the axle tube to ensure that the splines are properly aligned and remain undamaged. Once completed, the axle seal rubber boot should be greased, using the integrated zerk fitting.

6

The brake caliper and ABS sensor are the final components to be installed before the wheels are reinstalled.

7

Incorporating these tube seals provides a first line of defense against foreign materials and particulates, which can enter the axle tube and damage your driveshafts and gears.

PROJECT 29
Selecting the Proper Rod End

 Time: N/A

 Tools: N/A

 Talent:

 Applicable Years: All models

 Tab: Costs vary depending on the selected rod end

Parts Required: N/A

 Tip: Know the size and thread pitch of the rod end that you need, as well as where on the vehicle it will be installed. In some cases, if it will be placed where there is excessive heat, a certain type of rod end may not work adequately, given its method of lubrication.

 Performance Gain: Articulation

 Complementary Project: N/A

We've all heard the phrase that a chain is only as strong as its weakest link. This adage couldn't be any truer, especially when it comes to your Jeep's suspension and steering systems and their points of connection to each other and to the frame mounts. On some of today's more elaborate Jeep suspension systems, it is not uncommon for there to be at least 15 linkages between the pieces, all of which articulate. Depending upon the linkage, an extremely rigid articulating joint, commonly known as a spherical rod end or a Heim joint, may be necessary where precision is required. The most common types of precision linkages are found where wheel position and alignment are issues, such as a track bar linkage or a steering component linkage. The other reason for utilizing and choosing a rod end is to replace a rubber and poly bushing on a shock or steering stabilizer with a spherical rod end, which provides the owner the ability to maintain the joint better as well as increase the life of the joint.

While rod ends may look the same, the similarities stop there. Depending upon its intended application, placement on the vehicle, and model of Jeep, the material of the rod end's body, insert, and ball assembly may vary considerably. The way they are lubricated may vary as well. Some units may be self-lubricating via a Teflon insert, others may require zerk fittings for a periodic greasing, and some may not require any lubrication at all. It all depends on the manufacturer and model.

We have assembled a few of today's most popular and most widely used rod ends and joints for your review,

in hopes that you'll find one that appeals to you and your application.

KARTEK RSMX SERIES HEIM JOINT

Photo courtesy of Kartek

- Available in right or left thread directions
- Durable metal alloy, built to exact specs for racing and prerunning
- Stainless steel swivel joint with self-lubricating ball
- Variety of sizes ranging from $^3/_8$ x $^5/_{16}$-inch to $^7/_8$ x1-inch
- Rated up to 107,000 pounds.

CURRIE FORGED JOHNNY JOINTS

Photo courtesy of Currie Forged Johnny Joints

- Male rod end–style forging that features a ⁹/₁₆-inch through-bolt hole
- Right-hand threaded shank
- Accepts a ⁹/₁₆-inch greaseable through-bolt
- May be used in any Currie adjustable lower control arm, as well as in any type of universal application for those building their own arms
- Finished in gold zinc plating

EVO LARGE HEIM JOINT

Photo courtesy of Evo

- Rebuildable joint with a yield of over 100,000 pounds
- Large body design with a ³/₄-inch through-bolt hole
- Male rod end built from 4140 HTSR steel with a 303 stainless steel ball
- Delrin insert material provides ultimate wear resistance and performance
- Shank diameter of 1³/₄ inches
- Custom boltholes may be ordered

EVO REBUILDABLE HEIM JOINT BALL SOCKET

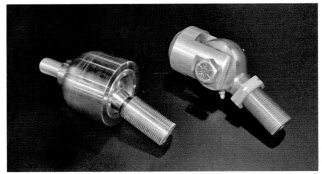

Photo courtesy of Evo

- Rebuildable Heim joint
- Combines a Heim joint with a clevis for one stand-alone unit
- Available in three different sizes from small (³/₄ inch) to large (1¹/₄ inches)
- All materials are 4140 alloy

RUBICON EXPRESS CARBON STEEL ROD END

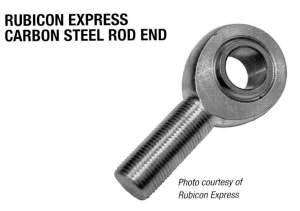

Photo courtesy of Rubicon Express

- ¾-inch right-hand threaded shank
- Precision ground, heat-treated, hard chrome-plated stainless steel ball
- Teflon and Kevlar self-lubricating insert
- Low carbon steel body that has been zinc-plated
- Corrosion resistant
- Additional mounting and hardware available separately

RUBICON EXPRESS SUPER-FLEX ASSEMBLY HEIM JOINT

Photo courtesy of Rubicon

- Originally designed to replace Heim joints in some early model suspension designs
- A direct replacement for factory lower rubber bushings used on Jeep XJ/MJ/ZJ/TJ/WJ models
- Utilizes a unique thread in side nut, which allows for easy tightening, installation, and conversion
- Fully rebuildable design
- Utilizes a ⁹/₁₆-inch through-bolt

RACING ROD ENDS XMR 12 ROD END

- 4130 chromoly steel heat-treated body
- Injection molded Teflon/Kevlar insert
- 52100 precision ground stainless steel ball bearing
- Shank lengths vary depending upon desired application
- Available in either a right- or left-hand threads

Photo courtesy of Racing Rod Ends

TELLICO 4X4 MORE ROD END

Photo courtesy of Tellico

- 4130 chromoly steel heat-treated body
- Injection molded Teflon/Kevlar insert
- Stainless steel ball bearing
- Shank lengths vary, depending upon desired application
- Available in either a right- or left-hand threads
- Locking nut included

FK HEAVY-DUTY PERFORMANCE ROD END

Photo courtesy of FK

- Steel heat-treated alloy body
- Injection-molded Teflon fabric insert
- Available in either a bright electrolysis nickel- or hard chrome-plated finish
- Shank lengths vary, depending upon desired application
- Available in either a right- or left hand-threads
- 52100 steel ball bearing

QA1 X ROD END

Photo courtesy of QA1

- Self-sealing and lubricating liner system
- 10 percent lighter than traditional rod ends
- Available in metric or SAE
- Shank lengths and thread patterns vary, depending upon desired application
- Internal zerk fitting
- Rebuildable insert

TERAFLEX TERA JOINT

Photo courtesy of TeraFlex

- Integrated zerk grease fitting
- Injection molded Teflon fabric insert
- Shank lengths and thread patterns vary, depending upon desired application
- Rebuildable insert

PROJECT 30
Install an Underbody Skid Plate

 Time: 1 Hour

 Tools: Socket set, open-ended wrenches

 Talent: 🔧🔧

 Applicable Years: All

Tab: $500

 Parts Required: Skid plate, mounting hardware

 Tip: For best results and ease of installation, the vehicle should be placed on a lift.

 Performance Gain: Provides protection to the underbody and key drivetrain components

 Complementary Project: Installation of aftermarket differential covers

The purpose of a skid plate is to act as a shield of armor between your key driveshaft components and the obstacles that are aiming to take them out and render your Jeep undrivable, often in the middle of nowhere. While there are numerous versions of skid plate systems that can cover every conceivable part of an undercarriage, the vast majority of them are fabricated from smaller pieces and together form the system. In our experiences driving off-road, we have found that the more skid plates installed on a vehicle, the more of an opportunity exists for there to be loose panels, additional hardware, and more of a logistical challenge to service the vehicle, since instead of removing one panel, several must be removed. Knowing this, we chose to

install one of American Outfitter's undercarriage skid plates, which is fabricated from a single piece of $^3/_{16}$-inch laser-cut steel plate and is CNC bent to follow the contours of the undercarriage, thereby avoiding taking up any ground clearance. Since the American Outfitter's plate covers more surface area than the factory skid plates, the factory units are removed and that their mounting locations are reused in conjunction with a few new ones for the new plate. Offered in either bare metal or a powder-coated finish, the skid plate is definitely the way to go if you want to make it off the trail in one piece and still moving. To assist us with the install, Dave Wever of Wever's Welding and Fabrication installed our skid plate.

1 One of the most important components to protect on any Jeep is the transfer case. Let this piece of machinery become damaged, and it's all over.

2 Aside from being easier to handle during the installation, a solid piece undercarriage skid plate reduces the amount of required mounting hardware, minimizes seams or gaps that can often get caught on rocks, and allows for better access to items that need to be maintained.

3

One of the great benefits to this unit is that the factory skid plate mounting locations are utilized, which reduces install time and ensures that the plate is mounted on a solid foundation, which in this case is a frame crossmember.

4

Since the skid plate will be doing battle with rocks, logs, and other obstacles, the factory mounting bolts should be torqued to factory specifications upon completion of the install.

5

In a few other locations on the skid plate, Grade 8 hardware supplements the factory mounting locations to guarantee solid and stable platform.

6

Once installed, there is a noticeable difference in the coverage area of the solid piece skid plate versus the multiple factory skids. One noticeable feature of the skid plate is that while it does not interfere with the front driveshaft's operation, it still protects the U-joints and a portion of the shaft.

PROJECT 31
Upgrade a Universal Joint

Time: 3 Hours

Tools: Allen head wrenches, socket set, hand tools, grease gun, impact gun

Talent:

Applicable Years: All

Tab: $150 To $230 (depending upon axle size)

Parts Required: Ox Joints

Tip: Be sure to grease the U-joints prior to their installation.

Performance Gain: Provides added durability to the front axle

Complementary Project: Installation of upgraded front axles

If you're looking for a quick and relatively easy upgrade to your Jeep that can be performed with a few hand tools but will yield a tremendous amount of strength to your drivetrain, then look no further than upgrading the universal joints on your rig. Given the extreme conditions that the front axle shafts face on a day-in-day-out basis, your universal joints are sure to feel the pain and will eventually break apart, literally. For numerous years, the train of thought for having a bulletproof front end was to replace the axle with a larger, stronger, more expensive unit, say, a Dana 60. While performing this swap is indeed the best way to go to achieve this goal, the costs can be somewhat prohibitive, especially when you're looking at spending $9,000 for a top-of-the-line unit like a Dynatrac Pro Rock 60, before the cost to install it is included.

Considered to be one of the weakest links of any axle, a universal joint is essentially a pair of hinges located close together and oriented at 90 degrees relative to each other, and are used to transmit rotary motion. A typical universal joint, or U-joint, as they are commonly referred to, is constructed of a steel body and feature end cups that have needle bearings inserted into them that are attached to trunnions. U-joint failures commonly occur due to a loss of lubrication at the needle bearings inside the end cups, which allows rust to build up and degradation of the trunnion to follow, which in turn causes the U-joint failure. Since the majority of U-joints do not have grease fittings or any other provisions for maintenance, the failures occur often, which is why they are defined as the weakest links.

One of the most durable and impressive U-joints that we have ever encountered and that is guaranteed to withstand the test of time is the Ox Joint. Once installed, the chances of a U-joint failure are pretty much diminished. Built by the same company that produces the ever-popular Ox Locker, these U-joints have been fabricated from 8620 alloy and heat-treated to endure 22,000 lbs-ft without breaking a sweat. As a comparison, a Spicer 760x cold-forged U-joint will withstand about 5,400 lbs-ft before failing; and a Spicer 297s U-joint is good for about 4,600 lbs-ft before failing. The multipiece design contains grease fittings, the body, retainers, and pins, all of which can be disassembled for service. Rather than having end caps, the Ox Joint utilizes pins that are inserted through the axle yoke ear into the body. They are retained inside a cavity in the body by a pair of 4340 alloy retainers. The pins are also 8620, but they get a different heat treatment than the body. The pins use an O-ring seal to keep water out.

The current applications for the Ox Joint include Dana 35, 44, and 60 models. One thing to keep in mind however is that in order for the axle to be the strongest it can be, in addition to the U-joint being replaced, the axles must be upgraded as well; even with both items replaced, it is still cheaper and easier than upgrading to a larger unit.

1

Traditional universal joints use end cups filled with needle bearings as their agents for turning the joint. Often the cause of a U-joint failure is due to the lack of lubrication, which cannot be monitored or maintained as there are no grease fittings installed.

2

Victims of the same failure as traditional needle bearing units, a bushed U-joint relies upon a bronze sleeve to turn the joint instead of the needle bearings. Notice there are still no provisions for greasing the U-joint.

3

Placed alongside each other, the basic concept of the U-joint end cap is the same, and susceptible to the same failures and pitfalls. The Ox Joint has been designed to take a different approach on this conventional design.

4

The body of the Ox Joint has been fabricated from 8620 alloy and heat-treated to endure 22,000 lbs-ft without breaking a sweat.

5

Rather than having the traditional end caps, the Ox Joint utilizes pins that are inserted through the axle yoke ear into the body.

6

The pins are retained inside a cavity in the body by a pair of 4340 alloy retainers. The pins are also 8620, but they get a different heat treatment than the body and use an O-ring seal to keep water out.

7

Once the pins and retainers have been installed, a protective cover with a built-in grease zerk fitting is secured in place.

8

Due to the fact that the Ox Joint has had the needle bearings eliminated from its design, it is not ideal for continuous-duty operation in certain applications, such as full-time four-wheel drive.

PROJECT 32
Install a Differential Cover

 Time: 1 Hour

 Tools: Socket set, torx head sockets, hex head sockets, scraper

 Talent:

 Applicable Years: All

 Tab: $300 per axle

 Parts Required: Silicone gasket sealant, differential cover, differential fluid, brake cleaner

 Tip: Prior to loosening the differential cover, make sure that a collection bowl or pan is located below the unit to collect all of the differential fluid

 Performance Gain: Provides additional protection to the differentials

 Complementary Project: Installation of new ring and pinion gears

The old saying about chains and their weakest links is no truer than when looking at an axle and its differential cover. For the most part, a Dana 35, Dana 44, or Dana 60 axle is a solid and bulletproof piece of equipment that can take numerous blows from rocks, debris, and other obstacles that are often encountered off-roading. However the same cannot be said for their differential covers. Typically, an encounter with a rock to the factory differential cover can turn your fun-filled day of adventure into a stranded nightmare. Known for being the weakest link on an axle, the factory differential covers can be easily replaced with units that have been designed to the same specifications as the axles that they are attached to.

One example of a bulletproof differential cover is Dynatrac's Pro Series differential cover. Fabricated from 100 percent high-strength nodular iron, these covers feature Dynatrac's exclusive webbing design, which adds strength and rigidity. In addition to the increased protection, the Dynatrac cover also features a raised fill plug, which increases fluid capacity. Recessed lower bolt heads are included for additional protection to the cover while rock crawling. It doesn't hurt that they give an aggressive look to your axle and are affordable. Any way you look at it, nothing but good can come from this replacement.

1

The weakest link of your axle is the factory differential cover. Prior to its removal, ensure that the floor is protected from the differential fluid that will be seeping out as soon as the cover is loosened and that a pan for the fluid is under the differential.

2

As the existing fluid drains from the differential, it is a good time to perform a quick inspection of your gears; examine the fluid for any metal shavings.

3

Prior to moving forward with the installation of the new cover, brake cleaner should be sprayed onto the gear set to clean away any remaining fluid and particles. The existing gasket should be scraped at this time, and the differential surface scraped with a razor blade until the surface is clean and ready for the new gasket and cover.

4

With the new cover having been cleaned and prepped for installation, a bead of black RTV silicone is applied to the cover at about 1/4 inch in width.

5

Once the new cover has been set onto the axle, care should be taken to minimize the amount of movement that is made. Too much movement could result in the gasket not being seated correctly and possibly leaking fluid.

6

Each of the new differential cover bolts is recessed for added protection. Each of the bolts should be installed in its correct mounting pattern and should not be overtightened as it could damage the axle housing.

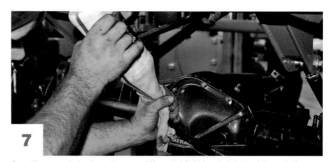

7

Once the cover is in place, the new differential fluid is administered through the new raised filler plug.

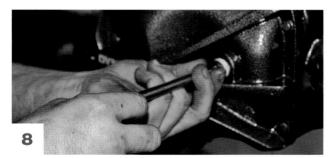

8

Install the new fill bolt that is provided with the Dynatrac differential cover. Tighten this bolt to 25 lbs-ft of torque.

9

Now that the new Dynatrac differential cover has been installed, the risk of causing serious damage to your axle and gears is greatly reduced, and the unit looks great.

PROJECT 33
Upgrade to a Dynatrac Pro Rock 60 Axle

 Time: 6 Hours

 Tools: Axle stands, socket sets, open-ended wrenches, hand tools

 Talent:

 Applicable Years: All

 Tab: $8,000 per axle

Parts Required: Axle, gear oil

 Tip: When performing this swap, it is necessary to have a forklift or some other apparatus available to move the unit around.

 Performance Gain: Aside from making your axles bulletproof to anything they come into contact with, they also provide additional ground clearance at the differentials

 Complementary Project: Installation of a suspension system

We all know the importance of a truck's engine, suspension, and transmission. However, these items are only as good as the drivetrain to which they are attached. When adding larger tires to the stock axles of a Jeep, the strength and durability of those axles must be considered. The ever popular Dana 35 and Dana 44 axles from the factory are more than adequate as stock, but as soon as 37-inch or larger tires are installed, a larger, more durable axle should be installed. The reason for the upgrade is that the construction of the components is much more adept at handling the increase in weight, stress, and force that is applied to the knuckles, axles, differentials, and axle tubes.

One of the most highly regarded axle manufacturers in the industry is Dynatrac. Their flagship model, the Pro Rock 60, was introduced in 2002 as the answer to the need for a bulletproof axle. They are built from Dynatrac's patented nodular iron, with housing and fittings of the highest quality. They are shipped "install ready," which means that the upgraded disc brake assemblies, SD 35 spline axles, Warn heavy-duty manual locking hubs, and selected ring and pinion gears are included. They also feature the highest ground clearance of any axle, including the Dana 44. Fully ABS compatible, they feature a one-year warranty with unlimited mileage.

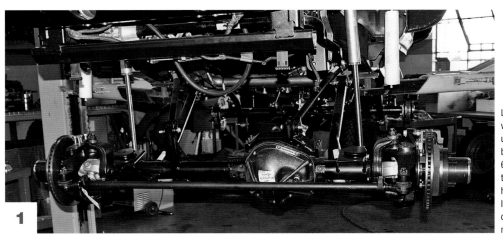

1

Legends in their own time, for those who can afford the swap from a factory unit to a bulletproof powerhouse, the buck stops with Dynatrac's Pro Rock 60 axle. Just one look and you can see the strength and craftsmanship that has been put into these works of art. In fact, they are almost too nice to take off-road. On second thought, no, they're not. Let's go!

2

A forklift is used to maneuver the axle around the shop and set it in place for the swap. Their weight and durable construction are just two reasons so many avid off-roaders decided to exchange their Dana 35 or Dana 44 units for one.

3

Built to the highest degree of quality, the nodular-iron steering knuckles and a high-steer arm allows for crossover and high-clearance steering systems to be used. Also worth mentioning are their upgraded disc brake assemblies and solid steel end forgings.

4

One of the advantages to installing a Pro Rock 60 is that the appropriate brackets are already installed, which saves a tremendous amount of fabrication time, not to mention that the brackets are actually in the correct location and attached at the right angles.

5

Each Pro Rock 60 axle is shipped with 35-spline SD, induction-hardened, alloy steel inner axle shafts and a 1480 axle joint.

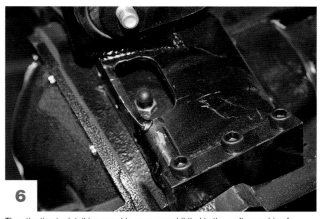

6

The attention to detail is second to none, as exhibited in the craftsmanship of the axle bridge that supports the driver's side upper control arm mount. Note the forethought of having an opening cut in place for the breather vent hose.

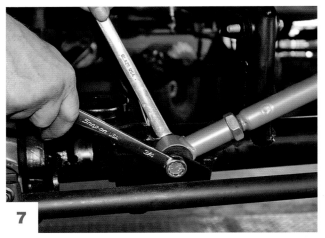

7

Regardless of the suspension manufacturer, virtually any suspension system can be bolted onto these units. In this photo a Rubicon Express track bar is being installed.

8

As we mentioned previously, the Pro Rock 60 axles have been set up to allow Dynatrac's high-steer kit to be used. This allows use of the factory pitman arm, so turning radius is not compromised.

9

The driver's side upper control arm is installed onto the axle bridge that spans the width of the center differential of the front axle.

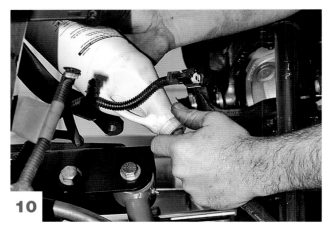

10

One thing that must not be forgotten is that all Dynatrac Pro Rock 60 axles are shipped without gear oil. Upon completion of the swap, fill the differential before moving the Jeep. Failure to do so may result in a costly repair.

11

The final items left to install are the shocks and other suspension components. Between the durability of the axles and the coil-over shock unit seen on this suspension, something tells me this rig will be able to go anywhere without so much as breaking a sweat.

PROJECT 34
Install a Differential Breather Hose Extension and Filter

 Time: 1/2 Hour

 Tools: Hand tools, side cutters

 Talent:

 Applicable Years: All

Tab: $225

 Parts Required: Vent filter, filter lubrication, hose clamp, metal coupler

 Tip: Be sure to lubricate the hose prior to installing the vent filter and coupler onto the hose.

 Performance Gain: Added protection from the elements to the differential

Complementary Project: None

Regardless of what size or type of axle that your Jeep has in it, it will have a vent at the top of it. The purpose for these vents is to equalize the pressure in the axle that builds up as the temperature within the axle changes depending on the amount of driving, as well as the style and place that the vehicle is driven. Typically, a vacuum hose connected to the vent extends only a few inches above the axle itself. While this is fine if the vehicle will not be going off a paved road, it may become an issue as soon as the dirt road begins or water crossings are stumbled upon. Since the stock breather hose has no way of keeping debris, dust, or water out of the differential, there is a good chance that a fair amount of damage could occur to the unit if the breather hose is not protected and extended. Also, if your vehicle has been lifted, there is a good chance that the breather hose has not been lengthened to make up for the increase in suspension lift, and when the vehicle is articulating, the hose may become detached from the vent.

Extending the breather hose is easily achieved by one of two methods. The first method is to remove the hose at the vent fitting and install a longer piece. The other method is to leave the factory hose in place and install a coupler upon which a longer section of same-size hose can be installed. Either method will work fine. Another issue that must be considered is the actual placement of the hose. In many stock configurations, the hose is left terminated somewhere inside the wheel well. Once again, while fine for street driving, this is detrimental to the vent hose when off-road

driving, given the amount of debris that is stuck and found in the wheel wells that could potentially be directed down the hose.

During our install, we extended the breather hose and relocated it to a space inside the engine compartment for better protection. The rear breather hose was extended and placed in a more shielded area. The final step is to install a vent filter at the end of each hose. We utilized filter units from K&N that are both durable and receptive to lubrication, which adds another layer of protection to the system.

1 The K&N breather filter will assist in keeping dirt and other contaminants from being sucked into the differential as the differential pressure changes due to driving conditions and related elements.

2

Once the breather hose is found, it can either be replaced completely with a longer piece or it can be extended. The new length of hose should take issues such as suspension height increase, suspension articulation, and exposure to the elements into consideration.

3

Our breather hose was relocated and routed along the side of the shock tower into the engine compartment.

4

Our breather hose was relocated and extended into the engine compartment of our Jeep for added protection. During the reroute, the factory breather cap was installed to help keep debris from falling into the new hose. It was then removed when the hose was installed in the new location.

5

The vent filter is attached to the breather hose to guarantee the highest level of protection possible from the elements.

6

It is important to relocate the breather hose and vent filter to an area that is easily accessed for service and inspection of the filter.

SECTION 4
SUSPENSION

Suspension is very important to a Jeep. While it may have the biggest and baddest engine and a bulletproof drivetrain, a Jeep will not go anywhere or over anything without a suspension. Considering its importance on the vehicle, this chapter reviews projects that will benefit a suspension system greatly. Items such as installing a lift kit, shock replacement, and coil-over conversions are addressed, with many other similar items as well.

PROJECT 35
Replace Shock Bushings and Grommets

 Time: ¹/₂ Hour (per shock)

 Tools: Hand tools, socket set, lubricant, open-ended wrenches

 Talent: 🔧🔧🔧

 Applicable Years: All

Tab: $25 (per shock)

 Parts Required: Shock bushings

 Tip: Be sure to lubricate the old shock bushing to aid in the removal of it.

 Performance Gain: Increases the performance and stability of the shock

 Complementary Project: None

Shock absorbers work hard, whether they are absorbing the potholes in a city street, absorbing a washboard road, or exploring off-road. After a few thousand miles of this abuse, things can get pretty ugly for some related components, especially the bushings and grommets. In addition to the shock vibration taking its toll on them, items such as road salt, oil, and an entire laundry list of contaminants will also destroy most common rubber units. While the shock may still continue to have some life in it, chances are that the bushings and grommets are destroyed, which is translated to the driver by a loss in vehicle control and damping abilities. To regain and firm the ride back up look no further than a new set of bushings and grommets to get the job done. While a variety of materials on the market cater specifically to shock absorber bushings, the most popular and longest lasting in our experiences has been Energy Suspension's HyperFlex polyurethane units.

Energy's polyurethane bushings and grommets, which have been awarded a total of nine patents, are created using a technically advanced chemical formula that resists contaminants. They are offered in a variety of durometers (firmness or softness) for either specific Jeep models or road conditions.

1 From the looks of things, these grommets and bushings need to be replaced with more durable pieces that can do a better job at withstanding the torque and forces that they are subjected to on a daily basis.

2 Energy Suspension's HyperFlex polyurethane grommets and bushings have been created from advanced materials that are resistant to contaminants. For a truly custom fit, the bushings are available for many of today's most popular shocks.

Depending upon its age and material, a bushing or grommet can either be easy or difficult to remove. Generally one will know within a few seconds. In the event that the bushing or grommet is difficult to remove, simply spray it with a lubricant and let it soak in before attempting again to dislodge the piece.

3

Once it has been determined that the bushing or grommet needs replacing, the shock is removed from the vehicle.

5

The new bushing and bushing sleeve are pressed into place with the use of a vise.

6

Once the bushing is set in place, the shock can be reattached to the vehicle.

PROJECT 36
Adok a Steer Stop
Adjust a Steer Stop

 Time: 1/2 Hour

 Tools: Open-ended wrenches

 **Talent:**

 Applicable Years: All

 Tab: None

 Parts Required: None

 Tip: None

 Performance Gain: Restricts the tires from hitting key suspension and steering components thereby causing damage

 Complementary Project: Install wheel spacers

Ever wonder what keeps your tires from turning all the way in and hitting your inner wheel well material and also what keeps them from taking out or rubbing against key suspension components? It's a little bolt called a steer stop. Consisting of a threaded bolt that is installed into the spindle of your front axle and locked in place with a nut, this small but effective item controls when your wheels stop turning in or out, a type of governor. Typically set at the factory in accordance with the OE-sized wheels and tires, there's a good chance that

it will have to be readjusted the minute larger wheels and tires are installed. Given their larger size and width, the steer stop must typically be adjusted further out to accommodate this increased size. In turn, when making adjustment for larger tires, the turning radius of the vehicle will also be affected since the wheels will not be turning in as tight as they did in the factory configuration. Failure to adjust the steer stop could result in the tires rubbing against or damaging key suspension components.

1 In this photo, the steer stop has been adjusted at the factory to fit the OE-sized wheels and tires. Once larger units are installed, adjustment is required.

2 Utilizing two open-ended wrenches, the bolt that makes up the stop and the lock nut are loosened so that a measurement can be taken for adjustment.

3

In cases where the bolt has never been removed, it is a good idea to back it all the way and apply a penetrating lubricant to keep it from seizing in the spindle.

4

Once reinstalled, the bolt and nut are adjusted to the point where there is no interaction between the tire and suspension components.

5

Once adjusted correctly, the chance of a tire rubbing a control arm, as exhibited in this photo, or causing other more serious damage to the suspension is highly unlikely.

PROJECT 37
How to Center a Steering Wheel

 Time: 1/2 Hour

 Tools: Hand tools

 **Talent:**

Applicable Years: All

Tab: None

 Parts Required: None

 Tip: None

 Performance Gain: Allows the steering wheel to be in alignment as it should be for proper orientation when driving

Complementary Project: Steering stabilizer install

Aside from being a nuisance, a misaligned steering wheel is a great indicator that your Jeep's steering system is slightly off kilter. There are numerous reasons for this misalignment to occur. Some of the plausible reasons address the toe settings of the vehicle, which are essentially responsible for setting the angle of the front wheels in relation to the rear. Another reason could be from a loose steering linkage that has received an impact from a possible rock while off-road driving, and yet another reason could be that there is a damaged component that is bent. To correct the issue, the cause for the condition must be determined first. Upon learning of the cause, the appropriate corrective actions and adjustment can be taken to correct the issue.

Noticing that our project vehicle's steering wheel was misaligned, we determined that it had been placed out of adjustment from the previous week's off-road trip and that the drag bar link had become loose. To resolve it and get things back in line with each other, the drag link bar bolts were loosened and the turnbuckle was adjusted, using a pair of pliers to recenter the steering wheel. The purpose of a drag link bar is to act as a connection to other linkages in the suspension system. It functions each time the steering arm operates, in a plane above other suspension links. During its movement, the sweeping arc of the steering arm is converted to a linear motion, which is transferred to the steering links.

While an easy fix, this is one condition that could have been identified on a routine inspection of the underbody components upon our completion of the trail.

What's wrong with this photo? The steering wheel is turned but the wheels remain straight. Often caused by hitting a rock or having the toe out of alignment, a misaligned steering wheel can be more than a nuisance. It can also be a safety issue, in that the wheel is positioned in one direction and the tires are going in another.

The alignment between the steering wheel and the front tires is performed by loosening each side of the drag link bar turnbuckle bolts.

3

Using a pair of pliers, by turning the turnbuckle either in a clockwise or counterclockwise rotation, the steering wheel alignment will be adjusted.

4

Depending on the type of front skid plate that is mounted on your Jeep, you may need to inspect the proximity of the drag link bar to the plate to make sure that when the tires are turned in either direction they do not interfere with each other. If they do, rotate the bolts on the drag link bar until clearance is achieved.

5

Once the drag link bar clearance has been resolved, the end bolts on the turnbuckle are tightened.

6

Upon completion of the alignment, the steering wheel is once again in alignment with the direction that the front tires are pointed.

PROJECT 38
Install a Long-Travel Front Coil-Over Suspension

 Time: 8 Hours

 Tools: Grinder, plasma cutter, welder, hand tools

 Talent: ✶✶✶✶✶

 Applicable Years: Jeep Wrangler JK (two-door and four-door models)

 Tab: $1,050 (Including coil-over shocks)

Parts Required: Coil-over shocks, brackets, mounting hardware

 Tip: Professional installation is highly recommended. A new front aftermarket CV driveline is required for proper installation and is not included with the kit.

 Performance Gain: Adjustable ride height and increased suspension articulation

 Complementary Project: Installation of a long-travel bolt-in cantilever coil-over rear suspension system

Suspension systems are interesting animals, in that you can install one that will raise your Jeep to the sky and allow larger tires to be installed, but it will not provide any additional suspension articulation or travel beyond the stock system that it replaced. On the other hand, some suspensions are so over the top that the mere thought of driving down a city street in a Jeep equipped with one would be terrifying. Regardless of what style of suspension your Jeep has installed on it, Off-Road Evolution's Evo Coil-Over Front Suspension system can be installed. One look at any purpose-built rock crawler or competition vehicle is all it takes to see that a coil-over suspension system is the choice to have when long travel and articulation is required. Installed as a preassembled package, the shock absorber and spring work together to provide optimal damping without torsional loads, the end result being the best suspension setup one can have for off-road driving.

Fabricated from laser-cut 3/16-inch plate steel, the front shock towers and lower mounting brackets are easily installed with a welder after careful preparation. Compatible with most 12- to 14-inch coil-over shocks, the ride height is fully adjustable and will allow the use of 35- to 42-inch tires.

1 The first order of business is to remove all of the stock front suspension brackets from the frame. Once this is completed, the frame is prepped for the shock tower by grinding and painting the affected area.

2 The shock tower is mounted in place along the frame rail, along with the optional Evo Airbump kit, which utilizes 2-inch bump stops to help dampen the suspension when under extreme compression.

3

The front shock towers are tack welded in place first to confirm their correct position in relation to the other mounting hardware. Once confirmed as acceptable, they are finished being welded onto the frame rails.

4

With no room to spare, the shock is bolted into the shock tower and torqued to the required specifications.

5

The lower shock mounts are attached to the front axle in preparation for the front coil-over unit. The lower shock mount is also fabricated from $3/16$-inch laser-cut plate steel; it features a built-in skid plate to protect the unit from any encounters with unfriendly rocks.

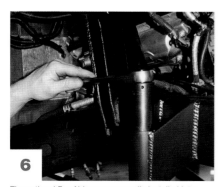

6

The optional Evo Airbumps are easily installed into their frame-mounted holders.

7

As we mentioned earlier, the coil-over units contain external reservoirs that must be secured somewhere in close proximity to the main shock body. A pair of clamps is being attached to the reservoir body so that they can be measured against the frame rail mounts.

8

The frame rail reservoir mounts are welded onto the frame and will hold the reservoirs securely in place. The finished product is quite impressive, especially since it has been designed for handling both on and off the road, a rarity to some other systems that feature the same technology.

PROJECT 39
Select a Suspension Lift

Time: Average 6–8 hours

Tools: N/A

Talent: 🔧🔧🔧🔧 to 🔧

Applicable Years: All models

Tab: Costs vary depending upon selected suspension system

Parts Required: N/A

Tip: Choose a system that will fit with your needs and requirements—do not buy a suspension to impress others on the trail.

Performance Gain: Increased ground clearance and suspension articulation

Complementary Project: Installation of wheels and tires

One of the first things that should be performed on your Jeep if you even remotely plan on taking it off-road is to install a suspension system. Given the new design of the Jeep Wrangler JK models, a very minimal amount of suspension lift is required to install a suitable-sized tire for off-road driving.

While there are literally hundreds of suspension companies out there that offer their own version of a suspension lift utilizing both new and old technologies, choosing the correct system for your needs can be confusing, to say the least. Features such as ride quality; dependability both on and off the trail; how it is installed, a bolt-on application or a full custom fabrication, are issues to consider when making your decision.

Listed below are some of the newest suspension kits on the market that range from mild to wild, depending upon how far you choose to take your build.

DEAVER LEAF SPRINGS

Deaver's progressive series springs are high-quality 9- and 10-leaf units fabricated from the highest-grade 5160 steel. Employing a higher leaf count spring allows for the use of a thinner leaf material that yields a more flexible progressive leaf stack, thereby producing a much smoother spring rate curve throughout the complete suspension cycle. The even, linear compression rate curve of the spring is the primary key to the excellent ride quality.

Other design features include diamond-cut inner leaf ends to minimize the shear points, antifriction pads inserted between the leaves for a smoother ride and quiet operation, full military-wrapped spring eyes for superior durability, and OEM bushings that are perfect for early model Jeeps.

RUBICON EXPRESS JK SHORT ARM SUSPENSION KIT

Rubicon Express' JK short arm suspension package utilizes the factory mounting brackets to achieve the desired lift height of 2 to 3½ inches. Each kit features rebuildable SuperFlex joints in both the upper and lower control arms. Adjustable heavy-duty track bars and brackets are also included, as well as front sway bar disconnects. The high-strength steel coil springs are tailored for either two- or four-door models. Due to the increased height, each kit contains lengthened stainless steel braided brake lines.

Photo courtesy of Rubicon Express

Photo courtesy of Rubicon Express

FULL-TRACTION 3-INCH "ULTIMATE" JEEP JK WRANGLER SUSPENSION SYSTEM

Full-Traction's latest Jeep JK system is nicknamed the "unlimited" kit because of the numerous components that make it up. Consisting of rebuildable, fully adjustable upper and lower control arms that have been manufactured from durable 2x0.250-inch wall drawn over mandrel (DOM) steel tubing with 4130 Cromoly Heim joints, the system allows for increased wheel travel and 35-inch tires.

Additional components of the kit include heavy-duty adjustable front and rear track bars, new generation front sway bar disconnects, rear links, bump stops, offset brake line relocation brackets, and ride frequency tuned coil springs for a comfortable ride.

Photo courtesy of Full-Traction

PRO COMP STAGE II X FLEX JEEP JK SUSPENSION SYSTEM

Pro Comp Suspension's new 4-inch Jeep JK Stage II X Flex suspension system has been designed for performance. Replacing the factory lower control arms are CNC-formed units made from $3/16$-inch A 36 plate steel that has been plated for additional strength with $1/8$-inch thick gusset plates. The replacement high-angle spherical ball end is rebuildable and features polyurethane bushings. The factory alignment specifications are retained, thanks to adjustable length front upper control arms. Heavy-duty adjustable front and rear track bars are made from 4130N chromoly tubing to retain proper axle alignment. Additional custom components to the kit include billet bump stops, offset brake line relocation brackets, replacement front and rear weight vehicle specific coil springs and a set of matching MX6 mono-tube gas shocks. The kit will allow a set of 35-inch tires to be installed with no clearance issues.

Photo courtesy of Pro Comp Suspension

SUPERLIFT ROCKRUNNER LONG-ARM SERIES SUSPENSION SYSTEMS

Superlift's RockRunner Long-Arm Series lifts are available in 4-inch and 6-inch heights for the Jeep Wrangler TJ and Wrangler Unlimited. Both kits utilize high-articulated RockRunner link arms at each corner to provide exceptional ground clearance, full steering, and incredible suspension flex. Built with quality and durability in mind, the RockRunner arms feature internal swivels at the Heim joint ends, steel-encased rubber bushings at certain link mounting points to ensure bind-free articulation, and vibration dampers. The RockRunner arms bolt directly to the TJ axles and are anchored to a two-piece skidpan assembly. The desired lift height is derived from taller-than-stock coil springs. The base model kits include compression-travel-control components, threaded-style sway bar quick-disconnects, and adjustable track bars with mounting brackets. Additional components included in the 6-inch kit are rear sway bar disconnects, a dropped pitman arm, and extended-length braided steel brake hoses.

Photo courtesy of Superlift

JKS MANUFACTURING'S ACOS PRO SUSPENSION SYSTEM

The original adjustable coil-over suspension system for Jeep Wrangler TJ, XJ, ZJ, and JK vehicles has incorporated an integrated bump shock into the coil-over system to help prevent the suspension from bottoming out when the vehicle is traveling at high speeds or supporting heavy loads. In addition to the bump stop technology, the system allows for quick adjustment of ride height without the removal of any components by a simple turn of the spring retention ring. An adjustment range of between $1\frac{3}{8}$ inches to a full $3\frac{3}{4}$ inches is achievable depending upon the type of terrain and tire and wheel sizes.

Photo courtesy of JKS Manufacturing

TERAFLEX JEEP JK 4-INCH SUSPENSION SYSTEM

TeraFlex's 4-inch JK suspension system contains everything needed for a weekend of hardcore trail running on 37-inch tires. Included in each kit are new upper and lower FlexArms, matched shocks at all four corners, front sway bar disconnecting brackets and an extended rear track bar bracket. Additional items included with the kit are new bump stops and new hardware. It is important to note that this system can be installed on both the Rubicon and Unlimited versions of the JK. Driveline modifications are required on all two-door versions.

Photo courtesy of TeraFlex

OLD MAN EMU JEEP TJ HEAVY-DUTY SUSPENSION SYSTEM

The name of this suspension system says it all. Named after one of the strongest birds on the planet, whose legs are able to handle extreme amounts of weight, the OME Jeep TJ kit follows suit. Consisting of custom replacement coil springs and matched shock absorbers, the OME heavy-duty suspension compensates for any heavy add-on items such as front bumpers, jacks, winches and lights. Each kit includes installation hardware, coil spring pads, and complete instructions.

Photo courtesy of Old Man Emu

BDS SUSPENSION'S 6½-INCH JEEP JK SUSPENSION

BDS Suspension's Jeep JK $6\frac{1}{2}$-inch suspension kit has been designed to allow 37-inch tires and increased capability on the trails. The heart of the system is the upper and lower control arms, which feature flex ends and are adjustable, allowing the pinion angles to be fine-tuned for increased performance. Included with the kit are new Pro-Ride coil springs that are capable of full coil bind, new pitman arm, adjustable track bars, and Department of Transportation–approved Kevlar-lined stainless steel brake lines for the front and rear. A front sway bar disconnect is standard, as are BDS' 5500-series shock absorbers.

Photo courtesy of BDS Suspension

GEN-RIGHT 3-LINK FRONT END KIT

Always at the forefront of off-road engineering, Gen-Right Off-Road introduces their new three-link front end kit for all Jeep TJ and YJ models. Whether you're looking to increase suspension performance or move the front axle forward to achieve a 100-inch wheelbase, this is the kit to do it. Included with each kit are heavy-duty 3/16-inch laser-cut and CNC-machined brackets and mounts. Currie-forged Johnny Joints have been used for ease of maintenance since they are rebuildable and greaseable, while the control arm tubing is crafted from thick wall 1/4-inch tubing that can be easily adapted to any length. The control arm inserts are machined specifically with left-or right-side threads for adjustments. Each kit contains chromoly Heim ends at the track bar ends and has Grade 8 hardware. The kit can be used with coil-over shocks, 2.5-inch air shocks or regular coil springs and may be used with 8-inch to 10-inch travel shocks, tires up to 35 inches in diameter, and vehicles with 12 to 14 inches of wheel travel.

Photo courtesy of Gen-Right

OFF-ROAD EVOLUTION EVO LEVER REAR COIL-OVER SUSPENSION SYSTEM

Off-Road Evolution's Evo Lever Rear Coil-Over Suspension system is based off of a subframe with two massive levers attached to the axle. The levers articulate at the command of two dual-rate 8-inch coil-over shocks with remote reservoirs, with an end result of 14 inches of vertical suspension travel. Fabricated from laser-cut 3/16-inch plate steel brackets and DOM tubing for the subframe, the system is easily installed and is a direct bolt-in that will function with most aftermarket short-arm and long-arm suspension systems for the Jeep Wrangler JK models, two-door or four-door. It is also compatible with most 12- to 14-inch coil-over shocks; the ride height is fully adjustable and will allow the use of 35- to 42-inch tires.

SKYJACKER 4-INCH JK SUSPENSION SYSTEM

Skyjacker's 4-inch suspension system for the JK is full of heavy-duty parts that can handle whatever is thrown in their path. Softride coil springs provide 4 inches of lift and all the control you need for any terrain or highway. In addition to the benefits and control of the front and rear coil springs is the built-in durability of the replacement heavy-duty lower links. Skyjacker's Single Flex lower control arms replace the factory units and have durable, greaseable polyurethane bushings at the frame mount ends for longevity and increased performance. At the axle end, the arm has Skyjacker's Next Generation (NG) rebuildable rod ends with a forged steel alloy housing that is CNC-machined for accuracy and gold zinc-plated for extreme duty rating. Also incorporated into the NG rod ends are separate ball joints with Pivot Plus bolt inserts. These distinctive V-shaped Pivot Plus bolt inserts allow more pivot or rotation of the joint; upward of 35 degrees of maximum rotation, which factors into more articulation for the entire suspension system. Other key features of the system are the sway bars that are reset to proper form and function, with front double-disconnect links and extended length rear end links. The track bars are locked into position with heavy-duty relocation brackets, while the transfer case is realigned to its proper angle. The bump stops are relocated as well for great travel on extension and rebound. Stopping is no problem either, because the brake lines are rerouted via extension brackets.

Photo courtesy of Skyjacker

CLAYTON OFF-ROAD JEEP TJ/LJ LONG ARM SUSPENSION SYSTEMS

Backed by a lifetime warranty against bending or breakage, Clayton Off-Road Manufacturing's TJ/LJ 4-inch and 5 1/2-inch suspension systems are fabricated from 1/4-inch thick square tubular arms and laser-cut weld-on frame brackets. The rear system is a four-link design. Best of all, either kit allows for the use of 35-inch-tall tires.

Photo courtesy of Clayton Off-Road

PROJECT 40
Install a Long-Travel Bolt-in Cantilevered Coil-Over Rear Suspension System

 Time: 8 Hours

 Tools: Grinder, plasma cutter, welder, hand tools, transfer punch, drill, drill bits

 Talent: 🔧🔧🔧🔧🔧

 Applicable Years: Jeep Wrangler JK (two-door and four-door models)

Tab: $3,200 (including coil-over shocks and skid plate)

 Parts Required: Coil-over shocks, evo lever, brackets, mounting hardware

 Tip: Professional installation is highly recommended.

 Performance Gain: Adjustable ride height and increased suspension articulation

 Complementary Project: Installation of a long-travel front coil-over suspension system

The mind never stops turning when it comes time to building a great Jeep. Mel Wade, owner of Off-Road Evolution in Fullerton, California, has such a mind when it comes to designing some of the most cutting-edge suspensions we have ever seen. His latest creation is called the Evo Lever Suspension. This state-of-the-art, rear cantilevered system has been designed to allow a perfectly street legal, daily driver Jeep Wrangler JK to posses the same amount of suspension articulation as competition rock crawlers, yet still retain the vehicle's drivability. A far cry from the stock coil spring suspension, the Evo Lever is based off of a subframe with two massive levers attached, which articulate at the command of two dual-rate 8-inch coil-over shocks with remote reservoirs, with an end result of 14 inches of vertical suspension travel.

Fabricated from laser-cut $^3/_{16}$-inch plate steel brackets and DOM tubing for the subframe, the system is easily installed and is a direct bolt-in that will function with most aftermarket short-arm and long-arm suspension systems. It is also compatible with most 12- to 14-inch coil-over shocks; the ride height is fully adjustable and will allow the use of 35- to 42-inch tires. For best results, the system should be combined with Off-Road Evolution's long-travel front coil-over system.

1

The Off-Road Evolution Evo Lever system's subframes and brackets are constructed in-house from DOM tubing and then powder-coated for a durable and chip-resistant finish.

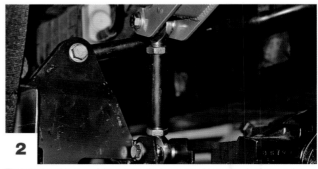

2

The actual workhorses of the system, the levers are able to absorb whatever the terrain can dish out and still provide a smooth and well-articulated ride. The levers are secured to the rear axle by using custom-fabricated linkages with Teflon-lined rod ends that are attached to the included rear track bar relocation bracket.

3

Each of the coil-over shocks has an external reservoir that is attached to the frame with custom brackets that must be welded onto the rear frame rail. The rear coil-over shocks are bolted directly to the levers. The shock valving determines the articulation of the lever.

4

Given the amount of travel that the Evo Lever system contains, limiting straps are installed to guard against any overextension of related components, such as axle breather vents and brake lines.

5

The rear brake line connection must be relocated from the vehicle frame onto the Evo Lever subframe. This is accomplished with a transfer punch and included hardware.

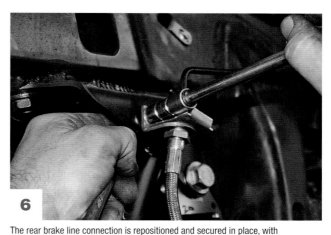

6

The rear brake line connection is repositioned and secured in place, with special attention being given to shield the brake line from being pinched by any moving components.

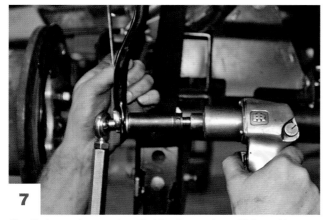

7

Given the increase in suspension articulation, the sway bar end links need to be lengthened. Using Off-Road Evolution's Hex Head Sway Bar End Links will allow them to be fine-tuned to just the right height that is need for optimal sway bar performance.

8

The finished product is quite impressive, especially since it has been designed to handle both on- and off-road duty, a rarity to some other systems that feature the same technology.

PROJECT 41
Install a Front Air Bump System

 Time: 30 Minutes per wheel

 Tools: Sawz-All, Allen wrenches, torque wrench, impact gun, ratchet, socket set

 Talent:

 Applicable Years: 2007–2008 Jeep JK Wrangler two- or four-door models

Tab: $300 per set

 Parts Required: N/A

 Tip: Apply a liberal amount of RTV silicone to the top and bottom bump stop mounting brackets.

 Performance Gain: Acts as a secondary source of suspension absorption, while minimizing the affects to the front suspension usually encountered when driving hard and fast over rough terrain

 Complementary Project: Suspension lift and shock upgrade

When traveling off-road, aside from the obvious obstacles that one may encounter that could render your vehicle inoperable, attrition of key suspension and driveshaft components is also a very viable issue to address and minimize. One of the contributing factors to the fatigue or failure of a suspension and its related components is the excessive recoil or lack of suspension absorption, which then reverberates throughout the entire suspension system and drivetrain; not a good thing to have going on.

While having the best or perfectly valved shocks on a vehicle helps to reduce the threat of damage and premature fatigue to these components and systems, to truly minimize the risk, air bump stops should be considered. Acting essentially as an additional shock, these air bumps serve as a secondary suspension absorption system. Long a staple on many of the high-end desert racing trucks, these items are worth their weight in gold to some hardcore enthusiasts.

Another area where the air bumps differentiate themselves from the OE rubber units is that they can be valved according to the specific type of terrain and driving style. Additionally, the air bumps absorb the deflections with greater smoothness, as they are typically nitrogen charged, rather than made from rubber or polyurethane that does not possess the same rebound factors.

Off-Road Evolution's air bump system has been fabricated from the countless years of experience that owner, Mel Wade, has under his belt in off-road racing and professional rock crawling. Beginning with a solid piece of billet aluminum, the top and bottom mounting brackets have been machined to exact tolerances and have been outfitted with retention bolts to guarantee safe and secure mounting points for the air bumps. The choice of Fox, King, or Bilstein 4-inch air bumps is available with each kit and all of the necessary hardware is included for an effortless install.

1 The first step in installing the air bump system is to remove the lower mounting bolts on the front shocks so that the front axle and front coil springs can be removed to allow access to the bump stop tower and bushing. The front sway bar linkages must also be separated.

2 In order to accommodate the 4-inch-long bump stop, the lower portion of the factory bump stop must be cut away to expose the hollow tube of the bump stop tower the new bump stop will slide into. The bump stop tower should be cut directly above the weld joint. Precautions should be taken to ensure that the cut is perpendicular to the tower; failure to have a flush cut will result in the bottom bracket not seating flush with the entire surface of the tower.

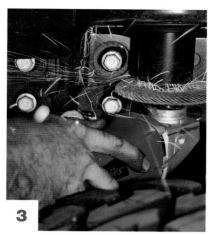

3

Once both sides of the towers have been cut, a grinder should be used to clean and remove any residual fragments that could become lodged between the air bump and tube. This step will also allow the mounting brackets to seat flush against the tower.

4

A liberal amount of RTV silicone should be applied to the flanges of the top and bottom mounting brackets prior to their installation on the vehicle. The RTV silicone will assist with the placement of the brackets in relation to the air bump mounting points.

5

Prior to installing the mounting brackets on the top and bottom, they should be aligned in such a fashion as to allow for easy access to the retaining bolts that will be securing the air bumps.

6

Once the RTV silicone has had an opportunity to cure, the air bump is easily slid into place between the two billet aluminum mounting brackets and the factory bump stop tower.

7

The new air bumps are secured to the vehicle through retaining bolts that are tightened down equally with an Allen head wrench. The top bracket bolts should be secured first; with the bottom units being last.

8

Once complete, the new setup will provide many miles of comfort by reducing the amount of recoil placed upon the suspension by hard-packed roads or overextension of the suspension at extreme approach or departure angles.

9

The final step of the install involves reinstalling the front coil springs and reattaching the lower bolt of the front shock to the axle. The sway bar links should also be resecured to the axle as well.

PROJECT 42
Install Front Axle Gussets

Time: 2 Hours

Tools: Welder, drill, wire wheel brush attachment

Talent: ✴✴✴

Applicable Years: All Jeep JK Wranglers

Tab: $90

Parts Required: Axle gussets, welding materials, spray primer, and paint

Tip: Prior to spray painting the new axle gussets, apply a coat of primer first to allow the paint to adhere better and resist coming off when washing the undercarriage.

Performance Gain: Provides additional protection and strength to the axle Cs

Complementary Project: Installation of front lower control arm skid plates

Jeeps are inherently tough vehicles, by most standards; however that is not to say that some aspects of them are not weak. As an example, the inner Cs on the front axle of the new Jeep Wrangler JKs are prone to bending when subjected to minimal amounts of force or stress during off-road driving. In the event that one of them should break, your day would be pretty much over and you would be headed home sitting shotgun with the tow truck driver. To strengthen these parts of a JK axle, Off-Road Evolution's C2 Evo axle gussets are $3/16$-inch laser-cut steel plates that have been fitted to the exact contours between the Cs and the axle tube. Once welded into place the probability of the Cs flexing and possibly breaking is alleviated. There are two plates per side, an upper and a lower, which must be installed separately.

They are easily installed. The only preparation required is that the existing paint between the Cs and the axle tube be removed with a wire brush that is attached to a drill. Once the paint is cleaned off and the surfaces are ready for the weld, the mounts are identified for each side and welded in place. After a few minutes of cool down, they are shot with primer and then spray painted for a factory finish.

1 The area of concern, the factory Cs of the front JK axles are susceptible to bending, flexing, and even breaking due to the amount of stress and force placed upon them by larger tires and off-road driving.

2 Each of the Evo C2 axle gussets is fabricated from $3/16$-inch laser-cut steel plates that have been fitted to the exact contours between the Cs and the axle tube.

3

Using an air drill with a wire brush attachment, any paint or debris is removed from the Cs of the front axle in preparation for the C2 axle gussets to be welded in place.

4

It is extremely important to get into the corners of the axle tube and Cs to ensure a solid and stable weld.

5

Prior to completely welding the C2 gussets in place, each piece should be test fitted for proper alignment.

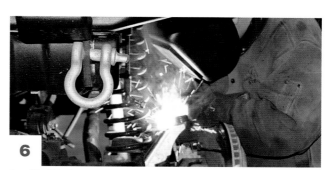

6

Once fitted into the correct location, the gussets are welded into place. Special care should be taken to protect the rubber bushings of the related components. To ensure their protection, they should be removed and reinstalled upon completion of the welding.

7

8

Looking as though they rolled off the assembly line with the rest of the axle, the gussets' fit and finish are not only durable, but unobtrusive.

9

For protection from the elements, the gussets are primed first and then spray painted black so that they blend in with the rest of the axle brackets.

10

While the gussets are not the flashiest or most easily noticed add-ons, once their performance is tested and your axles are in one piece, your enjoyment of them will come into play.

PROJECT 43
Replace a Shock

 Time: 1 Hour

 Tools: Socket set, impact gun

 Talent:

 Applicable Years: All

Tab: $500 to $1,500 (depending upon the shock type and brand)

 Parts Required: Shock and lubricant

 Tip: Prior to removing the rear shocks, make sure that the rear axle is supported. Failure to do so will make it harder to remove the shocks since they are holding the axle of the vehicle when it is on a lift.

 Performance Gain: Increases ride quality and performance both on and off the road

 Complementary Project: Installation of a lift kit

Believe it or not, a shock is considered to be a maintenance item on anything that has wheels. Just like needing to have an oil change or an engine service, shocks can become ineffective with the more miles that are placed upon them. In some cases, depending on the type of terrain or driving style that you may have, shocks may need to be replaced or serviced more often than one would think. Their primary role is to absorb and dissipate kinetic energy that is delivered to the vehicle as it travels down the road. The faster a vehicle drives on a bumpy road, the more kinetic energy is dissipated, which means that the shock must work that much harder.

Depending upon your type of Jeep, the type of shock absorbers used on it may vary. Whether the shock is a monotube design or a reservoir style depends on the terrain that it will be used on. As a rule of thumb, the harder the surface and faster the speed of the vehicle, the hotter a shock gets, which is why so many off-road race vehicles use external reservoir shocks.

The difference between the two styles of shocks, mono tube and external reservoir, is that with a monotube design shock, there is an internal reservoir that contains the shock fluid. This type of shock is the most common and widely used of all shock types. They do not perform quite as well as an external reservoir–style shock due to aeration, which is oil in the shock foaming due to the heat generated by the piston of the shock moving up and down so quickly. Aeration results in the shock losing its ability to dampen, causing the vehicle to ride rough and bouncy. A remote reservoir style of shock features an external reservoir that provides for greater oil capacity. The greater oil capacity allows the shock to operate at a much lower temperature, which means the Jeep can to be driven at higher speeds over rough terrain without the shocks fading or overheating. External reservoir shocks come in two types. A piggyback shock is so called because the external reservoir is attached to the main shock body. The other type has the reservoir separated from the main shock body, allowing it to be installed anywhere within the limits of the connecting hose. Remote reservoir shocks offer other benefits besides cool operation. For instance, they can be valved for specific vehicle applications and terrain, unlike most regular shocks that use generic valving, and they are easily rebuildable.

For our install, we are removing the factory Rubicon shocks from a Wrangler and are replacing them with a set of Rancho RS9000X Pro Series shocks that feature an anodized aluminum reservoir with a high-pressure stainless steel braided hose. To make mounting the external reservoir easier, a pair of reservoir cushions and clamps is provided with the shock. One of the big features to these models is that they can be adjusted to nine different settings, depending on the terrain and whether towing is being performed, all with the turn of a knob.

1

While the factory shocks on all Rubicon models of Wrangler are fine for the street, a few miles of hard off-roading can convince you otherwise, which is why we are replacing them with the Rancho RS9000X Pro Series units.

2

Part of the RS900X's durability and performance come from the external reservoir, which is connected to the main body of the shock by a braided stainless steel hose.

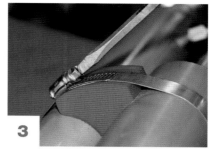

3

Included with each shock is a pair of reservoir cushions and hardware, which will allow the external reservoir portion of the shock to be mounted onto the main shock body, minimizing having to locate another area for the reservoir.

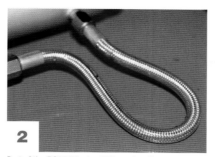

4

Typically shipped already filled with nitrogen, a Schrader valve is attached to the end of the external reservoir to allow additional adjustments to be made to the ride quality, if needed. As the sticker notes, only trained professionals should touch the valve.

5

Specific to this make and model of shock, the RS9000X Pro series is able to be adjusted to nine different settings, all with the turn of this knob, which is located at the top of the main shock body.

6

Allowing for an easy installation, the upper shock mounts and bushings are easily inserted into the factory location.

7

Prior to tightening the shock down, make sure the bushings are seated properly and that they are in the correct positions.

8

The lower shock bushing may be difficult to insert into the shock; we recommend applying a liberal amount of grease to help things slide on easier.

9

Aside from appearing beefier and looking like we mean business, the Rancho RS900X Pro series shocks are formidable components when rough roads are ahead.

PROJECT 44
Install Sway Bar End Links

 Time: 2 Hours

 Tools: Open-ended wrenches, socket set, impact gun

 Talent:

Applicable Years: All

Tab: $80 Pair

 Parts Required: Sway bar links

 Tip: If the links you need measure within the length gap, use the larger size.

 Performance Gain: Increases stability of the suspension system

 Complementary Project: Installation of a suspension system

The role of a sway bar system on a vehicle is to keep it from turning or pitching excessively from one side to another while cornering or driving over rough terrain. Aside from the horizontal sway bar itself, other components, such as bushings and sway bar end links, assist in these duties. Typically, a sway bar end link is a solid, nonadjustable-length bar that is sized depending upon whether or not the vehicle has a raised suspension system or is stock. Regardless of the make or model of Jeep that you drive, your vehicle has a sway bar and sway bar end links. With so many suspension systems for Jeeps being able to be adjusted to within inches, the need to have a sway bar system that is able to match a suspension's adjustments was seen as a much-needed item by Mel Wade of Off-Road Evolution. Rather than having to settle for a link that was either too short or too tall, and with no in-between length, the Off-Road Evolution Evo HD Sway Bar End Links were created.

The Evo HD Sway Bar End Links are constructed from a solid steel hex bar that has been threaded to allow for the ultimate in adjustability. Attached at either end of the bar are $\frac{1}{2}$-inch studded Teflon-lined rod ends and a $\frac{3}{4}$-inch hex bar linkage. Offered in lengths ranging from $5\frac{1}{2}$ inches to 15 inches, the end links are sold as a complete pair. Upon installing them on our project Jeep, a big improvement to the system's performance was noticed, especially when going into a corner or traversing a large boulder.

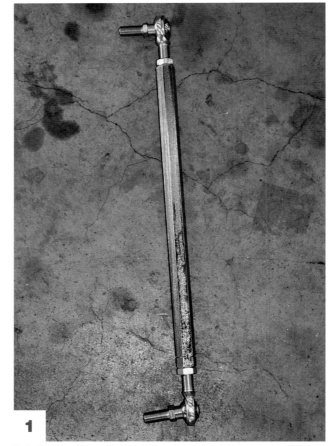

1

Each of the Evo HD Sway Bar End Links contains a pair of $\frac{1}{2}$-inch studded Teflon-lined rod ends and a $\frac{1}{2}$-inch hex bar linkage for the ultimate in both strength and adjustability.

2

Looking more like a component from an off-road race vehicle instead of from a Jeep, the HD rod ends featured on the sway bar end linkage are valuable not only for their ability to support such load forces, but their ability to be constantly moving, which is where the Teflon inserts come into play for quiet and maintenance-free service.

3

While completely adjustable, the end linkages are not any more difficult to install than a normal pair of linkages.

4

The new linkages should be installed onto the vehicle before any adjustments are made. This allows for both sides of the sway bar to be on equal footing so that each side has a base line to start from.

5

The first step in adjusting the linkage is to use an open-ended wrench to begin turning the shaft to the desired height. One of the main features of these linkages is that they can be adjusted to such a fine degree of precision.

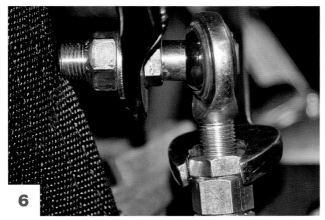

6

Once the desired height and adjustment has been made, a retention nut located on the stud of the rod end is tightened to the hex bar, theoretically securing the adjustment to the bar. Each side of the linkage has a retention nut that must be tightened.

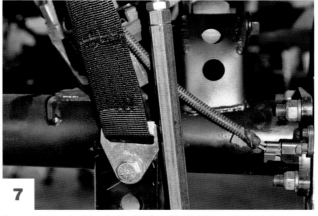

7

Strong and fully adjustable, the Evo HD Sway Bar End Links will not only improve your cornering ability, but they will also reduce the wear and tear on your suspension components by minimizing the excessive shifts in weight from one side to another.

PROJECT 45
Install Extended Length Brake Lines

 Time: 1¹/₂ Hours

 Tools: Socket set, brake fluid bleeding kit

Talent:

 Applicable Years: 2007–2008 Jeep JK Wrangler two- or four-door models

 Tab: $75 per set

 Parts Required: Brake fluid

 Tip: Make sure that the new extended length lines do not interfere with any moving parts, including tires. Also make certain that upon suspension articulation, the lines do not become pinched or pulled by other components.

 Performance Gain: In addition to providing improved brake system performance, the extended length lines will allow proper suspension articulation on lifted vehicles without restricting the suspension's travel

 Complementary Project: Upgrade to synthetic brake fluid and high-performance brake pads

There are numerous reasons for adding a suspension lift to your Jeep. For some, it may be to boost the rig's overall aesthetics, while for some others it may be to gain additional ground clearance to conquer that difficult trail. Whatever the intent, the one thing that should always be kept at the forefront of this decision is the safety, performance, and reliability of the vehicle after the work is performed. One item that is often overlooked while adding a suspension system is the upgrade of the factory brake lines for extended length units. Having been sized at the factory to complement the factory ride of height of a vehicle, the factory brake lines, both front and rear, are all too often stretched to their limits after a suspension system is installed. Granted, many of the better designed and assembled suspension systems include drop-down brackets in proportion to their respective kit heights, but utilizing some of these items may be just as detrimental to the vehicle and its performance as not installing them.

Numerous times while off-roading, a broken or bent drop-down brake line bracket has been seen. When drop-down brake line bracket are installed, there is still a chance for the factory lines to become damaged, due to their construction, typically a rubber line with no sheathing to protect against off-road obstacles. By installing longer brake lines, the suspension is no longer restricted by the length of the factory line, which is an all too often occurrence.

When the factory lines are replaced with extended aftermarket lines, chances of a component failure are minimized, and safety for all involved is greatly enhanced. We chose to utilize a set of Currie Enterprises Rock Jock extended length brake lines to fit on a Jeep JK two-door model. The Currie extended-length brake lines are an additional 3 to 4 inches longer than stock units and mount directly to the stock location, eliminating the need to use extensions, drop-down brackets, or similar mounts. An additional benefit of these lines is their increase in performance to the brake system, in that the pressure differentiation is stabilized by the lack of flexing that occurs with a traditional rubber line. The Currie lines are manufactured as preassembled, direct bolt-on units that consist of braided stainless steel hose with Teflon inner liners that meet and exceed all DOT MVSS-571.106 specifications. The fittings are zinc-plated, and for additional protection, the lines are sheathed with 308 stainless steel outer braid with an additional layer of protective coating.

1 The Currie Enterprises Rock Jock stainless steel braided brake lines are available for both front and rear applications, are Department of Transportation–approved, and include all of the necessary mounting hardware.

2

In this scenario, the factory rear brake line has had a drop-down bracket installed to it, which has caused the line to interfere with the rear sway bar upon its rebound and compression while off-roading. The interference is caused by the angle and increased size of the bracket in that specific area of penetration between the frame and sway bar.

3

To begin the exchange, the factory line and drop-down bracket are removed from the frame rail with open-ended wrenches.

4

Once the top of the line has been removed, the lower portion of it is removed from the inner caliper using an open-ended wrench. Caution should be taken to avoid exposing any parts or components of the vehicle to the brake fluid, which may cause etching, finish removal, or damage to the components (e.g., brake fluid on the brake pads).

5

Prior to installing the new extended length line to the caliper, care should be taken to ensure that the copper washer included in the kit is seated onto the fitting, as this washer will provide the seal between the caliper and line.

6

A gentle force should be applied to the caliper bolt when reinstalling the part. An excessive amount of force used to tighten the bolt may cause damage to the caliper or brake line fitting, which could cause the system to leak.

7

The upper portion of the new brake line will attach to the new frame-mounted tabs that have been installed in the factory locations.

8

Once the frame-mounted tabs have been installed, the top portion of the extended length brake line is slid into position and secured by the supplied banjo washers.

9

The final steps of the install involves attaching the factory bridge (hard) line, which originates from the master cylinder to the extended length line, and realigning the two components to ensure that their contours and unions are secure and not stressed. The newly installed lines must be bled to allow any trapped air to exit and to fill the lines with brake fluid.

PROJECT 46
Install a Steering Stabilizer

 Time: 1 Hour

 Tools: Impact gun, socket set

 Talent:

 Applicable Years: All

 Tab: $250

 Parts Required: Steering stabilizer, tie rod bracket

 Tip: Depending upon the type of lift, if any, that you have installed and the front track bar bracket (if the vehicle has been lifted), it may be necessary to turn the stabilizer around so that the body of the stabilizer does not interfere with the track bar bracket bolts and damage the stabilizer.

 Performance Gain: Allows the vehicle to be turned with minimal effort and reduces steering vibration and movement

Complementary Project: Installation of new shocks

It is a component that is used daily when driving down the road, but one that gets very little recognition for the hard job that it does. We're talking about a steering stabilizer. Just like its close relative the shock absorber, a steering stabilizer essentially performs the same task as a shock absorber but serves the steering system rather than the suspension system. By minimizing vibration and providing some level of control when the steering wheel is being turned, which in turn pivots the front wheels, a steering stabilizer increases the longevity of tires, ball joints, and other steering components.

For our install, we chose to use a Fox Racing Shox damper, given its $28\frac{1}{2}$ inches of extension, 8 inches of travel and 19 inches of collapsed length, not to mention the fact that it has a 2-inch diameter monotube design with an internal floating piston that is driven by a $\frac{5}{8}$-inch hard-chromed shaft. An added bonus is that the nitrogen-charged and oil-filled damper is fully rebuildable and tuneable, making it the last stabilizer we'll ever have to buy. A Poly Performance tube clamp with a custom bolt was used to attach the stabilizer to the tie rod. Manufactured from high-quality 1018 steel and CNC-machined for a precise fit, this is one of the best-performing and best-looking mounts on the market.

1

Out with the old and in with the new. The previous steering stabilizer was damaged by the track bar bolt head, because the body of the stabilizer was too big for the tight space it was placed in.

2

An important item to keep in mind when removing the old stabilizer is to check where on the unit the damage occurred, so that when installing the new unit the same areas can be checked to make sure there are proper clearances.

3

Since we were installing the new Poly Performance tube clamp mount, the previous stabilizer's tie rod mounting bracket was removed.

4

The new Fox stabilizer and Poly Performance mount will make steering duties of any large tire Jeep a treat. Included with the system are various-sized bolt spacers.

5

Before the coil spring spacer can be installed, the entire spring must be removed to allow access to the upper spring seat.

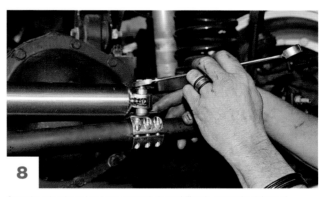

6

The tie rod bracket bolt is installed through the stabilizer and onto the tie rod tube clamp while the proper measurements for stabilizer pitch and distance are marked.

7

With the measurements completed, the Poly Performance tube clamp is secured in place with six mounting bolts. When tightening these bolts, a crisscross pattern should be used to minimize any warping or inconsistent gaps at either side of the clamp.

8

Once the tube clamp has been secured, the stabilizer is next to be tightened.

9

Literally a night and day difference in the way the vehicle steers and responds, which is why professional racers have been using Fox Racing Shox since the early 1970s.

PROJECT 47
Install Rear Coil Spring Spacers

 Time: 1 Hour

 Tools: Impact gun, socket set, axle jacks

 Talent:

 Applicable Years: All

Tab: $100

Parts Required: Lubricant

 Tip: Apply a liberal amount of lubricant onto the rubber coil spring spacer prior to seating it back onto the vehicle.

 Performance Gain: Allows the vehicle to be raised in the event that it is sagging, due to heavy loads, and levels the suspension

Complementary Project: Installation of new shocks

If you're anything like us, a day of off-roading begins the night before when we load everything but the kitchen sink into the back of our Jeep and head for the hills. While it is great to have all (and we do mean all) of the necessities from home, there is a hefty price to pay in the form of the rear end of our rig sagging, due to the added weight of our gear in conjunction with the added weight of a larger spare tire, tire carrier, and ¼-inch-thick steel plate bumper. All this weight causes us to lose valuable rear wheel travel, which in turn causes our tires to rub the inner rear fender wells. The same scenario is true if you tow a trailer off-road as well.

Given the soft suspensions on many of today's most popular Jeep models, utilizing a set of coil spacers to compensate for this rear end sag is an easy and cost-effective way of keeping the rear level when it is fully loaded or when you are towing and still retain the ride quality. Available in a variety of heights and materials, we chose a set of 1-inch TeraFlex coil spacers that have been made from rubber. The required height of the coil spacer was determined by measuring the vehicle height prior to the installation of the rear bumper, tire carrier, spare tire, and load, and then measuring it once all of the aforementioned items were installed. The end result was 1 inch. The TeraFlex spacers are solid performers and have been designed to literally fall into place with minimal effort. Once the ancillary attachments have been removed from the rear axle and the coil springs have been removed, the remainder of the install is a snap, as you will see. Assisting us with our installation was Dave Wever of Wever's Welding & Fabrication San Marcos, California.

1 The rear tires are removed for a few reasons, the first being to reduce the amount of weight on the axle when working on it. The second reason is to allow access to the rear sway bar brackets and track bar bolt.

2 Since the axle must be dropped to remove the coil spring and insert the spacer, the axe is supported by an axle jack.

3

In order to gain the travel needed from the axle, the rear sway bars are disconnected at the joints and moved up and out of the way until their reinstallation.

4

Part of the preparation includes removing the rear shocks at the bottom bracket only, which will allow them to be removed out of the way, but not require a complete removal and reinstallation.

5

Before the coil spring spacer can be installed, the entire spring must be removed to allow access to the upper spring seat.

6

Place the rear spring rubber isolator on the rear spacer and pop it into place.

7

Install the rear spacer by pushing the spacer into position. It will pop into place and will hold itself in position. To make installation easier, apply a liberal amount of lubricant to the top portion of the spacer to allow it to slip more easily into the mounting piece.

8

With the coil spacer in place, the coil spring is reinstalled, making the spacer rest atop the spring.

9

Once all of the shocks, sway bar linkages, and springs have been reinstalled, the last item to reattach is the track bar. When reinstalling this item, it is necessary to pull the Jeep together by using a heavy-duty ratchet strap. When the track bar is relieved of its tension, the vehicle spreads a minimal amount.

10

When the track bar and track bar mounting hole are realigned, insert the bolt and tighten. There you have it; an inch in an hour.

SUSPENSION

PROJECT 48
Install Front Lower Control Arm Skid Plates

  Time: 4 Hours

 Tools: Welder, drill, wire wheel brush attachment

 Talent: 🔧🔧🔧

 Applicable Years: All

Tab: $100

Parts Required: Skid plates, welding materials, spray primer and paint

 Tip: Prior to spray painting the new skid plates, apply a coat of primer to allow the paint to adhere better and resist coming off when washing the undercarriage.

 Performance Gain: Provides additional protection to the control arm brackets and strengthens them as well

Complementary Project: Installation of axle gussets

Every adventure off-road is usually highlighted by a few really technical encounters on the trail, the type of encounters that when you have driven through them leave you on your back and under your rig wondering just where that terrible noise came from. For us, one such run identified the fact that our lower front control arm mounts had been bent and damaged as a result of a run in (literally) with a rock that thought it was bigger than us. While Jeep and rock decided to part ways amicably, our Jeep was a little worse for wear. Since the lower control arm mounts are located so close to the ground and in the direct path of any obstacle, repeated abuse and encounters with rocks, logs, and other solid material can cause damage to them. This, in turn, could affect the rig's ride quality, suspension performance, and overall safety. A quick trip to see Mel Wade, owner of Off-Road Evolution, was all it took to give our mounts a one up on the obstacles.

Off-Road Evolution's Evo Front Lower Control Arm skid plates are fabricated from 3/16-inch laser-cut steel and are CNC-bent for a perfect fit around both mounting brackets. Each skid plate is fabricated to fit each side of the vehicle specifically, which further guarantees their performance. Easily installed, the only preparation required is that the existing paint on the mounts be removed with a wire brush that is attached to a drill, and that the edges of the control arm tabs are chamfered to allow more surface area to bond with the skid plates when being welded. Once cleaned off

and ready to be welded on, the mounts are identified for each side and welded in place. After a few minutes of cool down, they are shot with primer and then spray painted for a factory finish. Amazing how something so small can make all the difference on the trail.

1 Using an air drill with a wire brush attachment to remove any paint or debris from the material, Mel Wade of Off-Road Evolution in Fullerton, California, begins to prep the factory lower control arm mounting tabs for their meeting with the skid plates. Once he has completed the scuffing, a die grinder is used to chamfer the edges of the mounts to allow for more surface area to be exposed to the skid plates.

126

2

The ³⁄₁₆-inch laser-cut steel and CNC-bent skid plates are fabricated to fit the driver and passenger sides of the vehicle specifically, which allows for a more accurate fit, given a few discrepancies with each side.

3

Prior to completely welding the skid plates in place, each plate should be tack welded and checked for proper alignment. Once the green light has been given that things are in alignment, the welding may resume.

4

Once the skid plates have been allowed to cool down from the welding, a coat of spray primer should be applied and allowed to dry before the final coat of flat black spray paint is applied.

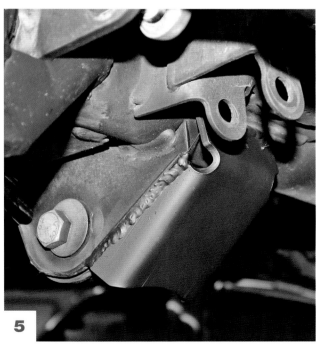

5

The new skid plates look as if they had rolled off the assembly line with the rest of the vehicle. Your lower control arms will thank you for the added protection, as will your wallet, since now you don't have to worry about really damaging key suspension mounts or components.

PROJECT 49

Install Rear Lower Control Arm and Shock Relocation Brackets

 Time: 1 Hour

 Tools: Plasma cutter, drill bits, socket set, die grinder

 Talent:

 Applicable Years: Jeep Wrangler JK (two-door and four-door models)

 Tab: $125 pair

 Parts Required: Mounting hardware, evo rock star skids

 Tip: It is recommended that you cycle your suspension before and after installation and check for travel and interference issues. This kit may require new (shorter) rear sway bar end links and/or coil spring retainers.

 Performance Gain: Provides protection to the rear shocks and increases ground clearance by 1½ inches

Complementary Project: Installation of front lower control arm skids

Chances are that if you own a Jeep Wrangler JK and have taken it off-road that you have noticed how easily the rear shocks come into contact with rocks and other obstacles while on a trail. Often when the shocks encounter a rock, their lower mounting tabs become damaged; sometimes to the point of cracking the factory weld on the tab at the axle. The same is true for the rear lower control arm brackets.

To alleviate these problems, as well as to provide a skid plate to the rear lower control arms, Off-Road Evolution's Evo

Rock Star Skids were created. Each Evo Rock Star Skid has been fabricated from laser-cut and CNC-bent ³/₁₆-inch steel plate. Incorporated into the skids' design are the rear shock relocation brackets, which provide an increase of 1½ inches of ground clearance, which translates into an additional 1½ inches of shock travel under articulation. The skids are fully boxed on the bottom and feature a durable black powder-coated finish. The attention to detail can be seen by the laser-cut Evo logo on the sides of the brackets.

1 Fabricated from laser-cut and CNC-bent ³/₁₆-inch steel plate, the Evo Rock Star Skids serve two functions, to act as a lower rear control arm skid plate and to act as a rear shock relocation bracket.

2 The rear shocks are impediments while on the trail. The Evo Rock Star Skids will effectively raise their mounting locations 1½ inches, helping to tuck them up and away from any future damage.

3

The rear shocks and sway bar end links must be removed from their lower mounting brackets and secured out of the way during the installation of the new brackets.

4

The stock lower rear shock brackets are removed with a plasma cutter to make room for the new brackets. Prior to cutting the mounts off, a measurement of the new brackets should be transferred onto the lower rear control arm mounts.

5

The lower brackets should be removed slowly and carefully so the lower control arm brackets are not damaged. This is why we are removing the shock mounts piece by piece.

6

Once the lower shock bracket has been removed, the area is ground to smooth out any imperfections and to make the cut level, so the new bracket fits as flush and solid as it can. This will help in the alignment of the boltholes with the lower control arm bolt.

7

The lower control arm bolt was removed and threaded through the new Evo Rock Star Skid bracket with an impact gun.

8

An additional bolt is required for the install, which requires that a hole be drilled through the factory bracket; this will help to minimize the vertical movement of the skid plate.

9

The factory sway bar end links are reattached and the shocks are bolted into their new mounting locations.

10

Upon completion of the install, an additional 1½ inches of shock travel is gained during rear suspension articulation, as well as an additional 1½ inches of ground clearance. And, of course, the lower control arms have a skid plate to protect them.

SECTION 5
EXTERIOR

The exterior of a Jeep is very important, especially if there are numerous accessories that have been added to it. Aside from improving the overall aesthetics of the vehicle, some of the items we feature in this chapter can also protect it. A few of the items that are addressed in this chapter include installing front and rear bumpers, side rock guards, and steel fenders.

PROJECT 50
Install a Front Winch Bumper

 Time: 7¹/₂ Hours

 Tools: Socket set, impact gun, torque wrench

 Talent:

 Applicable Years: All Jeep Wrangler JK models

 Tab: $1,300

 Parts Required: Factory fog lights, winch, winch fairlead, front bumper

 Tip: When drilling the required ¹/₂-inch holes into the frame for the tow hook brackets, it is easier if an ¹/₂-inch pilot hole is started first.

 Performance Gain: Replaces the factory plastic bumper with a stronger and more attractive unit that has the option of integrating a winch

Complementary Project: Installation of auxiliary lights

The front bumper of your Jeep is the first line of defense between you and off-road obstacles. It also serves to set the tone and image for your rig, whether it is to be a true rock crawler or just a daily driver. So how does one go about choosing the correct bumper for their Jeep? To start with you must ask yourself what you want to get from it. Do you desire a bumper that is just stronger, but keeps the factory appearance or do you want one that will allow you to install a winch on it and some accessory lights? Once these parameters have been defined, your search can begin.

Bumpers range from full width, midwidth and short width—each one having a specific purpose. Typically, with wider bumpers, your ability to clear and traverse larger rocks, etc. is somewhat limited. With shorter bumpers, your ability to clear the same obstacles is increased, if only because you have less bumper between you and the obstacle. The material of the bumper can also make a difference as well, with regard to overall appearance and strength. Obviously, steel is the material of choice for any replacement unit, given its ability to take a beating and not be compromised.

We enlisted Mel Wade of Off-Road Evolution in Fullerton, California, to assist us with the install of an American Expedition Vehicles front bumper on our 2008 Jeep JK project vehicle. Not just a pretty face, AEV's unit is the only bumper on the market to be constructed of heavy gauge steel and stamped to create its unique design.

The process of stamping the bumper eliminates the need for multiple pieces of steel to be welded together. The stamping also allows the bumper to be formed with a radius and to flow better with the vehicle's body line, as opposed to the angular features of some other units. With regard to safety, the unit retains the factory airbag "crush cans" and factory fog lamps. Additional provisions for off-road lights can be found via two heavy-duty light tabs, which are housed inside the steel tube hoop in front of the optional winch mounting area. A pair of 6-inch off-road lights can be fitted onto the bumper with room to spare.

Continuing with the custom appearance, a perforated stainless steel mesh insert allows winch users the opportunity to view the winch cable while spooling in or out. Speaking of winches, the bumper is able to fit Warn winches up to 9,500 pounds without modifications. For our installation, we chose to incorporate a Ramsey Patriot 9000 winch, which required some minor modification to the winch mounting plate.

As durable as its construction, the AEV bumper is available in two finishes—one finish a paint-ready primer finish and the other a multistage coating that consists of a layer of zinc coating, an epoxy coating, and then a textured black powder-coated finish. All hardware is included with the bumper, including tow loops that work with standard shackles and a MOPAR tow bar for hassle-free flat towing when needed.

All in, the AEV bumper weighs in at a respectable 116 pounds, including the hardware, bumper winch mount, and tow loops. A true bolt-on installation, the unit does not require any additional cutting of the factory frame rails. Upon completion of the install, we were excited with the high quality of craftsmanship and design that has been incorporated into this piece. If a bumper could be called a work of art, the AEV unit would definitely be it.

1

The factory plastic front bumper and skid plate must be removed to prepare the vehicle for the American Expedition Vehicles front bumper. Note that the front factory fog lights must be removed from the stock unit so that they can be modified for use in the AEV unit.

2

With the stock bumper removed, the stock fog lamp lighting will need to be repositioned, since the fog lights will be mounted further apart in the AEV unit. This is accomplished by removing the factory conduit and rerouting the harness above the frame rails and along the bottom of the grille, with it being fastened to the power steering line using tie straps. It is important to note that the factory harness does not require cutting.

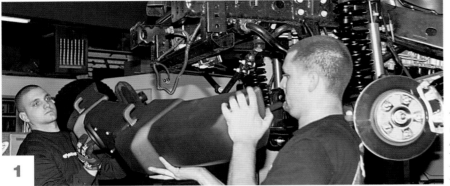

3

Depending upon your application, you may need to enlarge the two outermost upper holes in the factory frame rail. To determine if this is necessary, insert a large bumper mounting bolt into the holes. If it does not pass freely through the holes, drill them out, deburr, and apply rust inhibitor or touch up paint to prevent rusting.

4

In addition to the factory frame rails, the supplied winch mounting plate may also need to be drilled. The same method used in the determination to drill the frame rail should be followed.

5

Due to the fact that we used an alternative brand winch other than Warn, the winch mounting plate required a minor modification in order for the winch housing to fit without interference.

6

Prior to installing the tow hook bracket, it must be placed against the frame, so that a center punch can mark the vehicle frame and it can be drilled with a $1/2$-inch drill bit. The drilled holes should be deburred and painted with a corrosion inhibitor or touchup paint to minimize rusting.

7

With the holes drilled into the frame for the tow hook brackets, place the tow hook bracket back into position and install the $1/2$-inch hex head bolts into the front attachment point. Place two washers between the tow hook and frame at this point to ensure a flat mounting surface. Install the bumper mounting brackets to the tow hook mounting holes; tighten the bolts, beginning with the lower outside. An open-ended wrench should be used to access the nut from the top of the frame rail. Install the upper bolt, using the thin locking nut supplied in the kit and torque all of the bolts.

8

Distinguishing items of the AEV bumper kit include factory fog light relocation brackets and air bag crush canister covers that install onto the bumper for a seamless appearance.

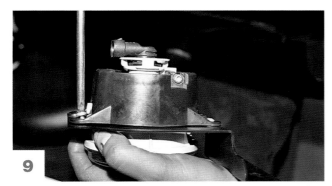

9

In order for the factory fog lights to fit into the new AEV bumper, they must be removed from the stock bumper mounting hardware, and the new AEV brackets must be installed.

10

As we have previously mentioned, the AEV bumper utilizes the factory "crush cans" that are specifically tuned for the vehicle air bag performance in low-speed impacts. The "crush cans" are integral to the factory bumper beam and must be removed and reinstalled on your AEV bumper. The crush cans are removed from the bumper beam by using a plasma cutter. A paper template is supplied with the bumper so that the outline of the required cut can be transferred to the bumper beam. Once removed, the crush cans are then bolted onto the bumper and hidden with formed plastic covers.

11 A perforated stainless steel mesh insert allows winch users the opportunity to view the winch cable while spooling in or out. The mounting bolts for the mesh insert have been welded to the inside of the bumper and are secured with the supplied nuts.

12 Once all of the required brackets, mounts, and accessories have been installed, the Off-Road Evolution crew lifts the bumper to the vehicle for the final fit and attachment.

13 Access to the outer mounting bolts is achieved through the inner fender well, which exposes the mounting bolts.

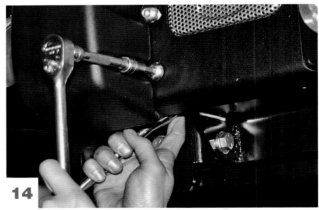

14 The inner mounting bolts are accessed along the sides of the crush can covers. All of the bolts should be hand-tightened to allow room for alignment prior to final tightening.

15 One of the best-looking front bumpers on the market, the AEV unit has the accommodations to install a winch and auxiliary lights, all without detracting from its appearance.

PROJECT 51
Install a Rear Bumper

 Time: 2¹/₂ Hours

 Tools: Socket set, impact gun, torque wrench

 Talent:

 Applicable Years: All models

 Tab: $1,000 Average

Parts Required: Bumper, mounting and latch hardware

 Tip: Prior to installation of the new rear bumper, make sure that a large work table is available so that the new bumper can be placed on it. This will bring the unit closer to the vehicle, minimizing the height that it must be lifted for alignment and placement.

 Performance Gain: Increased protection to the vehicle body

 Complementary Project: Installation of a tire carrier

One of the challenges associated with off-roading is to see whether or not we can avoid destroying our rigs by chance encounters with rocks, boulders, and other hazards. In order to triumph in this battle between vehicle and nature, the appropriate body armor is required. Just like any battle, the stronger your armor, the better the chance you have of walking away unscathed and with minimal damage; the same goes for our vehicles. One of the most important pieces of armor that you can add to your vehicle is a new rear bumper that is designed and fabricated to handle whatever it encounters without sustaining damage. On some of the newer model Jeeps, the rear bumpers are manufactured from plastic, which, when taken on the trail, can become damaged instantly. The plastic bumpers do not provide the necessary body protection to the rear of the vehicle, which if damaged could be quite costly to repair.

Some things to keep in mind when choosing the type or style of bumper are the type of terrain you will be driving through, the abuse level you want it to stand up to, and the weight of the new piece. Bumpers are made in numerous styles; the three most popular types are full width, midwidth, and short. A full-width bumper will extend the full width of the vehicle, from the outer edges of your rear fenders. These types of bumpers are good for street driving and light off-road driving, as they do not allow for additional clearance while crossing over obstacles. A midwidth bumper is one that does

not extend the full width of the vehicle, but stops at the actual body panels, leaving the fender flares unprotected. These types of bumpers are adequate for street driving and medium to difficult off-road driving where some rock obstacles will be encountered. A short bumper is one that does not extend beyond the frame rail width. Often seen on some of the most extreme rock crawlers, these bumpers have been designed for extreme trails where large obstacles are encountered.

The weight of the bumper will also need to be considered in your selection as well, since some suspensions may sag, causing you to lose valuable wheel travel. The weight increase can often be 100 to 200 pounds, depending upon the manufacturer, material, and size of the unit.

One of the industry leaders in bulletproof aftermarket bumpers for Jeeps is Rock Hard 4x4. Built as a full replacement piece, the Rock Hard 4x4 rear midwidth bumper that we installed has been constructed from solid ¹/₄-inch thick plate steel. It features an integrated Class 2 receiver hitch, CB antennae mounts and a horizontal Hi-Lift jack mount. For extrication duties, two ⁵/₈ x 2¹/₂-inch CNC D-ring shackle mount tabs have been integrated into the unit as well.

Designed with tapered ends for increased departure angles, the look is clean and functional. One look at the rear bumper from Rock Hard 4x4, and you know it means business.

1

The stock rear plastic bumper is easily removed from the two factory mounting locations with an impact gun and socket.

2

Aside from the stock side mounting brackets, additional bumper supports along the rear frame crossmember must be removed prior to the bumper being removed.

3

The stock receiver hitch or tow hook is attached separately to the rear frame crossmember and must be removed to accommodate the new bumper, which has an integrated 2-inch receiver hitch installed.

4

The three bolts that attach the stock receiver hitch or tow hook must be removed prior to installing the new bumper.

5

The Rock Hard 4x4 Parts rear bumper requires that the stock license plate assembly be removed from the vehicle and minimally trimmed to accommodate the new unit and its mounting hardware.

6

Given the increased weight of the new bumper in comparison to the stock unit, the new bumper is placed on a large worktable to bring the unit closer to the vehicle, minimizing the height that it must be lifted for alignment and placement. If a lift is available, the vehicle can be lowered to the exact height as the table to further reduce having to lift the unit.

7

To keep the frame mounting locations aligned with the bumper mounting points, the bumper was strapped to the frame via ratchet straps until all of the bolts were installed. This method also reduces the chances of the bumper falling off the vehicle.

8

Upon completion of the install, the increased clearances on each side of the vehicle are obvious, as well as the sheer strength and durability of the unit.

PROJECT 52
Install a Rear Tire Carrier

 Time: 2 Hours

 Tools: Socket set, open-ended wrench, tape measure, dead blow hammer

 Talent:

 Applicable Years: All model Jeep CJs, YJs, TJs, and JKs

 Tab: $450

Parts Required: Tire carrier, grease, lug nuts (3)

 Tip: Apply a layer of anti-seize compound and extreme pressure lubricant that has been formulated with copper, graphite, aluminum, and other ingredients to protect carrier pivot against rust, corrosion, and seizure.

 Performance Gain: Reduces the weight of a larger wheel and tire being placed on the tailgate and tailgate hinges

 Complementary Project: Installation of a spare tire mounted third brake light kit

As with all things, there are causes and effects. Building a Jeep is no different. As soon as the suspension system is modified, larger tires and wheels are typically installed, which requires that a larger spare tire be on hand in the event that it is needed. And that is where a spare tire carrier comes into play. In the stock configuration, all model Jeep CJs, YJs, TJs, and JKs, have the spare tire mounted on brackets that are secured onto the tailgate. While this type of mounting is convenient with a stock-sized tire, numerous issues arise when a larger wheel and tire combination is added to a stock mounting location. Items such as the tailgate becoming warped or damaged, the tailgate hinges becoming misaligned, the simple fact that the larger tires will not fit on the stock brackets due to bumper clearance, which then requires them to be modified. And the additional amount of weight of the new wheel and tire combination all become solid reasons to install a tire carrier that transfers all of the weight from the tailgate onto a separate frame that is independent of the tailgate. Offered by numerous manufacturers, tire carriers are often sold in conjunction with an aftermarket rear bumper or are sold as add-on accessories.

We chose to integrate a Rock Hard 4x4 Parts spare tire carrier, built from heavy-duty steel tubing in the design of an A-frame for ultimate durability, with Rock Hard's bulletproof rear bumper. Designed as a self-latching design, the carrier can be closed by simply pushing it shut. Also included is a double-safety latch with a hard plastic rest and a rubber bump stop to ensure rattle-free operation at any speed. The key component to the carrier's effortless operation is the 1¼-inch steel shaft and 2¾-inch hub with sealed upper and lower tapered roller bearings. For ease of maintenance to the shaft, a zerk fitting has been incorporated into the design to allow the shaft to be greased. Another high-quality feature is the spring-loaded autolocking pin system. When the carrier is opened, it allows a solid steel pin to drop into a predrilled hole, allowing the carrier to remain open regardless of the vehicle's position or how long it is left opened. As the carrier is spring loaded, to close the carrier all that must be done is for the steel pin to be pulled up on and the carrier to be swung closed. There are also built-in provisions for a CB antenna and a Hi-Lift jack. Providing further isolation between the carrier and the tailgate of the Jeep it is installed on is a tailgate isolator bar that attaches directly to the factory spare tire mounting location.

1

The single most important item that defines the durability of a tire carrier is the hinge pin. The Rock Hard 4x4 Parts hinge consists of a ¼-inch steel shaft with a 2¾-inch hub. To begin the installation the sealed lower tapered roller bearing and shims are slid onto the shaft.

2

With the lower bearing and shims installed, the tire carrier frame is placed on the shaft. It is important to ensure that the bearings and shims are seated properly in the groove of the pivot. Failure to seat them properly could result in the top bearings and shims not being able to be seated correctly, which would affect the hub installation.

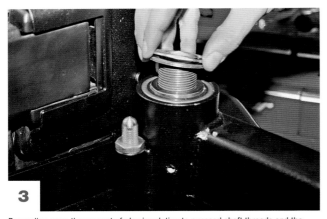

3

Depending upon the amount of play in relation to exposed shaft threads and the hub, the amount of shims may need to be adjusted until the proper fit is achieved. For this reason numerous shims have been included with the kit.

4

Tightening the hub onto the shaft requires an aluminum open-ended wrench to avoid damaging the aluminum hub.

5

In addition to the carrier frame requiring installation, there are numerous other parts, such as this latch pin, which keeps the carrier secured to the bumper. The quality of the latch pin is equal to those that are used as door latch pins on automobiles, proving that safety and durability concerns have been addressed.

6

Prior to the latching mechanism being slid into the lower portion of the frame and bolted in, it must be assembled. Similar to the mechanism used on car doors, the carrier's mechanism is a double-action design, meaning that even if it is not closed entirely, the secondary latch will at least catch and hold onto the carrier.

7 Sealing the latch mechanism into the carrier frame is a custom solid piece of billet aluminum that is tapped into place with a nonmarring dead blow hammer. The latch from the mechanism extends through the plate for ease of opening.

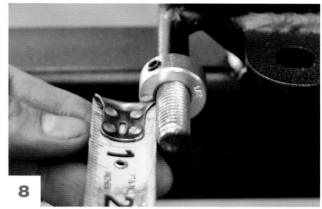

8 As an added feature, there are provisions to mount a Hi-Lift jack to the bottom tube of the carrier. The bolts are adjustable two ways—one way depending upon the length of the jack and the other depending upon the depth of the unit, which is shown being adjusted.

9 The spare tire wheel studs are included in the kit and are pressed into the wheel plate. There are numerous mounting holes on the plate to allow the various types of wheel bolt configurations to be accommodated.

10 A rubber bump stop that attaches to the bumper is secured into place to minimize any unwanted movement or rattles while driving.

11 A tailgate isolator bar with a center-mounted rubber bump stop is installed onto the tailgate to serve as yet another buffer between the carrier and the tailgate. Best of all, the bar utilizes the factory mounting hole locations on the tailgate, which means no additional penetrations to the sheet metal are required.

12 The completed tire carrier allows a larger wheel and tire combination to be installed with little or no adverse effects to the rest of the Jeep's body panels or hinges—not to mention the fact that it looks good too.

PROJECT 53
Install Rock Guards

 Time: 5–6 Hours

 Tools: Medium socket set, drill bit, high-speed drill, open-ended wrench (2), transfer punch, ball-peen hammer, torx driver, Phillips head screwdriver, masking tape, file or deburing tool

 Talent:

 Applicable Years: All

 Tab: $550–$650 per pair, depending upon manufacturer

 Parts Required: Utilize the new bolts and nut inserts that are included with each pair of corner guards

 Tip: Apply a liberal amount of masking tape to the surrounding body panels and fenders prior to installing the rock guards for fitment in order to avoid denting and/or scratching the painted surfaces of the vehicle. Also, use a blow gun with compressed air to blow off the metal fragments derived from drilling the body panels that will be resting on and around the vehicle. This will help eliminate any excess scratches.

 Performance Gain: Helps eliminate body damage to the side of the vehicle by rocks. The rock guards also provide a strong and solid surface that acts as a slider when having to hug a rock or other impeding obstacle without causing damage to the side of the vehicle.

 Complementary Project: Corner guards and underbody skid plates

Depending upon the make and model of your Jeep, it either may or may not come equipped from the factory with a set of side steps or rocker guards. For the 2007–2008 Jeep Wrangler line, there are numerous variations from the factory depending upon the vehicle's trim level. The base X model is not equipped with either a step or rocker guards. The Sahara model is equipped with a side step which is made of plastic, while the Rubicon model is equipped with rock sliders made from steel. Depending upon your intended use for your vehicle, these OE options may not accommodate your needs. This was the case with our project vehicle, a 2008 Jeep Wrangler Rubicon. While the factory rocker guards were sufficient to deflect small rocks, we found them to be inadequate when going over larger obstacles. To alleviate this issue and provide more structural rigidity and protection to the body of our Jeep, we installed a set of PUREJEEP's formed crawler rocker guards.

Fabricated from heavy-walled DOM steel tubing and laser-cut ³⁄₁₆-inch steel plate, the end result is a pair of rocker guards that can slide, hit, or be driven over anything in their path without being fazed in the least. The distinguishing factor between these rocker guards and the OE versions is that they represent a perfect blend of side step and rocker guard into one compact and clean package. Essentially they are two items merged into one. As previously mentioned, the OE units are offered as either a step or a rock guard, but not both. By combining the guard and step, the ability to enter and exit the vehicle becomes easier, access to the roof is better achieved, and general off-road performance is increased.

Designed for durability, the attachment locations of the PUREJEEP units to the body are plentiful and have been evenly distributed along the entire rocker guard for the purposes of keeping any impact loads or stress points from compromising the units. In addition to the factory mounting locations being retained, there are also numerous holes drilled through the lower doorsill and front and rear fenders.

Having the PUREJEEP rocker guards installed will not only add strength and support to the body of your Jeep, but is will also add to your off-road peace of mind, knowing that you can now slide from rock to rock without worrying about caving in the entire side of your rig.

1

The stock rocker guards on our 2008 Wrangler Rubicon are adequate for light trails. However, for the more technical trails, a pair of stronger and more protective guards are required. The factory guards must be removed prior to the fitment and installation of the new PUREJEEP rocker guards. The lower mounting bolts are easily removed with hand tools.

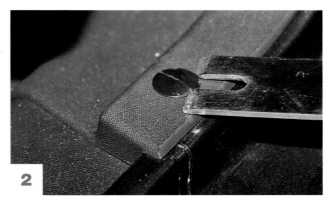

2

As part of the installation of the new guards, the two front doors must be removed. Special care should be taken to protect the doors from being damaged while off the vehicle. One unique feature of the PUREJEEP guards is the way in which the mounting hardware passes through the lower portion of the doorsill. In order to access this area for drilling and bolt installation, the plastic trim pieces surrounding the doorsill and lower quarter panels must be removed.

3

Protecting the body panels and fenders from damage is achieved by applying layers of protective tape to any surface that is within the immediate vicinity of the guards. Small strips of tape should be overlapped roughly 1/2 inch to provide a thick enough layer of protection. It is also recommended that a tape that is compatible with automotive finishes is used to reduce any damage to the vehicle's finish.

4

A floor jack and block of wood is essential to the correct alignment and markings for the mounting locations. Each corner guard weighs roughly 40–50 pounds, making for holding the units up to the vehicle all but impossible. Once aligned with the factory mounting locations, the additional mounting points in the fenders and lower doorsill should be transfer punched.

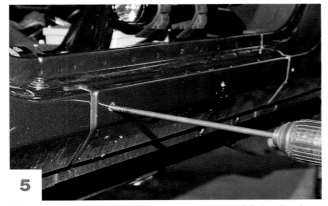

5

Following the transfer punch markings, the lower doorsills are drilled to allow the supplied bolt and support sleeve to pass through the body panels. Specific care should be taken when performing this task; if the holes are not drilled straight through, aligning them up with the guards becomes virtually impossible.

6

The front lower portion of the fender also has mounting locations that pass through the body panels into the interior cab of the vehicle.

7

Riv-nuts are included with the set of rocker guards and should be installed with care, making sure that they are fully seated against the body panel. Failure to install them correctly will result in them not fastening the guard to the body, as required for the appropriate distribution of load impacts.

8

The lower doorsill mounting locations are supported internally with heavy-walled steel sleeves to minimize any unwanted play between the body panels and the mounting bolt. During the process of installing the guards onto the vehicle, additional support may be required to hold one side up while the mounting locations are aligned. To assist with this task, guide rails are inserted into the steel sleeves and then pushed out of the way by the mounting bolt.

9

The lower doorsill mounting bolts require an exact fit. When tightening them down, an open-ended wrench on the exterior and a ratchet and socket on the interior is the correct combination to make the install easier.

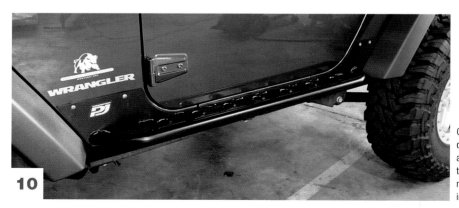

10

One look at the new rocker guards and instantly their durability and functionality make them a hit. The additional support and protection that is provided to the front and rear fenders by the steel plate, not to mention the integrated step will prove to be invaluable on the trails.

PROJECT 54
Install Steel Fenders

 Time: 6 Hours

 Tools: Drill, drill bits, threaded nut insert install tool, marking pen, transfer punch, hammer

 Talent:

 Applicable Years: Jeep JK Wranglers (two-door and four-door models)

Tab: $900 pair

 Parts Required: Steel fender flares

 Tip: To protect the adjacent paint around the new fenders, use two layers of blue masking tape. Also, have the fenders painted off the vehicle so that the backsides can be painted as well.

 Performance Gain: Increased ground clearance and protection to the body

 Complementary Project: Installation of side rock rails

Let's face it. If you own a Jeep, regardless of the model, one of the first encounters your rig will have with the elements, other than with your tires, is with the fenders. While the plastic factory fenders are good for street and some light trails, nothing can even compare to the durability provided by Off-Road Evolution's Evo Armor front steel plate fenders with built-in flares. Fabricated from 3/16-inch laser-cut steel plate and 1 3/4-inch 0.120-wall DOM tubing these units have been engineered to take a beating and still look like new. The fenders offer a bolt-on installation to all four-door and two-door Jeep Wrangler JK models. Attached to the factory sheet metal using the provided threaded nut inserts and hardware,

the steel plate fenders also feature cutouts to accommodate the radio antenna on the passenger side of the vehicle. A signature Off-Road Evolution skull logo is laser-cut into the fender sides to add to the already imposing appearance.

The front flare of the fenders offers 7 to 8 inches of tire coverage and is tapered toward the front to create a narrower vehicle approach. Given the amount of built-in flare on the fenders, there is more than ample room for 40x3.50-inch tires or larger. The fenders are unfinished so they can be painted to match the vehicle that they are being installed on. If desired, they can be powder-coated black to match the factory units.

1 The factory plastic front fenders will distort and bend when confronted with a stationary obstacle such as a rock or tree. The Evo-Armor steel plate fenders will hold strong and slide across the stationary surface so the vehicle can continue forward motion without sustaining major body damage.

2 Constructed from 3/16-inch laser-cut steel plate and 1 3/4-inch 0.120-wall DOM tubing, these units are the real deal and are easily installed without any modifications to the existing sheet metal.

3

While installing the fenders, there are a few key mounting locations that require a nut and bolt to be used for added stability and strength instead of the threaded nut inserts.

4

The tapered and raised fronts of the fenders allow for greater approach angles when off-roading.

5

The majority of fasteners for the fenders are threaded nut inserts that have been measured and transferred onto the sheet metal with a transfer punch. The marks are then drilled, and the insert is secured in place with a special tool.

6

A hex head socket is used to drive the nuts into the previously installed threaded inserts. This method of fastening the fenders onto the sheet metal is stronger than just using a sheet metal screw, as they are prone to pull out or becoming stripped or loose from impacts with rocks, etc.

7

The passenger side front fender features a cutout for the factory radio antenna, yet another detail that has not been overlooked in the design or fabrication of these units.

8

The factory hood latches are not compromised by the addition of the fenders; in fact they are protected, given the amount of steel plate and tube surrounding them.

9

Ready to hit the road and anything else in their path, the Off-Road Evolution Evo Armor front steel fenders look as though they belong more on a tactical assault vehicle than a trail runner.

PROJECT 55
Install a Cargo Divider

 Time: 1 Hour

 Tools: Open-ended wrenches

 Talent:

 Applicable Years: Open-ended wrenches

Tab: $250

 Parts Required: Cargo divider, installation hardware

 Tip: The built-in bottle holders can be filled with key vehicle fluids or accessories for emergency repair situations.

 Performance Gain: Provides stability and organization within your cargo area

 Complementary Project: Installation of a roof rack

Tell me if this has ever happened to you: You've loaded your Jeep's cargo area with either groceries from the supermarket on your way home from work or with some tools for that quick trail run, and the minute you head down the road and apply your brakes, everything that once was seated nicely in the cargo area has moved forward toward you and is now residing under both front seats. Your salvage mission has begun. To alleviate this problem with load shift and to provide a platform for some essential vehicle fluids that will keep them protected and away from damage, the crew at Magnum Off-Road has provided all of us Jeep owners with a solution, a bulletproof cargo divider.

While there are numerous cargo dividers already on the market, a few distinguishing factors to the Magnum Off-Road version is that it is not a full height divider, which means that the cargo area is still accessible from the front seats. Also, the unit is easily installed and has provisions for mounting an air bottle to it for easy access when you need to air your tires up, as well as the ability to hold vital engine fluids, such as brake fluid, steering fluid, and engine oil. Constructed from DOM tubing and perforated steel mesh, the divider is easily installed and can be removed with no adverse effects to the space.

1 Constructed of DOM tubing and perforated steel mesh, the cargo divider is available either powder-coated or as bare material. The divider is easily installed within a few minutes and stops your cargo from barreling forward and resting under your seat.

2

3

Keeping functionality in mind, the cargo divider has the option of holding vital engine and vehicle fluids out of harm's way, ensuring that the containers will not be squashed or compromised. They are also great for holding duct tape and other trail necessities.

Weighing in at roughly 25 pounds, a loose air bottle can become a dangerous missile if left unsecured. An added benefit to the cargo divider is that it has the provisions for an air bottle and mount to be installed on it.

4

5

Using the factory rear seat attachment points, the cargo divider is installed easily and quickly. Best of all, the seat attachment point is not compromised in any way.

The mounting hardware is Grade 8 for durability, and it contains four attachment points to guarantee a solid and stable unit.

6

Once the divider has been installed, loading and unloading cargo on and off your Jeep will be an entirely new experience, since you will no longer have to hunt for the smallest items that escaped their bag or box.

PROJECT 56
Install Rear Corner Guards

 Time: 1½ Hours per side

 Tools: Medium socket set, drill bit, high-speed drill, open-ended wrench (2), transfer punch, ball-peen hammer, torx driver, Phillips head screwdriver, masking tape, file or deburring tool

 Talent: ✕ ✕ ✕

 Applicable Years: All

 Tab: $300–$400 per pair, depending upon manufacturer

 Parts Required: Utilize the new bolts and nut inserts that are included with each pair of corner guards

 Tip: Apply a liberal amount of masking tape to the surrounding body panels and fenders prior to installing the corner guards for fitment in order to avoid denting and/or scratching the painted surfaces of the vehicle. Also, use a blow gun with compressed air to blow off the metal fragments derived from drilling the body panels that will be resting on and around the vehicle. This will help eliminate any excess scratches.

 Performance Gain: Helps eliminate body damage and crushing to the rear corners of the tub when off-road

Complementary Project: Rear bumper and rear taillight guards

A typical day of off-roading on your favorite trail is usually not without a few bumps and bruises to your rig, that is if you're doing it right; at least according to some hardcore off-road enthusiasts. With this said, one of the most susceptible areas on your Jeep for damage is the rear corner panels. Aside from housing your rear lights, gas fill location and license plate, it is also a critical area where the side and rear body panels join together. Needless to say, a good run-in with a rock or other obstacle could mean a couple of thousand in expensive bodywork.

Tasked with protecting this critical area of your Jeep are rear corner guards that are typically fabricated from a high-grade piece of steel that has been shaped to fit securely over the rear corners of your Jeep. While there are a number of manufacturers, finishes and materials used for these guards, the most durable and attractive units we have encountered are manufactured by American Expedition Vehicles. The AEV units are stamped from a solid piece of ⅛-inch thick steel and powder-coated in a durable finish to resist trail scratches and other environmental hazards. Each piece has had the mounting locations predrilled and the necessary cutouts made for the license plate, rear taillights, and fuel filler door.

Rest assured that by installing these guards, not only will your nerves be at ease when in a tight spot, but your pocketbook will also feel the ease, thanks to the thousands of dollars saved on bodywork.

1 Prior to the installation of the corner guards, it is necessary to remove the ancillary items that are attached to the affected area of the vehicle. These items may include the rear taillights, license plate holder and light, and the fuel filler door or trim ring (whichever your vehicle is equipped with).

2

The first step in the installation involves test fitting each corner guard to the respective side of the vehicle to ensure that the mounting holes in the guards are not misaligned with the body. Check all the gaps and adjust the guard as necessary to achieve uniform margins.

3

Once the fit has been confirmed between the body and guards, a pair of locking pliers is used to hold the guards on to the Jeep so that the mounting locations may be marked with a transfer punch and ball-peen hammer. It is important to note that only a light tap from the hammer is necessary to transfer the mark. An excessive amount of force may damage or dent the body panel, causing the mounting holes to become off-center and making it impossible to align the holes with the guard.

4

With the mounting holes marked, a $1/8$-inch drill bit set at $1/2$-inch depth stop is used to drill the pilot holes. After completion of the pilot holes, the mounting holes are then completed with a 10mm drill bit. A deburring tool or metal file should be used to clean the hole. A rust preventative primer or touch-up paint should be used around the exposed metal of the holes.

5

The supplied riv-nut inserts should be applied with minimal pressure into the mounting holes and should be seated fully onto the body. Failure to ensure that the riv-nut has been seated will prevent it from expanding later.

6

Included with the AEV corner guard kit is the necessary riv-nut installation tool. Holding the nut portion of the tool with an open-ended wrench, and slowly turning the bolt portion of the tool with a ratchet will torque the bolt and cause the riv-nut to seat fully and expand for permanent installation.

7

Once all of the riv-nuts have been seated, realign the corner guards and begin the process of attaching them onto the body with the supplied mounting bolts. The mounting bolts should be started by hand, with special attention being taken to avoid cross-threading the riv-nut inserts.

8

The final steps to completing the installation involve reattaching the taillights, license plate holder and light, and fuel filler door to the vehicle. In the event that one of the items being reattached does not align correctly or is coming into contact with the guard, simply loosen the corner guard mounting bolts, align the ancillary items, and then tighten the guards.

9

A successful installation of the corner guards will provide many miles of damage-free sides to your trail vehicle. In addition to their usability, they also add a certain ruggedness to the overall appearance of any Jeep.

PROJECT 57
Install Rear Taillight Guards

 Time: ½ Hour

 Tools: Philips head screwdriver

 Talent:

 Applicable Years: All Jeep Wranglers

Tab: $130 (black), $195 (chrome)

 Parts Required: Taillight guards

 Tip: None

 Performance Gain: Provides protection from the elements to your rear taillights

 Complementary Project: Steel corner guards

Any time you are headed off-road there is a possibility of encountering a piece of brush that can wreak havoc on your windshield, headlights, and taillights. Being constructed of plastic, the taillights are one of the most common items broken when off-road driving. This is largely due to a condition called branch slap, which is when the branch's energy from being recoiled backward as the vehicle moves forward is released and hits the taillight, causing catastrophic damage to the lens. One way to add the necessary protection to the taillights is to install a set of brush guards. Easily installed in a few minutes, these metal guards not only protect the lenses, but they also lend an aggressive look to the rear of the vehicle. We chose to install a set of Mopar taillight guards to our Jeep Wrangler. Made from the highest-quality metal, these guards are available in either a black satin powder-coated finish or as chromed units. Either way they do a great job at protecting the lenses.

1 Without any protection from branch slaps, the factory taillights are sitting ducks for wayward branches and other harmful elements.

2 In order to install the Mopar taillight guards, the four taillight mounting screws must be removed from the taillight. When removing the screws, be sure to pay special attention to where each screw came from, as there are two different types of screws installed. One set is installed on one side of the light and the other on the opposite side. One set of screws is for sheet metal inserts, and the other set is for insertion in plastic. Mixing the screws up may cause damage to the other screws threads.

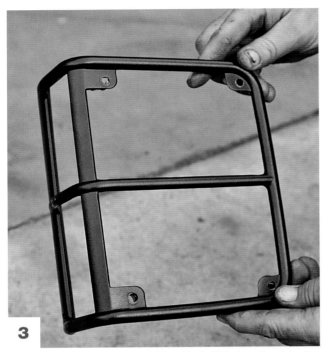

3

The Mopar taillight guards have been fabricated for the highest-quality metal and are a perfect fit onto the taillights. Also note the wraparound design to further protect the sides and corners of the lights.

4

With the screws removed from the taillight, the new taillight guard is placed atop the taillight and centered with the mounting holes.

5

Holding the taillight and guard with one hand, the screws are started by hand and tightened with the screwdriver. Do not use an electric or cordless drill for this installation, as the power and torque from these tools could break the plastic taillights, exactly what we're trying to avoid.

6

Once the guards are in place, the opportunity to break them is greatly diminished. From an aesthetics point of view, they add a rugged and strong look to the rear of the vehicle without compromising visibility.

PROJECT 58
Install a Fuel Door Hatch

 Time: 1 Hour

 Tools: Socket set, Allen head sockets, pry hook

 Talent:

 Applicable Years: All Jeep Wranglers

 **Tab:** $110

 Parts Required: Fuel door hatch

 Tip: None

 Performance Gain: Provides protection from the elements to your fuel filler and fuel cap

 Complementary Project: Steel corner guards

The design of the Jeep Wranglers is such that the fuel access area—where the fuel filler hose and fuel cap are located—are uncovered and exposed to elements such as rocks, dust, sand, mud, and other debris that could become retained in the bucket and could be potentially introduced into the fuel system upon refueling. To alleviate this condition and protect these vital components, a fuel door hatch is a highly suggested accessory. In addition to its function, a fuel door hatch would also increase the aesthetics of the vehicle by hiding the fuel cap and fuel filler hose.

One of the cleanest and best-fitting fuel door hatches on the market is a factory Mopar part that is available at all Jeep dealerships or through numerous Jeep parts websites. Fabricated from 6063 T6 aircraft-grade billet aluminum, the fuel door hatch is easily installed in less than 30 minutes, and utilizes existing mounting locations and hardware. Concealed in the hinge of the hatch is a unique cam-action hinge that provides smooth and hassle-free opening and closing. The included hardware for the hatch is corrosion-resistant for durability. The item is available in either a chrome finish or satin black finish. Given our project vehicle's color we chose to install the satin black unit.

1

Prior to installing the new fuel filler bucket, the original unit had to be removed. The difference between the two buckets is that the new bucket contains the predrilled mounting holes for the fuel door hatch to be attached onto.

2

A gasket is used to fill in the gap between the fuel bucket and the filler neck.

3

It is easier to get the gasket started onto the fuel bucket before the bucket is installed on the vehicle. Once in place, make certain that the entire gasket is seated along the bucket and that it is aligned properly and not twisted.

4

Using equally distributed pressure, the fuel bucket is placed into the opening bottom first and the pushed into the opening. Two plastic clips will catch the lip of the sheet metal and hold the bucket in place.

5

The fuel cap lanyard is reattached to the newly installed fuel door and secured onto the filler neck to protect any screws from falling into the fuel tank.

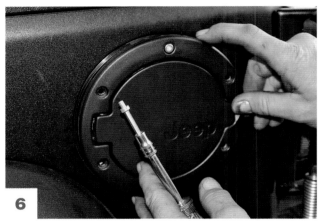

6

Once the bucket has been set into place, the fuel door hatch is aligned with the mounting holes and secured into place. It is important to note that while there are numerous bolts along the perimeter of the fuel door hatch, that only four are used to secure it onto the vehicle. The remaining bolts are decorative only.

7

Care should be taken when attaching the screws into the bucket, as it is plastic and if the threads become cross-threaded, it could cause a bit of a mounting issue.

8

With the installation complete, the fuel cap and filler neck are protected from the elements. The new door is also quite attractive against the American Expedition Vehicles steel corner guards.

PROJECT 59
Install an Aftermarket Hood

 Time: 2 Hours (without painting and prep)

 Tools: Socket set, torx head sockets, hand tools

 Talent:

Applicable Years: Jeep Wrangler JK

Tab: $749 (without painting cost— approx. $400)

 Parts Required: Replacement hood

 Tip: Be sure to have an assistant help with the removal and installation of the factory hood and the new one. Also, the wiper blades and cowl should be removed for ease of installation.

 Performance Gain: Provides additional cooling capabilities for the engine

 Complementary Project: Installation of a snorkel.

Keeping an engine's operating temperature as low as possible is essential to having a reliable Jeep, especially if it is used in adverse conditions and at slower speeds where there is not a sudden influx of fresh air moving through the compartment to aid in the process. For off-roaders who are always looking for new ways to keep the temperature down, the American Expedition Vehicles Heat Reduction Hood, made for all Jeep Wrangler JK models (both two-door and four-door), does just that. And it does it with style. The stamped steel hood is built with the same equipment that the factory uses to produce their body panels. The all-steel construction hood weighs considerably more than the factory unit and appears to be more stable at highway speeds, as the buffeting effect found on the factory hood is all but eliminated. Incorporated into the design are openings that allow fresh air to enter the compartment and then exit it. These openings are covered with custom-fabricated perforated stainless steel inserts that are truly a work of art. The unit comes epoxy-coated and ready for paint.

The installation is time consuming but relatively straightforward. The factory components of the original hood must be removed and transferred onto the AEV unit. Some additional time may be spent in the alignment of the new unit in relation to the existing body panels, but is nothing too difficult.

Even though the factory hood is being removed, some factory parts need to be removed from it to be used on the new AEV heat reduction hood. These items include the washer nozzle hose, the ground strap from the hood to the vehicle, and all latches, hinges, and hardware.

3

Replace all under hood components in their stock location. Exhibited here is the stock latch assembly being reinstalled onto the AEV hood. One of the benefits of this unit is that all of the attachment points align perfectly with the factory hood, making the reinstallation easy.

4

5

Aside from adding to the vehicle's aesthetics, the new AEV heat reduction hood features openings in the sides and top of the hood to allow engine heat to escape. Custom-fabricated perforated stainless steel inserts are attached to the inner portion of the hood.

6

Prior to the final tightening of the mounting hardware, the hood should be opened and closed a few times to align it with the body panels and to ensure that there are no spots that are rubbing or sticking to the fenders, etc.

7

The completed hood adds to the vehicle's aesthetics, and it serves a functional role in that it allows additional heat to dissipate from the engine compartment. We can attest to its function, since we have seen the thermals emanating from the steel mesh insert on the top of the hood as we are stopped at a signal or stop sign.

PROJECT 60
Refinish Side Body Moldings and Fenders

 Time: 1 Hour

 Tools: Razor blade

 Talent:

 Applicable Years: All

Tab: $30

 Parts Required: Blue masking painter's tape, paper, trim paint (spray)

 Tip: Make sure the vehicle is clean of debris prior to applying the masking tape to the body panels so the tape will stick to the surface better.

 Performance Gain: Aesthetics

 Complementary Project: Detail of vehicle

If you own an older-model Jeep with black plastic side moldings and fenders, chances are that after a few trips off-road and just general wear and tear they begin to get discolored and rather unsightly, which then detracts from your vehicle's overall appearance. While it is somewhat expensive and time consuming to replace these items for new pieces, a quicker and much more affordable method can be to refinish them. The key to refinishing these pieces is to take your time with the preparation of the parts prior to painting them and to use the correct paint for the job. Just because the spray paint can says it is satin black, does not mean that it will work for this application. Given the abuse and exposure these pieces are subjected to, a specialized paint is required for the job, if it is to be done correctly. Since all of the pieces are plastic, we used a satin black trim paint that is manufactured by Wurth. This paint has been specifically developed for parts such as these, since it is flexible and is equivalent to the finish currently on the factory pieces.

1 After numerous trips to the desert and sitting in the sun, the factory fender flares and side moldings were beginning to show some signs of wear and tear.

2 Painting is faster and cheaper than replacing the parts with new units; blue painter's masking tape is used to protect the paint during refinishing.

3

When the vehicle has been taped and protected, a towel that has been soaked in acetone is used to clean and remove any surface contaminants from the piece. The acetone will allow the trim paint to adhere better and minimize the chances of the paint peeling off.

4

It is important to protect as much of the vehicle as possible from any overspray that may occur as a result of the spray painting. Remember masking tape, masking paper, and time are all cheaper than overspray removal.

5

Once masking the vehicle is finished, it gets a final pass with the acetone-soaked towel.

6

The Wurth satin black trim paint has been specifically designed for pieces such as these. This paint is flexible and will match the finish on the rest of the plastic components on the vehicle.

7

8

Even coats of paint are sprayed onto the fenders and side moldings. It is best to apply a thin first coat and then a heavier second coat. This will allow the paint to adhere better and stronger to the material, rather than applying one heavy coat that may not dry evenly and may have spots where the application was not evenly applied.

9

Prior to removing the masking tape and paper, the areas should be allowed to dry for 30 minutes to allow the paint to set up.

10

An hour later, the vehicle's fenders and moldings look better than new and for a considerable amount less.

PROJECT 61
Install a Front Skid Plate

 Time: 1 Hour

 Tools: Socket set, impact gun, transfer punch, open-ended wrench

 Talent:

 Applicable Years: All

 Tab: $299

Parts Required: Self-threading metal screws

 Tip: Check for clearance between the drag link adjuster clamps and the skid plate. It may be necessary to place the bolts vertical and rearward.

 Performance Gain: Provides protection to the front suspension and steering components of the vehicle

Complementary Project: Installation of additional underbody skid plates

Adding a high-quality and durable front skid plate to replace your factory unit, if your vehicle is equipped with one, will protect key components of your front suspension system and help protect your steering components. Depending on your model of Jeep, there may be rather expensive components in the front of your vehicle, which if damaged, could be costly to replace. An example is the automatic disconnecting sway bars on the Rubicon model JK Wranglers. In the event this component is damaged by a rock, it could set you back $1,500 to replace, making the investment in a front skid plate a much better bargain.

Complementary to our American Expedition Vehicles front JK Wrangler bumper, we have selected to install the optional front skid plate onto the bumper. While this skid plate is specific to the AEV bumper, the general concept of the installation remains the same for the majority of aftermarket front skid plates that attach to front bumpers.

Stamped from $1/8$-inch-thick steel plate, the 23-pound unit looks like a factory part and, as we mentioned, protects the vehicle's sway bar, impact beam, suspension components, and steering system. The unit is multistage-coated and finished with a layer of zinc coating, an epoxy coat, and a textured black powder-coated finish.

Since holes will need to be drilled into the underside of the front bumper, the vehicle has been placed on a lift and raised to make the measurement and alignment easier. The AEV skid plate is offered as an option to the AEV front bumper. It has been designed to take the front tow hook mounts into consideration by having slots cut through it so the plate slides over them. *Photo courtesy of American Expedition Vehicles*

2

Holding the skid plate in place, a self-threading screw is secured at the front of the plate to the bumper. For safety purposes, it is recommended that the two outer mounting locations be started first, so that the plate is supported while the remaining mounting locations are identified. The screws should remain loose at this point and not tightened. *Photo courtesy of American Expedition Vehicles*

3

The rear portion of the plate is secured by four mounting locations. Being held in place at the front, a transfer punch is used to mark the locations. Upon completion, the skid plate should be removed in preparation for the holes to be drilled. A 3/8-inch drill bit is used to make the rear mounting holes. Once completed, the holes should be deburred and a treated with a rust inhibitor. The skid plate is reinstalled to the bumper with the front two screws being resecured, while four nuts, bolts, and washers secure the rear.

4

Following the installation of the rear bolts, the remaining four self-threading screws are installed. Once all of the bolts and screws have been installed, they should be torqued to ensure that they can withstand the impacts that they will soon encounter.

5

Upon completion of the install, the automatic sway bar disconnect coupler should be inspected to ensure it is not being interfered with by the skid plate. *Photo courtesy of American Expedition Vehicles*

6

Looking as though it rolled off the factory floor, a front skid plate will pay for itself multiple times throughout the vehicle's use. *Photo courtesy of American Expedition Vehicles*

PROJECT 62
Install Billet Aluminum Door Handles

 Time: 1 Hour

 Tools: Screwdriver, trim removal tool

 Talent:

 Applicable Years: Jeep Wrangler JK (two-door and four-door models)

Tab: $320 (two-door) $530 (four-door)

 Parts Required: Door handles

 Tip: Once the factory handles are removed, clean away any debris that has been lodged behind them.

 Performance Gain: Improves the appearance of the vehicle

 Complementary Project: Installation of rear tail-light protectors

Sometimes it's the attention to little details that can set your Jeep apart from someone else's. This is especially true when a group of Jeepers gets together and before you know it, the old "mine is better than yours" game starts. While perfectly capable of doing their job as the factory designed them, the door handles on the JK Wranglers leave a lot to be desired. When off-road driving many objects can be brushed against or come into contact with the sides of a vehicle. On more than one occasion, we have seen the factory plastic door handles become damaged, scratched, and even broken in half. To add some durability and bling to your ride, Off-Road Evolution's Evo Handles were created.

Fabricated from solid 6061 T6 billet aluminum, these handles have been CAD drawn, CNC-machined, and hand polished to a brilliant finish. A direct replacement to the factory door handles and tailgate handle, these units also feature stainless steel hardware. Available for either the two-door or four-door JK Wranglers these units scream durability and toughness, especially the available units with a machined iron cross embedded in them. The ease of installation is also a great feature, as they can be installed in about 20 minutes per door. Definitely worth checking out!

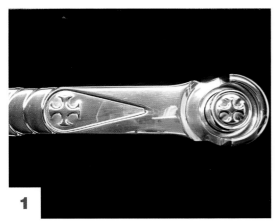

1

The Off-Road Evolution Evo door handles are fabricated from 6061 T6 billet aluminum and feature a hand-polished mirror finish. They are currently available for both two-door and four-door models of the Jeep Wrangler JK. *Photos courtesy of Lisa Wade*

2

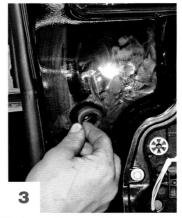

3

To remove the factory handles, the interior panel of the door must be removed. Once removed, the rubber grommet on the door must also be removed so the mounting hardware may be accessed. *Photos courtesy of Lisa Wade*

4

The hardware for the handle is accessed with a long-shaft screwdriver, used to loosened it. *Photos courtesy of Lisa Wade*

5

As you can see, the factory plastic unit is somewhat frail when compared with the solid billet replacement. Do not get rid of the factory handle just yet, as there will be some parts reused on the replacement handles. *Photos courtesy of Lisa Wade*

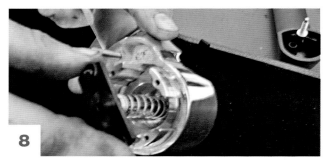

6

The factory rubber seals that are placed between the handle and the door sheet metal are removed from the factory handle to be reused on the billet unit. *Photos courtesy of Lisa Wade*

7

The inner spring mechanism and brace are removed from the factory unit and reinstalled on the new handle. *Photos courtesy of Lisa Wade*

8

When reinserting the spring button, make certain that it is seated properly against the button. *Photos courtesy of Lisa Wade*

9

When reattaching the crossbrace of the spring, care should be used when starting the threads so that it does not become cross-threaded, especially since it will be under pressure from the spring. *Photos courtesy of Lisa Wade*

10

The new handle is ready for to be installed now that the spring mechanism and gaskets have been installed. *Photos courtesy of Lisa Wade*

11

Once the handle has been installed, there is a considerable difference in the level of quality and appearance between the stock units and the Evo handles.

INTERIOR

A good majority of your time with a Jeep is spent inside the cab, as rock over rock is negotiated or as you drive to your next destination. While the suspension, exterior, and engine have all had attention paid to them, the interior should be no different. Items such as new seats, replacement center consoles, and cargo dividers are just a sampling of the number of items that can be improved or upgraded that this chapter addresses.

PROJECT 63
Install MasterCraft Racing Baja RS Seats

 Time: 3 Hours

 Tools: Socket set, open-ended wrenches, impact gun

 Talent:

 Applicable Years: All Jeep models and years

Tab: $550.00 per seat

Parts Required: Baja RS seat, seat rails, and zip ties

 Tip: Having a clean and clear area to work in and around will facilitate a quicker installation, since items will not be getting in the way upon removal and reinstallation of the seats.

 Performance Gain: Replacing the factory units for the aftermarket seats not only provides additional comfort, but also provides a safer platform to off-road in based upon the specific design and construction of the units

Complementary Project: Installation of a harness bar and set of five-point harnesses

Driving off-road is not for the faint of heart, as we all know, which is why safety should always be at the top of your list, not only for the driver, but for others on the trail as well. One highly overlooked safety component of driving off-road is the seat that drivers and passengers sit in. Stock units that came with the vehicle when it was new lack a great deal of support and comfort when riding off-road. While perfectly functional for street driving, when put on the dirt they become insufficient.

Designed for off-highway driving, MasterCraft seats are a fine example of aftermarket seats that have been designed to meet the needs of both driving on the street as well as off-road by providing additional support and strength to the rider. Starting with a mandrel-bent and mig-welded ¾-inch mild-steel tubing frame, the heart of the seat is a suspension liner system that is attached to the frame with high-strength parachute cord and made of a nylon-coated textile mesh that provides extreme strength, durability, and resistance to the movements encountered while on the trails. In addition to its cradling effect, the porous mesh material is breathable and allows moisture to pass through. Atop the suspension system, layers of polyurethane foam of differing thickness and density are glued to the liner and built up to achieve the seat's desired shape. The cover for the seat is just as functional as the unit for which it is covering; it is made from high-quality Rogue Naugahyde with a center insert of close-weave nylon fabric and slots for a five-point harness

system. Grommets on either side of the seat provide a bellow action to promote air circulation and rider comfort.

One of the distinguishing features of the Baja RS bucket seats is their ability to be fully adjustable, which provides a best of both worlds scenario: They remain functional like the stock units while providing additional support and comfort, not to mention a better appearance as well.

Upon replacing the factory seats with the aftermarket units, a noticeable change for the better is experienced due largely to additional side bolster support increasing driver control as well as the suspension system diminishing rider fatigue.

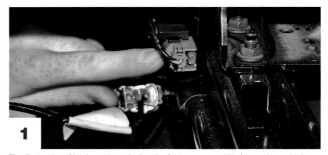

The first order of business in replacing the factory seats with aftermarket units is to remove the seat bolts with an impact gun. On the passenger side seat of newer model Jeeps, an airbag sensor is built into the seat and will need to be disconnected to remove the seat from the vehicle. The new Baja RS seats incorporate the same sensor into their design, making them compatible with the factory units.

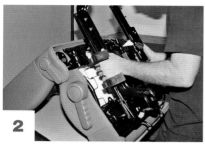

2

With the bolts and electrical connections separated, the factory seat is removed from the vehicle. Placing the seat on a waist-high worktable will make the process of removing and reinstalling key components such as the seat rails, seat belt latch, and electronics that much easier. The seat rail assembly is being removed from the stock unit.

3

Once removed from the stock seat, the seat rail assembly is test fitted with the Baja RS mounting locations to determine if any modifications are necessary.

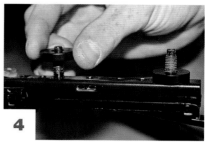

4

For our application, a set of shims needed to be installed between the seat and the rail assembly to insure proper seat height and adequate clearance for the seat slider assembly. Depending on the model of Jeep, shims or other aftermarket seat rails may be required for proper seat height and seat adjustment.

5

The seat belt latching mechanism is removed from the factory seats and installed onto the aftermarket seats. Special care should be taken to ensure that the retaining bolt is torqued to specs and that the bracket is positioned appropriately in relation to the seat.

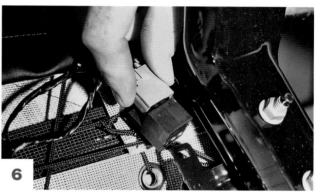

6

With the mounting bolts installed and set at the correct height, the seat rails are attached. Once the seat rails have been attached to the new seat, the trigger mechanism that allows the seat to be adjusted along the sliders is installed. With the new seat reinstalled into the vehicle, the electrical connections for the air bag sensor and seat belt latch are reconnected. It is important to ensure that any excess wiring is attached to either the underside of the seat bottom or to the seat rails so that the wiring does not get damaged with seat adjustments.

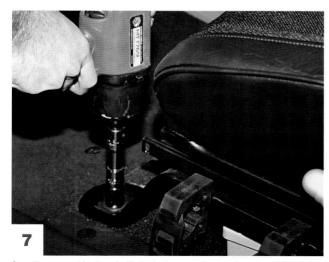

7

Once the new seat is aligned with the factory mounting locations, the retainer bolts should be reinstalled using an impact gun.

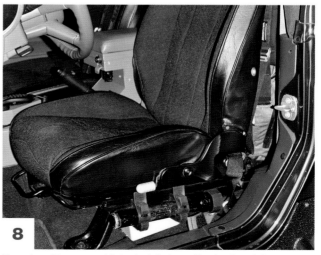

8

The end result is a new seat that not only looks good but is substantially more supportive, comfortable, and safer than the stock unit.

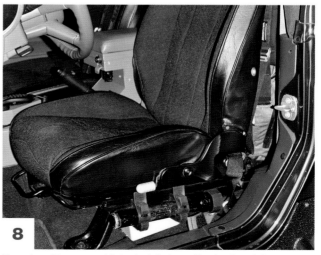

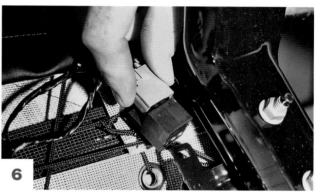

INTERIOR

163

PROJECT 64
Install Restraints

 Time: 1 Hour

 Tools: Socket set, Allen head sockets

 Talent: ✦✦✦

 Applicable Years: All

Tab: $200.00 pair

 Parts Required: Harness system

 Tip: Remove the seat that the harness will be installed on to allow for quicker installation of the harness components to both the seat and the harness bar.

 Performance Gain: Comfort and safety

 Complementary Project: Install a pair of MasterCraft Baja RS adjustable seats

Restraint systems are worth their weight in gold. Normally only found on pure race vehicles or extremely customized or competition rock crawler rigs, a high-quality restraint system will work for you every time you have it on. While the factory seat belts are more than adequate for street driving, a restraint system is a necessity while off-highway driving, given the amount of dangerous conditions, speeds, and hazards that are often encountered, not to mention the extreme angles that occupants are placed in while traversing obstacles.

MasterCraft restraints are some of the safest units in the industry. Given the countless number of off-road race teams that use their restraints, they are real-world proven. For our purposes, we utilized their 2-inch restraint system. SFI-approved, the restraints are manufactured from military-spec webbing and feature sheet alloy steel or drop forged hardware. The restraint systems are available in three versions depending on your desired method of installation: bolt-in series, snap-in series, or wrap-around series. We chose a combination of their bolt-in series for the lower restraints, as we were attaching them to the factory seat belt latch locations, and the wrap-around series for the upper restraints, as they were going to be wrapped around our harness bar.

The installation of the system is easily achieved. The upper restraints simply wrap around the harness bar and are secured by a steel buckle. The lower restraints are bolted on piggyback to the factory seat belt lath on one side of the seat and to the pivot bolt on the other side. The center latching mechanism is easily secured and unsecured as the upper restraint ends are paired together and the fed through the latch, which is secured by a hook and latch device.

Keep in mind that the restraints have a typical life expectancy of two years, which means that they should be either replaced or re-webbed to keep their performance up to par. There are some exceptions when restraints should not be used, as when a vehicle does not have the proper safety support system of a full roll cage. The reason to avoid installation in this condition is because in the event of a rollover or other accident, the occupants will become trapped in their seats and will be unable to move to avoid being crushed when the roof structure collapses. When a roll cage is installed, the integrity of the roof structure is retained, therefore eliminating the issue of roof failure and the occupants not being able to move to safety. Chances are, if your Jeep has a roll cage and restraints installed and it rolls, you and your occupant have a better than average chance of walking away unharmed.

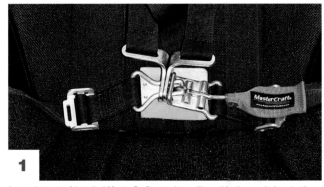

A complete set of installed MasterCraft restraints will provide the needed protection to off-road drivers, who often face dangerous situations that may leave their rigs turned upside down or possibly worse.

2

The side restraint belts are attached to the factory seat belt restraint latch on one side of the seat and to a mounting bolt on the other side.

3

Depending on the style and manufacturer of your Jeep's seats, there may be an opening to pass the restraint belts through. If your seat does not have an opening, simply route them along the top of the seat and then onto your shoulders.

4

Prior to wrapping the upper restraint belt around the harness bar, the drop forged alloy steel buckle must be laced through the restraint.

5

Once the buckle has been laced through the restraint, an under and over approach should be used to place the restraint belt around the harness bar. As a side note, the harness bar should not be placed any lower than 4 inches from the point where the restraints are at the driver's shoulders.

6

The buckle is laced with the restraint belt. The method used to lace the restraint through the buckle allows for quickly and effectively adjusting the restraints depending on a driver change or different seat adjustment.

7 **8**

The restraint should be pulled tight against the harness bar to become set it in place. There should be some level of slack available for fine tuning of them for driver comfort and related safety concerns.

9

With the driver sitting in his seat, the restraints are adjusted for length, proper height in relation to the buckle mechanism, and restraint pad placement, all to insure a perfect fit.

10

Once the restraints have been installed, an additional layer of safety covers the occupants of the rig in terms of staying in place while traversing those larger than life rock gardens.

PROJECT 65
Building a Roll Cage

 Time: Hours vary depending on the type and size of roll cage

 Tools: Welder, torch, tape measure, marking pencil

 Talent: to

 Applicable Years: All

Tab: $1,000.00 and up

 Parts Required: Tubing, welding materials

 Tip: Remember to include the necessary provisions for installing safety harnesses to the roll cage.

 Performance Gain: Could possibly save your life in the event of a rollover or other accident

 Complementary Project: Installation of safety harnesses

The single most valuable and important item that any Jeep can have installed on it is a solid and secure roll cage. Factory equipment on Jeep Wranglers for years now, a roll cage can literally mean the difference between life and death. On some other models of Jeeps, such as the Grand Cherokee, Cherokee, Patriot, Liberty, Jeepster, Commanche, Commander, and Compass, the body pillars have been designed to meet the safety requirements of the NHTSA while on the road. However, as soon as the tires of your rig hit terra firma, additional safety equipment should be installed for added protection to all of the vehicle's occupants. The terrain and obstacles you will be encountering can cause serious injury in the event that the vehicle is rolled, pitched sideways against a rock, or takes an unplanned trip down an embankment.

When building a roll cage, there are numerous issues to consider, ranging from the style of roll cage and the type of material to the method of attaching it to the vehicle.

STYLE OF ROLL CAGE

Not the easiest of items to install or fabricate, a roll cage can either be purchased in kit form (either to be bolted together or welded in place) or as a custom fabricated unit. There are numerous aftermarket companies that produce roll cage kits for a variety of Jeep vehicles. Often these kits are purchased because of their ease of installation and the lack of fabrication skills required on behalf of the vehicle owner. These types of kits usually have the option of either being bolted into the vehicle in pieces or being welded into the vehicle for a more semi-custom look. From a performance point of view, if installed correctly, both will do the job just fine.

The other alternative is to build a roll cage from the ground up. Typically these types of roll cages are found on custom-built vehicles that have been stripped of their interiors and are specifically designed for off-road driving or rock crawling. Given the endless possibilities of designs for such an item, a professional fabricator is often tasked with building these units. A few benefits to this type of roll cage include being able to attach the seats directly to the cage for additional occupant safety, selection of the material and finish color, and the ability to include attachment points for items such as harnesses, panels, and occupant handles.

MATERIAL

Depending on your budget and the intended use of the vehicle, there are three types of materials that a roll cage may be fabricated from:

Cold Rolled Electric Welded (CREW) tubing is produced in a mild steel carbon range, such as 1006 and 1008, and contains a seam along the length of the pipe. Given its relatively low cost and ability to be MIG welded, this type of material is often what roll cage kits are constructed from. Drawn-Over-Mandrel (DOM) tubing is also a mild steel product that can be MIG welded, yet features a higher carbon range of 1020 and has usually been treated with a process like Stress Relief Annealing (SRA), whose primary purpose is to reduce the material's hardness and increase ductility in order to facilitate subsequent manufacturing operations without distortion or cracking. The cost for this material is higher than the CREW material but lower than 4130 chromoly.

4130 chromoly. Known throughout the motorsports world as the best material to build anything bulletproof, this material consists of a combination of chromium, molybdenum, and carbon, and it is heat treated, which is why it is at the top of the material list. While certainly not the cheapest material, it is definitely the way to go if money is no object and performance and durability are the only things that matter. This material cannot be MIG welded, but TIG welded only.

ATTACHMENT METHODS

Depending on your level of skill and the intended use of your vehicle, the method of how your roll cage is attached may vary. There are three common methods used to attach a roll cage to or incorporate it into a vehicle. The first and second methods are typically utilized when an off-the-shelf kit is used. The first method is to bolt the kit to the floor plate of the vehicle. The second method is to integrate the new kit and pieces with an existing roll cage structure. This method is typically found with Wrangler and CJ models, which already feature a partial roll cage. The third method is to penetrate the floor plate of the vehicle and attach it to the vehicles frame, often accomplished by welding it on. While all three methods are acceptable as long as they are preformed correctly, attaching it to the frame and through the floor plate is by the far the strongest and safest method. The only drawback to this method is that it exposes the cabin of the vehicle to exhaust fumes, road noise, and the elements, which, as we said earlier, may be fine if it is a purpose-built rig, but as a daily driver may take some time to get used to, if ever.

By custom building a roll cage, such as the unit on this vintage Jeepster, there is more opportunity for customizing items such as the seat tab placement, seat angle, and restraint bar height and cargo accessibility.

The three most popular materials used in roll cage construction are CREW (left), DOM tubing (center), and 4130 chromoly (right). While each material has its own advantages and disadvantages, having a cage made from any of the three is better than none at all.

It is important to measure twice and cut once, especially when some of the material being used can cost in excess of several dollars per foot.

4

Bends should be minimized wherever possible in the design of a roll cage for the simple reason that a bend reduces the strength of a roll cage since it is based on compression and tension. If a bend is required, bracing should be incorporated to make up for the reduction in strength.

5

The most common way of notching a tube so that it will fit with another to form a tight intersection is with a hole saw and a tube notching tool. A tight notch is extremely important for a strong weld joint.

6

The floor plate of this vehicle has been cut to allow the roll cage to be mounted directly to the frame for added strength and durability.

7

A triangular plate is used to gusset the intersection between the frame and the roll cage on both sides of the tubing. In this picture, the side rock rails are also incorporated into the design, making it an entirely integrated system.

8

When constructing a roll cage, triangulation should be used wherever possible, given the stability of the geometric structure of a triangle. Without triangulation, a square has no lateral support; also, every primary structural tube should be one leg of a triangle.

9

Anytime the roll cage can be welded together rather than bolted in place, additional strength will be added to the system. It also is easier to maintain, since hardware will not be required to be tightened and inspected.

PROJECT 66
Install Roll Bar Mounted Grab Handles

 Time: 1/2 Hour

 Tools: None

 Talent:

 Applicable Years: All Jeeps with roll bars

$ **Tab:** $40.00 pair

 Parts Required: None

 Tip: Make sure that the grab handles are securely fastened, as they will have force being applied against them.

 Performance Gain: Comfort

 Complementary Project: Roll bar pad and cover replacement

Anyone who has ever tried to get into the cab of a raised Jeep will tell you that it is not an easy task, especially since the majority of them do not have grab bars. One of most stable and supportive sets of grab handles is manufactured by MasterCraft. Constructed from 1 1/2-inch nylon webbing for strength and durability, the handles of the bars are 1/2-inch wide Thermo-Press rubber, which is resistant to collapsing on your hand. For even more strength, a third mounting strap has been incorporated into the design along with a wear-resistant rubber pad that protects the roll bar cover material. Definitely a much needed accessory for anyone who needs assistance when getting into their Jeep.

1 A much needed accessory on any Jeep with a roll bar, MasterCraft's grab handles are built to the same specifications as their race seats.

2 With the straps released, the grab handle pad is placed atop the roll bar with the handle aligned parallel to the roll bar.

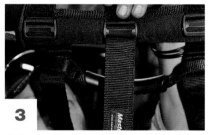

3 Starting with the center strap, it is laced through the buckle and secured in place. Installing the center strap first will set the angle of the handle in place.

4 The two end straps are laced through the buckles next. As you cinch the straps, the handle should align once again with the roll bar.

5 With the straps secured, the grab handle will provide additional support to anyone entering any Jeep equipped with a roll bar.

6 Once the grab handle is secured, grab the handle and apply a fair amount of pressure on it. If the handle and straps rotate, they need to be undone and re-secured for a tighter fit.

PROJECT 67
Install a Full Length Center Console

 Time: 2 Hours

 Tools: Torx head drivers, screwdrivers, socket set

 Talent:

 Applicable Years: All

Tab: $400.00

 Parts Required: Center console, mounting hardware

 Tip: Remove both front seats for added room and to minimize damaging any of the surrounding interior panels and pieces.

 Performance Gain: Safety and comfort

 Complementary Project: Installation of a CB radio or receiver

Owning an open top Jeep has its perks, especially when the sun is shining and you want to take a quick drive up the coast for some much needed relaxation. The only issue is securing items of value or importance inside the vehicle. One of the main ways to resolve this issue before anything is stolen is to replace the center console with a high-quality steel model that has been designed to be pick-proof and features additional storage areas and a high-security locking mechanism at the center console.

Tuffy Security Products is a company whose name is synonymous with security for open top Jeeps. Offering center consoles for virtually every model of open top Jeep, including the JK, the Tuffy Security products are as bulletproof as they come, which means that you can once again enjoy your day without worries of someone taking everything from your vehicle. You also won't have to carry around those additional unwanted items everywhere you go. The company also manufactures center consoles for other enclosed Jeep models as well.

The Tuffy Security Products consoles are constructed from 16-gauge steel and, in some cases, provide over twice as much storage as the factory console. A special bracket is included for mounting a stereo, CB, or other electronic equipment inside the lockable console with a hole on the side of console for the radio microphone, which eliminates the need to have the center console raised while driving. Inside the storage area, there is a 12-volt marine-grade power outlet and a removable utility tray for added creature comfort. The patented Pry-Guard II latching system secures the lid shut while a gas strut supports the lid when open. For added

convenience, front and rear drink holders are included with anti-rattle drink fingers. The console is taller than many OEM models, which provides a higher platform armrest for more comfort to driver and passenger. Each console includes brackets for both automatic and manual transmissions.

1 While completely functional by center console standards, the plastic factory unit left a lot to be desired when it came to security and comfort. In order to ease the removal and installation of the new unit, we took advantage of the seats being removed from our project Jeep.

2

The new Tuffy Security Products center console fits right where the factory unit did. One of the benefits to the new steel console is that the factory mounting locations are utilized and the unit is able to be purchased in a variety of colors to match the interior of each specific Jeep model for which they are made.

3

The factory hardware from the OE console is able to be reused.

4

Case in point: With the front seats removed from the vehicle, the installation will proceed much quicker and faster than trying to work around them.

5

Built to accommodate either manual or automatic transmissions, the only change that must occur at the console is that a trim ring is swapped for the correct transmission model. This unit is easily adapted by a few Phillips head machine screws.

6

One distinguishing factor of the Tuffy Security Products center consoles is their patented Pry-Guard II latching system for the center console lid. It contains a high-security lock and is pry bar–proof.

7

To assist with closing the center lid and keeping it open, a gas-charged strut is standard equipment on the console.

8

Every attention to detail has been addressed, as evident by the emergency brake opening gaskets that keep items from falling into the opening created by the brake handle.

9

Given their ability to have electronics mounted inside of them, an opening for a CB or other radio microphone has been provided to eliminate the need of having to keep the center lid open while in use. In this configuration, the CB radio channel is set and the lid closed, and the microphone is easily accessed. When not in use, a rubber grommet fills in the hole.

PROJECT 68
Install a Trail Table

 Time: 1 Hour

 Tools: Drill, drill bits, threaded insert installation tool, screwdriver, tape measure, level, Allen head socket

 Talent:

 Applicable Years: All Jeep Wrangler JK models

 **Tab:** $180.00

 Parts Required: Table, hardware kit

 Tip: None

 Performance Gain: Provides valuable space and a sturdy platform for various activities

 Complementary Project: None

Regardless of whether you are on the road or off of it, having access to a solid and flat surface is always needed for one thing or another, whether for use as a trail workbench or a picnic table. Given the tight space constraints in a Jeep, carrying a folding table in your rig may not make for the best use of space nor would it be very practical. So what's a person to do, you ask? Simple, just install one of Off-Road Evolution's trail tables.

Made in the United States from ⅛-inch steel and fabricated specifically for all Jeep JK Wranglers (two-door and four-door models) to maximize cargo space and still have enough clearance for the rear subwoofer, the folding trail table contains 348 square inches of surface area when opened and occupies a mere 1½ inches of cargo area when closed. Easily installed, using the supplied threaded nut inserts (the perfect choice for supporting heavy loads on the table), Allen head bolts, and washers, the table can be mounted in two positions—one position that allows the table to be folded down and the other position that allows it to be folded up. Each configuration has its own advantages and disadvantages; it just depends on what is being placed on it and how it will be used. One thing is for sure though: Once you install it, you'll never know how you lived without one.

1 With the tailgate open and secured from closing, the plastic panel that covers the tailgate wiring is gently removed.

2 The rear ⅛-inch steel back panel of the Off-Road Evolution trail table is lifted onto the tailgate.

3

Another set of hands is required to hold the rear panel onto the tailgate so that measurements can be taken to center the table onto the tailgate. A level should be used to confirm the balance of it as well.

4

Once the table has been centered and leveled, a transfer punch is used to mark the mounting locations from the table onto the tailgate. Not much force is required when transferring the marks—too much force and the tailgate metal may become indented, which may cause an issue as the installation progresses.

5

Once the holes have been marked, the tailgate is drilled to prepare for the threaded nut inserts that will be used to secure the table onto the tailgate.

6

The threaded nut inserts are secured with a specialty tool that has been designed to set them into place at the correct depth and with the correct amount of pressure. Special care should be taken when putting in these inserts, as too much pressure could cause them to seat improperly; the best method is a slow and steady pull of the trigger.

7

The equal spacing of the table mounts combined with the threaded nut inserts ensures that the table will be able to support heavy objects without failing.

8

The table back is once again placed onto the tailgate with the mounting locations aligned, and the included hardware is used to secure it to the tailgate.

9

Some assembly is required of the support struts and actual tray panel. Depending on its intended usage, the table tray can be mounted to either fold down or fold up.

10

Upon completion of the install, our new trail table will be used to hold tools, parts, and, yes, even a lunch or two. Destined to be one of the most useful items we've installed on our Jeep, we're sure once you get one, you'll agree.

PROJECT 69
Install Roll Bar Padding and Covers

 Time: 1 Hour

 Tools: None

 Talent:

Applicable Years: All Jeep Wranglers

Tab: $500.00 per complete set

 Parts Required: Roll bar covers, roll bar padding

 Tip: None

 Performance Gain: Provides safety and protection to occupants

 Complementary Project: Install a roll bar

Owning an opentop Jeep definitely has its perks. It also has its drawbacks, in that there are a few more items that need more attention and maintenance than those of other Jeep models. Roll bar pads and covers are one of these items. If the top is left off your Jeep for any period of time, the roll bar padding becomes faded, dirty, and somewhat worn rather quickly. Add a weekend at the local mud hole and suddenly you're in need of a new set of pads and covers. In the majority of cases, a new set of pads and covers can be purchased through the dealer or on dedicated Jeep parts websites. If, however, you are looking for a set of

pads and covers that are more durable to the elements and can be customized, your best bet is to have an automotive upholstery shop make them specifically for your vehicle. Going this route will allow you the freedom to choose your material and fastening method—zipper or Velcro. For our installation, we utilized a set of pads and covers that were custom fabricated from the same material, Cordura, used in outdoor backpacks. The pad material used is a highly engineered open-cell EA urethane foam material that would provide the ultimate head impact protection to whoever was in the seated areas.

1 After months of exposure to the elements, the factory roll pads and covers were ruined. Once removed, the roll cage structure is cleaned and inspected for any deterioration such as rust or other damage.

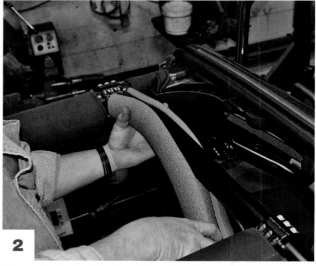

2 The new roll pad material used is a highly engineered open-cell EA urethane foam material that provides the ultimate head impact protection in case of an accident or a rollover.

3

It is important to install the roll pad seams facing upward for better protection to the occupants. In the event of an accident, occupants' heads will not come into contact with the seam, but a solid piece of padding.

4

The Cordura roll pad cover is first test fitted to make sure that the piece belongs in this exact location.

5

When installing the pad, place the seam facing upward for the same reasons as placing the roll pad material upward.

6

Velcro was chosen as the fastening method for the roll pad covers, given its ease of installation, its ability to absorb impact, and the ease of working out wrinkles when installing the covers.

7

Once completed with the installation of the new pads and covers, any intersections where one bar meets another is inspected for proper fit and protection from the bar.

INTERIOR

175

INTERIOR

PROJECT 70
Install Soundproofing

  Time: 3 to 4 Days

 Tools: Scissors, razor knife, tape measure, pen, trim tools, ratchet, socket set, steering wheel puller

 Talent:

 Applicable Years: Any Jeep model

Tab: $600–$900 (depending on the manufacturer and density of the material)

Parts Required: Cleaner/degreaser and shop towels

 Tip: To ensure the best adhesion, the surface upon which the soundproofing material is to be applied should be thoroughly cleaned and degreased using a manufacturer-approved cleaning agent.

 Performance Gain: Provides a night and day reduction in the amount of wind and road noise encountered, especially while at highway speeds; it also allows for better performance of audio/video systems

 Complementary Project: Installation of a hardtop liner or a new soft top

Anyone who has ever driven or owned a Jeep Wrangler knows that once inside the cab and driving at highway speeds, the odds of hearing oneself think are slim to none. Being able to take only so much, the decision to install soundproofing throughout our Jeep was made. Aside from the obvious auditory benefits, applying an insulating membrane to the interior of your Jeep will also increase the performance of your stereo system, as well as assist in heat reduction from the engine and transmission.

While there are numerous manufacturers of soundproofing materials for vehicles, our choice was Dynamat's Xtreme material based on its rated loss value of sound as well as its construction, which includes an aluminum coating designed specifically for high temperature applications such as firewalls and floors.

Knowing what it takes to install this material and have the job done correctly, SoCal Customs was tasked with essentially gutting the interior of the Jeep and applying numerous layers of the material to create our own quiet room. Each kit contains nine sheets of 18x32-inch material, 4$\frac{1}{2}$ square feet per sheet, or 40$\frac{1}{2}$ square feet per kit—just enough to line a Jeep Wrangler floor. Additional sheets are required for the firewall and wheelwells.

1

The first step in installing the soundproofing requires that the entire interior of the vehicle is gutted to the point that people begin to think the vehicle was either stolen or stripped or is a salvaged unit. Spencer Stewart of SoCal Customs is in the process of removing the factory center console and passenger side carpeting in preparation for the soundproofing material.

176

2

Once the interior has been removed from the Jeep, special care should be taken to ensure that none of the factory wiring connections have been disturbed by the process and that they are safely out of the way. Prior to the installation of the elastomeric butyl and aluminum material, the manufacturer recommends that a cleaner/degreaser agent be applied to the surface to remove any contaminants that may inhibit the materials ability to bond with its surfaces.

3

Prior to starting the actual installation, a few minutes should be taken to consider the best layout and usage of the materials. When ready to install the sheets, measure their place, trim the panels with scissors or a razor knife, test fit, and then simply peel back the release liner and apply it to the surface with firm and consistent pressure.

4

Throughout the floor of the vehicle, there are drain holes and service access points that should be worked around, but never concealed.

5

Once the material has been applied o the surface, a wooden roller is required to complete the adhesion to the surface as well as to assist with the contour shaping of the material.

6

It is important to begin the project from one main point and work out from that point. Following this method will reduce any unnecessary material overlap, as well as help reduce the number of small pieces of the material.

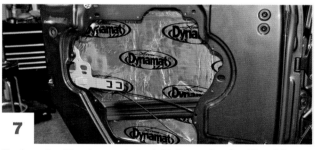

7

The doors of our Wrangler were also treated to the soundproofing. Although it was a bit more work, the benefits are immediately noticed even when closing the doors, which now sound like bank vault doors with the solid sound.

8

The firewall of our vehicle was also layered with the material to provide additional noise and heat reduction from the engine compartment.

9

Once the interior has been completed, the interior is ready to be reinstalled and conversations between passengers may resume.

PROJECT 71
Install Seat Covers

 Time: 1 Hour

 Tools: Head rest removal tool (if required)

 Talent:

 Applicable Years: All Jeep models and years

Tab: $75.00 to $100.00 per seat (depending upon seat configuration)

Parts Required: Factory seat and seat cover

 Tip: Prior to installing the cover onto the factory seat, make sure the seat has been cleaned and is free of debris; also, if the cover has vinyl or similar material incorporated into the corners or edges, place it in the sun for a few minutes to allow it to become pliable, which will ease the installation.

 Performance Gain: Covering the factory seats will provide a new appearance to the vehicle's interior as well as provide additional comfort and support to the riders

 Complementary Project: Installation of new roll bar padding and covers

As we all know, vehicles are a direct reflection of their drivers. Typically, the first items to be added to a Jeep are items that will make the vehicle climb a larger rock, drive through a deeper mud bog, or just look way cooler than it did in its stock configuration. These components are typically associated with the exterior of the vehicle, larger and wider rims, larger tires, lifted suspension system, etc. Equally as important, however, is the comfort of the vehicle and its passengers. One quick and cost-effective way to transform your interior in the matter of an hour or so is to install a set of custom seat covers.

Over the years the technology and construction of seat covers has improved tremendously. A fine example of today's new technology seat covers are the units that are made by MasterCraft Race Seats. Designed to mimic their popular racing seats, the MasterCraft units are constructed from the same durable woven fabrics and stitching and provide the level of comfort that is found on their race seats. The covers are available in a multitude of colors, designs, and fabrics that will allow you to compliment the vehicle's interior. The company provides covers for both bucket seats and bench seats on a vehicle-specific basis. Follow along as we install one of their seat covers onto the rear bench seat from a Wrangler. An additional benefit to utilizing seat covers is keeping a consistency in the interior as well, as evidenced by our project vehicle, which features MasterCraft Baja RS seats up front and a matching cover for the rear bench. The end result is a better-than-factory appearance that is not only comfortable, but protective of the original seats too.

1 To facilitate an easier installation of the seat cover, the rear bench seat from our Wrangler was removed and placed atop a table.

2 Prior to installing the seat cover, the factory headrests must be removed, as they too will have matching covers installed.

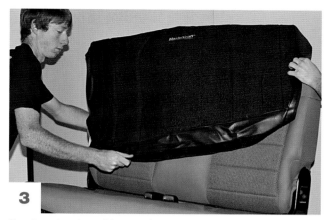

3 Given the awkwardness of the cover, the simplest method to beginning the installation is to start at the seat back and work down, which will allow the cover to be fitted tighter onto the seat.

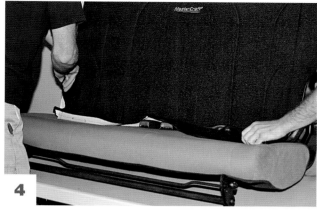

4 Once the cover has been fitted over the entire seat back, the excess material and fastening points should be routed through the gap at the bottom of the seat.

5 With the cover installed to the seat back, the seat should be turned with the seat bottom facing up, allowing the bottom portion of the cover to be installed easier.

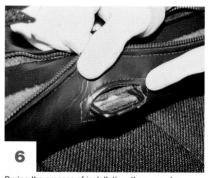

6 During the process of installation, there may be numerous attachment points or latch assemblies that the cover must either go through or around to insure the operational integrity of the seat.

7 Upon completion of the bottom and back portions of the seat cover being installed, the corners and sides should be pulled tight to eliminate any creases, wrinkles, or bulges that may be left over as a result of the cover being folded during shipping. Typically, these deficiencies will disappear after the cover has been installed for a few days.

8 Completing the transformation, the head rests have been removed for their covers to be installed as well. For the ultimate in durability, the head rest covers feature the same high-quality zippers as do the seat cover.

9 The final product—a seat that looks just as fast, comfortable, and stylish as the rest of the vehicle.

SECTION 7
ELECTRICAL

The electrical system of any off-road vehicle is truly something that should be marveled upon. This can be no truer than with Jeeps; just the fact that it is a Jeep is almost license enough to add winches, auxiliary lighting, and other wiring to it. This chapter addresses all of these items and a few more.

PROJECT 72
Install a High-Intensity Discharge (HID) Searchlight

 Time: 1½ Hours

 Tools: Allen wrenches, wire crimper, wire stripper, open-ended wrenches, ratchet, socket set, screwdriver

 Talent:

 Applicable Years: All Jeep TJ and JK Wrangler models

 Tab: $600 per light

 Parts Required: Wire connectors and switch assembly, if not ordered with light kit

 Tip: Prior to cutting the length on any of the wiring harness from the light to the switch, verify the wiring route so as not to come up short during the final installation.

Performance Gain: Allows for the driver to pivot and direct light to the exact location where it is required, while eliminating the need to hold a similar light by hand.

Complementary Project: Upgrade factory headlights and fog lights

In the realm of off-road driving there is a light designed for virtually any type of weather or driving condition that can be encountered. One of the tried and true staples within the industry continues to be a directional searchlight. Lights such as these are true multipurpose units that serve to illuminate work areas, obstacles on a trail, or a driving path. While this style of light has been around for some time powered by conventional bulbs, some of today's newer units feature cutting edge optics, housings, and bulbs.

One of the new guard units to this style of light is Delta Tech Industries high-intensity discharge (HID) searchlight. Aside from its rugged appearance given the polypro housing, night is turned into day by a 6,000K HID-rated bulb with internal ballast pack that is 105 percent brighter than daylight and 300 percent brighter than traditional halogen lights. Best of all, the light is installed alongside the windshield and is ready for use at the flip of a switch.

1 A tried and true staple within the off-road community, the new generation HID search light by Delta Tech Industries outperforms its predecessors by being 300 percent brighter than conventional halogen bulbs and 105 percent brighter than daylight and by being indestructible thanks to its polypro housing.

2 The first step in installing the HID search light is to remove the two factory Allen head driver's side A-pillar bolts.

3

Once the factory A-pillar bolts have been removed, insert the new A-pillar bolts that are included with the mounting bracket kit into the billet aluminum light bracket and prepare to reinstall the bolts into their original locations. It is important to note that the bolts included in the kit are longer to compensate for the thickness of the light bracket; because of this reason the factory bolts cannot be utilized.

4

Prior to installing the light onto its mount, the two bolts that secure the windshield wiper shroud need to be removed to facilitate the routing of the light wiring to the switch and point of power connections.

5

Once the path of travel for wiring has been determined and the mounting bracket has been secured to the A-pillar, mount the search light and align accordingly. Special care should be taken to ensure adequate clearance of the light in relation to any wiring as the light will be able to be rotated 360 degrees.

6

With the wires routed to the source of power, end connectors should be installed using a set of quality wire crimpers.

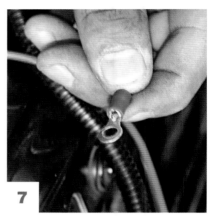

7

Prior to their installation, the end connectors of the wires should be inspected for proper connection to the wire and an uncompromised outer sheath.

8

For our application, we choose to install our search light onto our S-Pod power distribution block; however, any point of power is adequate, provided the point of connection is solid and secure.

9

The final step of the install involves aligning the searchlight to the desired position on the bracket and in relation to the other lights on the vehicle. Note that in some states, a light of this brightness and application may require a cover, given that it is forward facing.

PROJECT 73
Install Rock Crawling Lights

 Time: 2 Hours

 Tools: Hand tools, cable ties

 Talent:

 Applicable Years: All

Tab: $200

 Parts Required: Rock crawling lights

 Tip: Prior to final installation, the light locations should be tested to ensure maximum coverage.

 Performance Gain: Safety

 Complementary Project: Upgrade factory headlights

When off-roading at night, many things go bump in the night; hopefully most of the bumping will not be from the underbody of your Jeep hitting every conceivable rock or obstacle. A completely different perspective than when off-roading in the daytime, the same trail that you have memorized for years in the daytime is suddenly turned into the surface of the moon the minute the sun sets. For a few of us challenging souls who partake in night trail runs, small, compact, and extremely bright lights mounted in strategic points of the wheel wells and underbody are the only way to get though the trail in one piece. That is aside from the fact that they look cool and can usually scare someone enough into thinking that the aliens are finally landing to take over.

While a common set of driving or fog lights will do, they can be somewhat cumbersome in the wheel well of a Jeep, not to mention that they would last about two seconds once the tire and suspension began doing their dance. To solve this issue as well as make a kit that would be easily installed and bright enough to do their job, but not be a nuisance to other drivers, Vision X Lighting has created the Tantrum LED Rock Pod light kit. Each kit consists of eight 1-watt light pods, a master controller with built-in microphone for sound interface, a distribution block, a wireless remote with a 1,000-foot range, and a cigarette lighter adapter for a true plug-and-play installation.

Easily installed, the kit contains eight 3M high-quality adhesive pads that allow the pods to be mounted anywhere on the vehicle with mounting screws as well for a solid install. Once the pod wires are routed into the cab, the plug-and-play features of the kit are enjoyed by simply connecting all eight lights to the distribution block and the distribution block into the master controller. Once completed, the cigarette lighter adapter is plugged in, and the remote control button is pressed for instant daylight.

The Tantrum LED Rock Light kit includes everything needed to turn the trail into daylight from under your Jeep. A definite must-have when performing night trail runs.

2

Each of the eight pods has a 1-watt LED built into it. For stability and durability, the housing of the pods is CNC-machined billet aluminum.

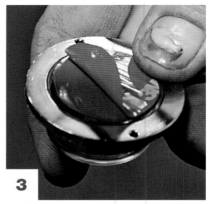

3

Included with the kit is a super-strong 3M double-stick adhesive pad that is used in conjunction with the included mounting screws to ensure that the pod does not fall off on the trail.

4

Prior to their final placement, the light pods should be mounted in such a way as to cast the light in front of and behind each wheel, thereby illuminating any obstacles that must be driven over. With the location selected, the light pod is installed and the wiring is routed into the engine compartment and through the firewall to gain access to the interior of the Jeep.

5

When penetrating the firewall, all of the front four-pod light wires should be combined, so it is easier to pull the wires. Once all of the wires are in the inside of the Jeep, the lights are connected into the distribution block, which then gets connected to the master controller.

6

When all of the lights have been connected to their respective boxes, the cigarette lighter adapter is plugged in to power the system. Understanding that the master controller can be an interference while off-road driving, we installed it along the front of the dash panel, where it is out of harm's way.

7

Included as a feature of the kit is a wireless remote control, which operates up to 1,000 feet away from the vehicle, making it great for approaching the vehicle in dark conditions. With the lights on, an even pattern of light can be seen both in front of and behind the wheel, which allows for spotters and drivers to see what rocks or obstacles are upcoming. This will allow the driver to select a path based on what is actually there, rather than what is thought to be there in the dark.

PROJECT 74
Install, Test, and Replace Fuses

 Time: ½ Hour

 Tools: Flashlight

 Talent:

 Applicable Years: All

Tab: None

 Parts Required: None

 Tip: None

 Performance Gain: Allows the specific electronics that are fused to operate while protecting them from overcharging or current spikes

 Complementary Project: General vehicle inspection

One of the most frustrating things that can happen when driving your Jeep is to have one of your key electrical components go out due to a bad fuse. Usually, this occurs, as luck would have it, when you are on your way home from a day of off-roading and your headlights, running lights, or some other necessary component is down for the count. Once your Jeep is pulled over, the lid on the fuse block is pulled and the hunt for the bad fuse begins. After a few minutes, the unit is identified, replaced, and you're back on the road. For a fuse to go bad is usually indicative of a larger issue with regard to your electrical system. Questions to ask yourself when replacing a bad fuse should be centered around topics like why the fuse went bad, what part of the component caused the failure, and was the vehicle's electrical system at its maximum capacity. All too often, especially with Jeeps, there are so many additional electrical components added that some of the other components are pushed to their capacity, and fuses go bad due to the inadequate charging and power capability of the vehicle.

In the event a fuse on your vehicle does go bad, the fuse block should be inspected to determine which fuse it is, the amperage should be determined (it is usually posted at the top or sides of it), and it should be replaced. Never replace a fuse with one of a higher rating than what is currently installed, as it could damage the electrical component that it is protecting. In some cases, if the component still does not function after a fuse is replaced, additional investigation with a test light or other device should be performed.

To test a fuse or circuit, a test light is used. This is a tool that features a metal pointed tip shaft on one end, and a wire with an alligator clamp on the other. In the handle of this tool is a low-wattage light bulb that illuminates as soon as current is detected from a wire or circuit.

Typically, your vehicle's owner's manual contains specific information regarding the type of fuses your vehicle has installed in it, as well as the types and amperages of the required fuses. For any aftermarket components, it's a good idea to identify the fuses yourself and carry a few extras in the glove box for those rainy days.

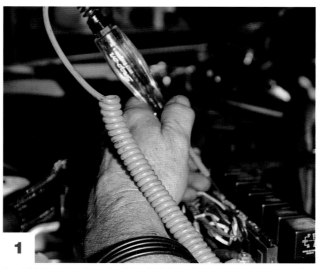

1

A test light is used to determine if the circuit is conducting an electrical current. Test lights are easily operated by attaching the alligator clamp end to ground, and the circuit is tested for power by either penetrating the wire with the point of the tool or placing it on the fuse holder bars. If power is being conducted, the built-in light in the handle will illuminate. If there is no power, the light will not illuminate.

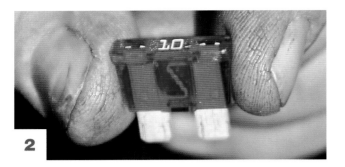

2

One of the most common types of vehicle fuses is called a blade fuse, due to the resemblance of the fuse ends to a razor blade. These types of fuses are available in a variety of amperages from 0.5 amp up to 150 amps. This type of fuse is blown if the internal bridge between the two blades is broken and not in the typical "S" pattern. The fuse shown has not been blown.

3

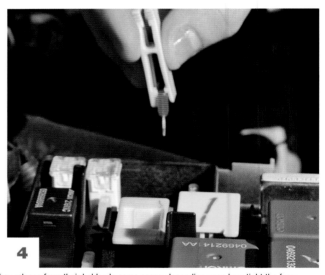

4

Blade fuses are easily removed and installed by simply pulling straight up on them until they release from their holder. In some cases, depending upon how tight the fuse holders are, a special removal tool may be required as shown. These tools can be found in the fuse block of your vehicle.

5

Depending upon the make and model of Jeep, the fuse block may be inside the vehicle in the region of the dashboard or it may be in the engine compartment. In some cases they may be in both locations, with the auxiliary fuses for items like the cigarette lighter, power adapters, and interior lights in the interior fuse block. Engine and vehicle specific fuses such as those for the air conditioning system, ECM, and headlights would be in the engine compartment fuse block.

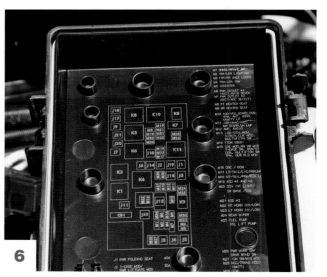

6

One look at a fuse block can be intimidating, especially since none of the fuses are labeled. To assist with the inspection and identification of the vehicle's circuits, the fuse block lids are usually inscribed with the schematic for the fuses and the required amperages for each fuse.

PROJECT 75
Install a Premier Power Welder

 Time: 6 Hours

 Tools: Socket set, pry bar, drill, screwdrivers, cable ties

 Talent:

Applicable Years: All

Tab: $1,000

 Parts Required: Premier power welder

 Tip: Install the unit in an area that is easily accessible.

 Performance Gain: Ability to weld and fix anything metal at a moment's notice anytime, anywhere

 Complementary Project: Installation of a dual battery system

It's not a matter of if you will break something on the trail as much as it is when you will break something on the trail. One way to be sure that you will be able to address any situation that requires welding to fix your problem is by having an on-board welder installed on your rig. One of the most widely known and used on-board welding systems on the market is the Premier Power Welder. For over 29 years these units have rescued countless off-roaders and enthusiasts from precarious situations in which they would have been helpless without the unit. Consisting of a high-output alternator, welding control box, and all of the necessary cables and hardware, these systems can be installed in virtually any location on your vehicle until they are needed. Premier Power Welders allow you to weld stainless, mild or high-carbon steel, and aluminum with no size or plate-thickness limits. Their high-frequency pulsating DC current allows you to use any AC or DC electrode up through 1/8 inch at 100 percent duty cycle. The system also allows both welding and battery charging by using No. 4 cable leads with up to 500-foot lengths with minimal loss of heat. The welding control box serves as the epicenter of the system by supplying power for Heli-Arc or tungsten inert gas or (TIG) welding for stainless steel and aluminum materials and metal inert gas (MIG) welding with up to 0.035-inch solid or 0.045-inch cored wire. As an additional benefit, the welding control box contains a 115-volt DC (maximum 2,300 watts at 20 amps) power-outlet jack for nonfluorescent lighting and brush-type power tools.

Like we always say, it's better to have it and not need it than to need it and not have it.

1

In order for the system to function, a high-output alternator must be installed that is compatible and wired to work in conjunction with the welding control box.

2

The Premier Power Welder alternator is easily installed and in most cases is a direct bolt-in replacement application unit. Once it is installed, the remaining components of the system follow.

3

Included with the system are all of the required charging cables and wiring that run between the alternator, regulator, and welding control box.

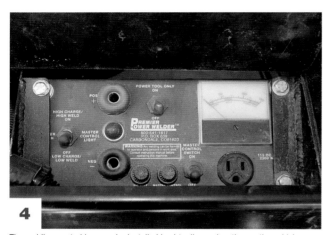

4

The welding control box can be installed in virtually any location on the vehicle, including in the dashboard. All of the key switches required to use the unit are mounted on its face for easy operation.

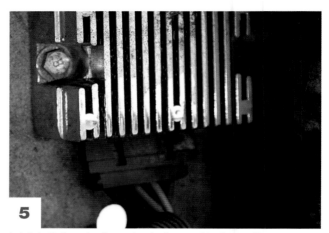

5

Included with the system is an external voltage regulator that provides surge protection to the system.

6

Proving that the system can be mounted anywhere, our welding control box was mounted inside our rear bumper's utility compartment, protected from the elements and unwanted visitors of the thieving kind.

PROJECT 76
Install an Auxiliary Switch Kit

 Time: 2¹/₂ Hours

 Tools: ³/₈-Inch socket set, T-20 torx bit, drill, ¹/₄-inch drill bit, screwdrivers, trim removal tools

 Talent:

 Applicable Years: All 2003–2009 Jeep Wrangler models

 Tab: $435 per kit

Parts Required: sPod, wire connectors, and auxiliary components

 Tip: Begin installing the components from the interior of the vehicle and work toward the engine compartment for ease of pulling the wiring through the firewall and manageable cable management.

 Performance Gain: The sPod system will alleviate numerous wiring connection and relay failures, given the circuit board design and aircraft-quality construction

 Complementary Project: Installation of auxiliary lights and components

Anyone who owns a Jeep Wrangler knows that dashboard space is at a premium, given the limited amount of space that is available for the installation of auxiliary electrical component switches, which poses a problem to the typical Jeep owner who may require up to six additional switches to control accessories such as lights, winch controls, air compressors, and differential lockers. An accompanying dilemma to the space constraints for the switches is the constraints for the numerous terminal connections at the battery, relays, and fuse blocks.

To alleviate virtually all of these issues, the sPod auxiliary switch kit was created for all 2003 to current Jeep Wrangler models. Consisting of aircraft-quality components, the system includes two main components: the circuit board (the source) and the switch console. Each source unit features six cube-style Bosch (Tyco) plug-in relays that have been rated at 30 amps each. Attached to the relays are ATO-style automotive fuse holders that are connected to protective diodes for accessory protection. Power to the source unit is achieved by a two-piece 8-foot-long, eight-conductor 18AWG wiring harness that has been wrapped with an automotive sleeve and 24 crimped-on ¹/₄-inch female terminals and a hot wire with inline fuse. All connectors to the kit are made in the United States and are military certified parts. The quick-release connectors used to join the switch console and the harness are made by Deutsch and have been designed specifically for critical applications in harsh environments where dust, dirt, moisture, salt spray, and rough terrain can contaminate or damage electrical connections and systems. An eight-gauge power lead with in-line manual resetting circuit breaker and ground provides the power to the sPod. The switch console houses six Contura III lighted rocker switches that are placed along the top of the windshield, thereby alleviating the need to drill into the dashboard for switch placement. For added durability, the rocker switches are resistant to dust, water spray, and submersion under pressure.

Upon installing this kit, all that is ever needed to connect auxiliary accessories to the source unit is a knowledge of which switch will control the accessory and a screwdriver to loosen and resecure the power and ground terminals.

1

Prior to installing any of the sPod components, the interior trim pieces surrounding the A-pillar and windshield surround must be removed, including both sun visors. With the trim pieces removed, the footman's loop that has been riveted onto the windshield frame must have the rivet heads drilled off. Special care should be taken when performing this task, due to the fact that overdrilling the rivet could result in the drill bit going through the windshield frame. When the rivet head is detached, the remaining rivet should be pushed into the windshield frame.

2

With the footman's loop removed, the sPod threaded adapter bracket bolt should be threaded through the two holes in the windshield frame. It is important to keep the nut attached to the right side of the bolt to keep it from being lost inside the windshield frame.

3

Once threaded through both holes, the adapter bracket bolt is ready to receive the switch console bracket. The supplied washer and nut should be attached to the assembly and secured, starting with the left side first and finishing with the right side.

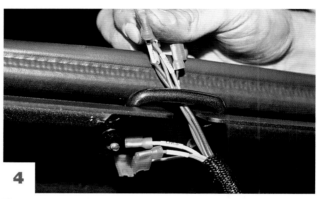

4

The wiring harness is fed through the footman's loop and the switch console bracket and should begin being routed to the firewall opening. Upon completion, the windshield header trim piece should be reinstalled in preparation for the switch console installation.

5

Once the connection has been made between the wiring harness and the switch console, the console is secured to the bracket by two screws on either side of the console.

6

The wiring harness continues to be routed down the driver's side A-pillar to the firewall penetration. Prior to penetrating the firewall, the grommet is cut to accommodate the wiring harness. This step is important to keeping the firewall sealed from the engine compartment and any related gasses or temperatures.

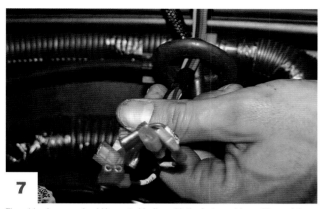

7

The wiring harness should be routed in-line with the factory wiring, with special care taken to keeping the wiring from being damaged by moving parts or pinch locations.

8

The circuit board or source, as it is called, is installed atop the factory ECM and shares the ECM mounting bolts. To begin the mounting process, the ECM bolts should be loosened but not removed. Once the bolts are loose, the source unit is placed behind the bolts and secured.

9

The end of the wiring harness, which contains the 24 crimped-on $1/4$-inch female terminals and a hot wire with inline fuse, is routed through the opening in the source and connected to the appropriately labeled terminals.

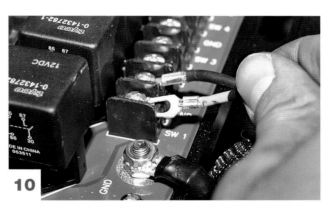

10

The final steps of the install involve connecting the auxiliary components and accessories to each of the labeled power and ground terminals that correspond to the switches inside the vehicle.

11

The power cable and ground for the source are secured along the firewall, using the supplied ties. One of the benefits of the kit is that while six accessories can be powered, only one connection must be made at the battery, eliminating the need for larger battery studs or additional connection points.

12

Upon completion of the wiring connections, the anodized aluminum cover is placed over the source to protect the components from the elements.

ELECTRICAL

PROJECT 77
Install a Lighted Safety Whip

 Time: 3 to 4 Days

 Tools: Hand tools

 Talent:

 Applicable Years: All

Tab: $75

 Parts Required: Wire, wire connectors, switch, in-line fuse, safety whip, bulb

 Tip: None

 Performance Gain: Provides additional safety and vehicle identification

 Complementary Project: Installation of auxiliary lights

Depending upon where you off-road, a safety whip may be a mandatory requirement and means of identifying your vehicle to other enthusiasts in the area. While typically found on quads, UTVs, and sand vehicles, a safety whip should be, if not already mandatory, a standard item on any off-highway vehicle for a number of reasons. Typical off-road trails feature numerous areas where there are blind corners, steep approach angles and other hazards that sometimes do not allow a vehicle to be seen until it's too late and a possible accident has occurred. Factor in night use on the same trails and it becomes disastrous.

Safety whips have been used as a reliable source in identifying a vehicle prior to it being seen. For our install we opted to use Buggy Whip's 10-foot-tall white fiberglass unit with a light head and attach it onto a spare mount that we had on our rear tire carrier. Since we would not be using the whip on a daily basis, a quick-release mount was also used, which allows the whip to simply be unscrewed as opposed to being installed with a nut and washer. While it may not look like much on the street, all it takes is one steep hill approach and someone on the other side, either in another car or on a motorcycle to find out that these items definitely have a place on your rig and are worth the time and cost to install.

A necessity when out four-wheeling, a safety flag and whip will alert unsuspecting riders and other enthusiasts of your whereabouts. These items are especially useful when cresting steep hills, as they are higher than the vehicle and are often the first item to be seen.

1

192

2

While clearly visible during the day, this particular model features a light head at the top of it for those night excursions. The bulb is a standard size 5-watt bayonet style unit; an optional LED bulb is also available.

3

The base of the trail flag is a quick-release style, meaning that it simply unscrews when not in use. We chose to mount the base onto one of the spare mounting tabs on our spare tire carrier.

4

A 12-gauge wire is routed from the mount into the engine compartment, where a power source is acquired for the light head. We chose to connect the flag to our sPod auxiliary power source unit. Ground for the light head is achieved at the base of the mount, through its connection with the metal frame.

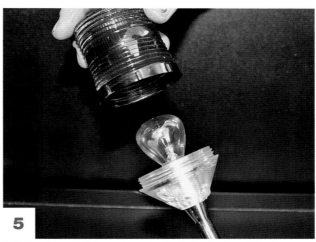

5

Aside from being able to be used as a signaling device, the Buggy Whip also provides a fair amount of campground light, thanks to its light bulb shield that has been designed to reflect 360 degrees and shine the light downward as well.

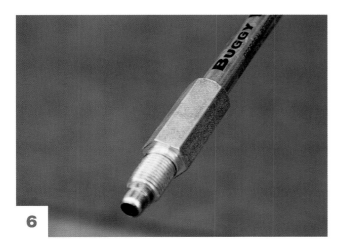

6

The shaft of the flag is fabricated from fiberglass and has all of the necessary wiring for the top-mounted light integrated into the shaft, reducing any wire connects at the unit's base.

PROJECT 78
Install Trailer Wiring

 Time: 1 Hour

 Tools: Screwdriver, pop rivet gun

 Talent:

 Applicable Years: All

Tab: $125

 Parts Required: Trailer wire harness, pop rivets, four-pin flat end adapter

 Tip: When routing the wiring, make sure to avoid any areas where excessive heat could damage the wiring or any parts that could pinch the wires.

 Performance Gain: Towing safety

 Complementary Project: Install a hitch receiver

If you are going to tow a trailer, lighting is a mandatory requirement in any state. For the majority of Jeeps that will be towing a trailer, the most widely used type of connector for the trailer lighting is a four-pin flat connector. This type of connector is best suited to the electrical systems of most Jeeps in that it provides turning signals, stop lights, and running lights for basic trailer lighting operation. Given today's technology regarding vehicle wiring and electrical systems, the days of having to splice into your vehicle's electrical system and tap the trailer wiring harness from these wires has been replaced by simple plug-in connectors that integrate directly with the existing connections. While we utilized a factory Mopar harness for our application, numerous other aftermarket manufacturers provide the plug-in style trailer wiring harnesses for a good majority of Jeep vehicles.

1 To begin the install, the driver's side taillight assembly must be removed so that the factory lighting harness can be accessed.

2 Once the taillight assembly has been removed, the new Mopar trailer light harness can be routed through the body panels and along the side of the frame.

3

The new trailer light harness is plugged into the factory lighting harness. To achieve this, the factory connector is removed from the taillight and plugged into one end of the new harness; the remaining end of the harness is then plugged back into the taillight assembly.

4

Resting alongside the driver's side inner frame rail, the trailer light wiring harness is routed to a predetermined location for final installation.

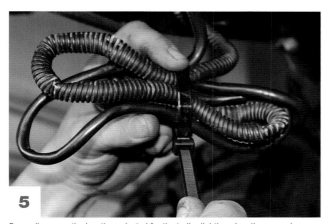

5

Depending upon the location selected for the trailer lighting plug, there may be excess wiring that needs to be bundled together and have a cable tie installed around it.

6

With a secure and safe location selected for the excess wiring, cable ties are used to secure them in place. These wires should be placed away from any moving parts or areas where excessive heat from the exhaust can damage them.

7

Not wanting to have the trailer light plug hanging below the bumper, an adapter was used that allowed the end connector to be relocated into the bumper for protection from obstacles when off-road driving. To keep the adapter securely mounted, pop rivets were used.

8

Once installed, all that is required for the trailer lights to function is for the four-pin flat connector of the trailer to be plugged into the harness.

ELECTRICAL

PROJECT 79
Upgrade Factory Headlights

 **Time:** 1–2 Hours

 Tools: Flat screwdriver, torx screwdriver

Talent:

Applicable Years: All Jeep TJ and JK Wranglers

Tab: $200 per set

 Parts Required: None required

 Tip: The new headlights do not require realignment from the factory specifications, so do not adjust the settings.

Performance Gain: Provides better illumination of the road and trails at night; enhances the appearance of the front of the vehicle

Complementary Project: Factory fog light upgrade

Keeping an engine's operating temperature as low as possible is essential to having a reliable Jeep, especially if it is used in adverse conditions and at slower speeds where there is not a sudden influx of fresh air moving through the compartment to aid in the process. For off-roaders who are always looking for new ways to keep the temperature down, the American Expedition Vehicles Heat Reduction Hood, made for all Jeep Wrangler JK models (both two-door and four-door), does just that. And it does it with style. The stamped steel hood is built with the same equipment that the factory uses to produce their body panels. The all-steel construction hood weighs considerably more than the factory unit and appears to be

more stable at highway speeds, as the buffeting effect found on the factory hood is all but eliminated. Incorporated into the design are openings that allow fresh air to entire the compartment and then exit it. These openings are covered with custom-fabricated perforated stainless steel inserts that are truly a work of art. The unit comes epoxy coated and ready for paint.

The installation is time consuming but relatively straightforward. The factory components of the original hood must be removed and transferred onto the AEV unit. Some additional time may be spent in the alignment of the new unit in relation to the existing body panels, but is nothing too difficult.

1 The comparison between the factory headlight and the new Delta Tech Industries unit is definitely noticeable. While there are numerous design differences, the most notable is the overall performance of the new units compared with their stock counterparts.

2 The factory headlights are manufactured from plastic and do not have the same level and quality of optics that the replacement units do.

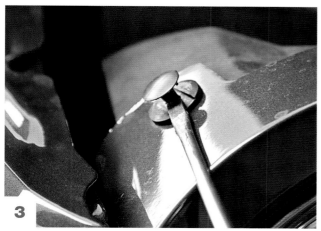

3

The factory grille mounting hardware and grommets must be removed using a flathead screwdriver to allow access to the retainer ring for each of the headlights. It is important to note that the entire grille need not be removed from the vehicle to access the headlight rings.

4

Once both sides of the grille have been loosened and access to the headlight retainer rings as been obtained, a torx screwdriver is used to remove the retainer ring that holds the light in place. Once the ring is removed, the unit can be removed from its housing.

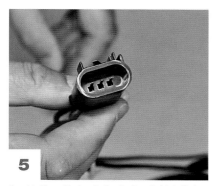

5

An added benefit of replacing the headlights is that the bulb is upgraded from the stock H4 style to an H13 xenon unit. This conversion is achieved through a new wiring harness provided with the kit.

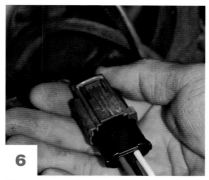

6

Prior to reinstalling the replacement unit into the factory location, the new conversion wiring harness must be attached to the factory plug.

7

Reinstalling the new lights is achieved by reinstalling the trim ring and tightening the torx head screws that hold the unit in place. It is important to note that the factory headlight adjustment settings should not be touched, as the new lights keep the same alignment as the stock units.

8

As a comparison between the two lights, the driver's side features the new unit, while the passenger side contains the stock unit, quite a noticeable change given the bulged plastic stock headlights versus the optic quality glass units that provide four times the light and are physically stronger as well.

SECTION 8
AUDIO/VIDEO/ COMMUNICATIONS

A Jeep just doesn't seem like a Jeep without a high-powered sound system, especially when resting at a trailhead. In this chapter, items pertaining to the installation of aftermarket speakers, public address and siren systems, stereo systems, and equipment racks are discussed.

PROJECT 80
Install a CB Radio

 Time: 2 Hours

 Tools: Hand tools, drill, drill bits, cable ties

 Talent: ✶ ✶ ✶

 Applicable Years: All

Tab: $150

 Parts Required: CB radio, microphone, microphone mount

 Tip: When considering a location to mount the unit, keep in mind other occupants and easy accessibility to the microphone.

 Performance Gain: Ability to communicate with your group while on a trail

 Complementary Project: Installation of a CB antenna mount

One of the basic pieces of equipment that every Jeep should have on board is a CB radio. Used for years as a tried and true method of communication between off-roaders who are on trail runs or require assistance, these devices come in a variety of sizes and shapes. CB radios have several other features, such as weather radios and emergency channel priority buttons, built in to provide an additional level of comfort and safety to their users.

For our installation, we chose one of the most popular CB radios in the off-road community, the Cobra 75 WX ST remote mount CB. Given its compact size and remote mount capability, the unit can be mounted virtually anywhere in the vehicle, without taking up valuable real estate. Featured in the 75 WX ST unit is Cobra's patented SoundTracker technology, which provides powerful transmissions with less static, the end result being clearer voice transmissions. Essentially consisting of two individual pieces, a transmitter box and the handset, the unit is portable and can be used in multiple vehicles, so long as an additional transmitter box is installed in the vehicle. The unit provides access to seven NOAA and three international weather channels help you avert bad weather and dangerous road conditions.

1 One of the most popular units in the off-road community, the Cobra 75 WX ST is a solid performer that takes up little space but delivers high-quality communications. It also features seven NOAA and three international weather channels for added safety.

2 The remote transmitter box is small enough to be mounted anywhere in the vehicle. For our application, we installed the box under the passenger side dashboard, up and away from debris often encountered while off-road driving.

3

The hand-held microphone is the heart of the system and allows the 40 channels to be tuned with one hand. The volume and squelch dials are also conveniently located to promote single-handed use as well. The large liquid crystal display (LCD) can be seen regardless of whether it's day or night.

4

The CB antenna is easily connected to the remote transmitter box with coax connectors.

5

A must for any CB radio, the fiberglass Firestick antenna has been tuned and mounted on a spring to protect it from damage when on the trails.

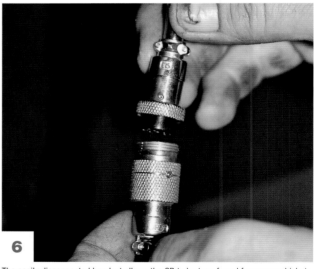

6

The easily disconnected handset allows the CB to be transferred from one vehicle to another, minimizing the costs associated with having two separate radios.

7

When not in use, the microphone is held in place with the included microphone clip that has been mounted onto our center console for easy access.

8

The wire connections to the unit were run to a power source while the ground was installed to the body. The connectors were then crimped together.

PROJECT 81
Install an Intercom System

 Time: 4 Hours

 Tools: Hand tools

 Talent:

 Applicable Years: All

Tab: $4000

 Parts Required: David Clark Intercom System, David Clark Behind-the-Ear Headsets

 Tip: Remove the front seat prior to beginning the installation; it will make routing the cable easier and quicker.

 Performance Gain: Comfort and communication

 Complementary Project: Install an Ipod mount and two-way radio

Anyone who has ever ridden in an open top Jeep will be able to relate to this installation. Between the road noise and the wind noise while doing 65 miles per hour down the highway in an open top Jeep, it is next to impossible to communicate with your passengers; let alone hear any music that may be playing on the stereo system. While used on numerous emergency vehicles and recreational sand cars as an effective means of communication, an intercom system would definitely be right at home in an open top Jeep. While there are numerous systems on the market that range from mild to wild, the best way to choose the correct system for your needs is to assess what features are important to you and what type of performance and sound quality you are expecting from the system. As with many things, there are systems designed for the budget conscious, and others that are top-of-the-line.

Some important features to look for and question regarding these types of systems are how the communication between the passengers is achieved. Are there push-to-talk buttons, or is the system an automatic voice recognition type, where the sound of an occupant's voice triggers the intercom? Also, you need to ask if auxiliary components such as two-way radios and MP3/iPOD devices be incorporated into the system, so that when not communicating with passengers, music can be heard through the headsets. The final item to be concerned with is the quality of sound from both the system and the headsets.

For our installation, we used a David Clark 9800 Series Marine Intercom System for numerous reasons that fit with our application. Having a reputation that spans decades, the David Clark 9800 Series is most commonly used for marine applications on speedboats or fishing boats that are continuously subjected to harsh working conditions, such as saltwater, dirt, sand, and other corrosive elements. When considering an intercom system for an open top Jeep, the similarities between the two conditions were surprisingly close, given the mud, dirt, and elements that a Jeep is subjected to on any given weekend. The 9800 Series system consists of a central master station and display panel to which all of the headset jacks, radio interface cables, and the power cable attach to, making the system one of the easiest to install, let alone use. Voice transmissions are self-activated, meaning that the need for a push-to-talk button is not required, all one must do is begin speaking for the transmission to occur. During those downtimes of conversation, an MP3/iPOD can be piped into the system for noise-free music. A two-way radio can be connected as well, which is great when on a trail. The final components of the system are David Clark's behind-the-ear headsets that feature gel-filled ear cups and noise-canceling technology, which further adds to the experience.

Looking as though they belong more on a helicopter or a high-speed go-fast boat, the David Clark behind-the-ear headsets feature gel-filled earpieces for the ultimate in comfort as well as noise-canceling technology for a truly quiet ride. They are also stereo quality units, which means that music and voices are free from any interference.

2

The heart of the system, the master station is responsible for all of the intercom's functions, including the voice activation, iPod interface, and distribution to the users through one central point.

3

Power to the control panel is delivered from the battery to the power cable, which attaches to the master station. For ease of installation and identification, the lid of the control box has each of the terminals marked for the components that should be installed.

4

The display panel features an LCD screen that allows the user to control the voice activation volume, system volume, and squelch levels. The panel also allows users to switch between two auxiliary inputs, such as an iPod or a two-way radio. The brightness of the screen can also be adjusted at the panel as well.

5

The ability to install and connect all of the components of the system to the master station couldn't be any easier. Each terminal is a plug-in style with a locking retaining ring to keep it from becoming loose while in punishing environments. They are also dust and weatherproof.

6

The headset jack was attached to our harness bar, and the wiring for each jack was routed through the bar directly to the master station mounted under the front seat.

7

Once the headset jacks are secured, the headsets can be plugged in and tested for voice transmissions, squelch, and listening volume.

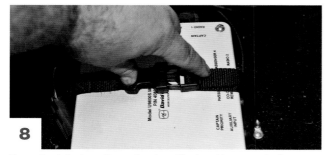

8

The master station is weatherproof, and we did not want to compromise the integrity of the box by drilling holes into it, so we installed footman's straps and secured it to the floor.

9

The end result is an intercom system that will allow each of the occupants to communicate with each other, regardless of the road noise or wind noise experienced when driving with the top down.

PROJECT 82
Install a PA and Siren System

 Time: 4 Hours

 Tools: Ratchet, socket set, drill, metal drill bits, wire cutters, wire crimpers, wire strippers

 Talent:

 Applicable Years: This system can be installed on any year and model jeep.

 Tab: $600 to $700, depending upon the type of speaker and PA/siren system

Parts Required: Battery terminal connectors, wire connectors, and flex loom

 Tip: Determine the pathway that your wiring will be run with regard to both the speaker placement and the siren control head to save on material cost and to make sure the lengths of wire are adequate.

 Performance Gain: Provides an additional level of safety while on the trails by alerting oncoming vehicles around blind corners and for communicating with spotters or other off-roaders. The siren will also aid in assisting rescue personnel in pinpointing your location in the event you become injured or stranded and can access the system controller.

 Complementary Project: Auxiliary lighting

Many times throughout my off-road experiences I have wished I had a PA and siren system on my trail rig to assist me with communication. All too often I have been either spotting another driver or have been being spotted by someone with no way of properly communicating due to the distances involved, conditions of the trail, etc. That has all changed now that a PA and siren system has been installed in our rig. In addition to opening a channel of communication with a fellow off-roaders and spotters, a public address system also allows one to broadcast any important messages to oncoming vehicles or to groups that have possibly organized for a trail run. Having a siren on board as well provides an added level of security, since it can be used to signal other vehicles that we are approaching, possibly a blind corner, or it can be used to assist with pinpointing one's location to rescuers should you become lost. On countless occasions, we have all heard that someone who was lost could identify their rescuers, but the rescuers could not identify them; having this added piece of equipment may just save your life.

The system that we chose to install on our rig is manufactured by Carson Manufacturing and is the SC-550 Stealth model. We chose this system because of its compact design and ease of use. It offers a fully enclosed and splash-resistant rubberized face, hand-held controller with a built-in PA microphone, and a volume control dial that also turns the siren on. The unit is easily installed in even the most constricting of interiors, while the remote control box can be mounted under a seat or in the cargo area. Designed to work with either a single or double 100-watt (one or two 100-watt speakers), the siren includes a six-position rotary switch and siren override push button switch for tone control selection. A slide switch controls the vehicle's primary lights, and four additional push button switches for the auxiliary lights. In total, the system has the capability to control up to 140 amps of light. While it may not be an item that would be used in daily driving, the benefits of having such a system could be recouped in just one situation on the trail.

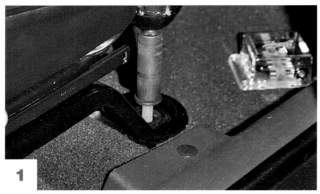

1

The first order of business is to determine where the remote unit for the system will be located. For our installation, we determined that area to be under the front passenger side seat. For ease of installation, we removed the seat and hardware with a cordless impact gun.

2

Prior to cutting any lengths of wire, their paths of travel should be determined to save on both materials and the possibility of having the length be too short. Running from the battery to the under seat location, our 1/0 gauge feeder wire was routed under the vehicle and secured in place along the factory wiring trunk. Special care should be taken at the entrance and exit points for the wire. In our application, a few wraps of electrical tape will ensure that the wire will not be damaged at the grommet intersection.

3

Once the wire has been secured, the weather-resistant rubber floor grommet was resecured and just enough slack was left in the wire to accommodate the remaining installation.

4

When utilizing a feed off the battery, it is a good practice to install a fuse block as close to the battery as possible to avoid any fire or wire shortages. The 60-amp fuse block is being installed along the passenger side inner front fender; the fuse block should be installed in a somewhat dry and secure location away from harm's way.

5

The 1/0 feeder wire was stripped and had a terminal connector placed on the end so that it could be installed on the positive side of the battery. When making high-current connections from a battery such as this, the connector should be soldered onto the wire to reduce any chances of vibration causing it to become loose.

6

Prior to the positive terminal being connected, the negative side or ground should be installed first to prevent the installer from becoming the vehicle's ground.

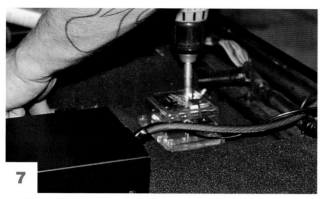

7

Our 1/0 gauge feeder wire from the battery must be split at an additional fuse block that will step it down into two No. 6 feeders. Due to the high-current capacity of the PA and siren system, the control unit requires two No. 6 feeder wires to its power source.

8

The two No. 6 feeder wires that supply power to the control box are installed separately and have a dedicated terminal lug each. Note the bank of circuit breakers that is available for up to 140 amps of auxiliary lighting.

9

For our intended use, a single 100-amp compact speaker was installed behind the front grille with the wiring routed along the same path as the 1/0 gauge feeder wire where it too terminated at the control box under the seat.

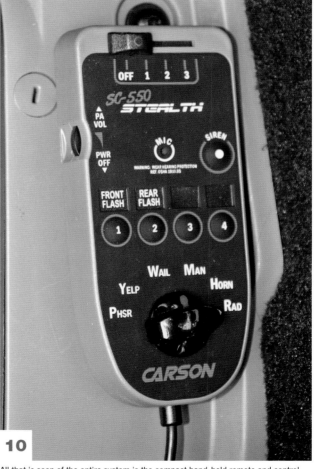

10

All that is seen of the entire system is the compact hand-held remote and control panel, which allows both the PA system, sirens with various tones, and auxiliary lights to be controlled. The remote was mounted along the side of the center console to keep it from getting in the way of daily driving duties.

PROJECT 83
Fabricate Audio/Video Equipment Racks

 Time: 3½ Hours

 Tools: Allen head wrenches, threaded insert installation tool, hand tools, cut-off wheel, level, tape measure, MIG welder

 Talent:

 Applicable Years: All models

Tab: $200

 Parts Required: Metal tubing, threaded insert rivet, miscellaneous mounting hardware

 Tip: Prior to installation, determine what equipment you want to install and mock up the placement to make sure the mounting locations of the equipment are accounted for during the fabrication of the frame.

Performance Gain: Allows the specific electronics that are fused to operate while protecting them from overcharging or current spikes

 Complementary Project: Installation of audio/video products

Regardless of the type of Jeep you own, chances are that interior space is at a premium. As we continue to acquire the latest and greatest in mobile audio/video for our vehicles, the amount of places to install this equipment becomes minimized rather quickly, especially since virtually every piece of equipment is supported with auxiliary components such as digital video disc (DVD) drives, control modules, etc. A typical solution for years has been to place everything under the seats and hope that they remain working and don't get damaged by passengers' feet. While this is a great place to keep prying eyes from seeing what equipment you have, it is one of the worst places if you plan on doing any type of off-road driving. Issues such as dust, water, and vibration can all be transferred directly to the equipment and wreak havoc on them in these locations.

While installing our audio/video system in our project vehicle, a 2008 Jeep JK two-door Rubicon, we quickly ran out of space for the satellite phone control unit, the navigation system DVD drive, a 1,750-watt sine inverter, the control module for the siren/PA system, and the light controls for our strobe system, not to mention the numerous relays and wiring harnesses. With numerous years of experience building custom show vehicles and manufacturer display vehicles in the industry, Spencer Stewart of SoCal Customs in Encinitas, California, came up with the idea to utilize the wheel wells of the JK as a foundation for custom-fabricated equipment

racks. Needless to say, this was one of the best options, if not only one, we had for installing so much equipment in such an efficient manner and have it remain unnoticeable.

Beginning with ½-inch-square steel tube, the measurements and mounting footprints of each piece of equipment was considered while he formed a quick skeleton of the rack. Once it was determined that the rack would be able to accommodate our audio/video system equipment, numerous support bars and tabs were welded into place. Mindful of the need to reduce penetrations into the tub of the vehicle, which would allow exhaust fumes, water, and dust to enter, Stewart chose to drill the mounting locations and insert a threaded rivet nut. Using this mounting method guaranteed a secure and sealed fit, which could withstand numerous years of off-highway driving without being compromised. After a quick trip to be powder-coated, all of the equipment was installed and a custom-carpeted medium density fiberboard (MDF) enclosure was fabricated to cover the equipment and racks.

One of the benefits of fabricating a set of racks such as this is that they can be custom fitted to whatever model Jeep you own and tailored to support whatever equipment you are installing. Given the differences between us all, it is a guarantee that no two sets of racks will ever be the same. Just like our Jeeps—similar in application, but so different in customization.

1

Often compared with trying to put 50 pounds of stuff in a 10-pound bag, finding an efficient and stealthy way of holding all of this equipment was the task given to Spencer Stewart of SoCal Customs.

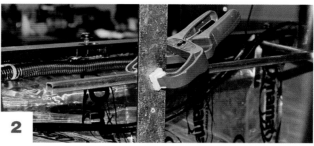

2

Beginning with the placement of a few key components, the skeleton of the soon-to-be audio/video equipment rack is fabricated from 1/2-inch steel square tube. The main support beam is measured for the correct height in relation to the top of the body panel and clamped in place.

3

Once it was determined what audio/video components were to be installed, numerous support braces and mounting tabs were fabricated and welded onto the rack, with each piece being strategically aligned to maximize the space.

4

The mounting locations were determined and holes were drilled through the upper wheel wells of the JK, with special attention given to avoiding hitting any hoses or lines that were underneath the mounting location with the drill bit.

5

A threaded rivet nut is installed as the anchor for the mounting bolts. The sound dampening material placed onto the inner tub and surrounding the hole will act as a seal between any exhaust fumes, dirt, or water that could enter through the penetration. This type of mounting will also guarantee a secure foundation for years of off-road abuse.

6

Prior to final bolt-in, Stewart checks to see that the equipment rack is level and on the same plane as the top of the body panel.

7

The audio/video equipment is installed similar to the way jigsaw pieces are connected, each piece having its own unique location where it will be mounted.

8

When installing items such as DVD drives, it is essential that their mounting location be as level as possible for them to perform correctly, not to mention shielded from dust, water, and other damaging elements.

PROJECT 84
Install an Aftermarket Three-Way Component Speaker System

 Time: 5½ Hours

 Tools: Socket set, wire crimper, hand tools, heat gun, cut-off wheel, hole saw, drill

 Talent:

 Applicable Years: All models

Tab: Depending upon the quality and brand of speakers, between $300 and $2,900

 Parts Required: Heat shrink tubing, wire connectors, MDF, cut-out template

 Tip: The exact placement of the speakers should be determined prior to work being started; and the power requirements of the speaker system should be addressed to ensure that the head unit or amplifier is capable of producing the required wattage.

 Performance Gain: Increase in sound quality

Complementary Project: Installation of an amplifier

Jeeps have never been known for their award-winning stereo systems, especially the open air CJ and Wrangler models that essentially have the interior of a square box when it comes to acoustics, let alone the lack of surface area for the sound waves to reflect off of when the tops are down. So what is a driver who wants to be able to hear their sound system to do, you ask? Easy; install a three-way set of stereo speakers that will provide some added level of balance and acoustics, given the sheer increase in the number of speakers, but also the efficiency to deliver sound from either the factory head unit or aftermarket unit with more accuracy and direction.

Included in the system is the newly designed MT-24LE tweeter, which employs a 1⅛-inch (28mm) diameter aluminum Hexatech voice coil, hand-coated Acuflex soft dome and a powerful neodymium magnet. The new MT-24LE tweeters deliver the same known "sweet and warm" sound characteristics with an unprecedented transience and dynamic range. Morel's top-of-the-line CDM-88 midrange was optimized to meet the new Elate SW 6LE woofer and the MT-24LE tweeter sound qualities, with improved acoustical parameters and enhanced overall dynamics and clarity. The CDM-88LE features a large 2⅛-inch (54mm) diameter aluminum Hexatech voice coil, driving the soft dome membrane with a larger than normal sound radiating

surface. The low resonance point provides the full midrange frequency spectrum and an exquisitely clear, deep sound. The Elate SW 6LE woofer features a large 3-inch (75mm) diameter Hexatech voice coil that supports a newly developed carbon fiber sandwich cone. This integrated sandwich-structure prevents cone breakup distortion at high output levels and delivers the low end of the sound spectrum with extraordinary crispness and definition.

In addition to the high-end speakers, top-grade crossover components offer a variety of customization capabilities, including frequency slope selection, level attenuation for all of the components, biwiring and biamping. With a power handling capability of 200 watts, the Elate LE assures optimum adaptability of the speakers' performance to any Jeep environment.

To ensure a seamless and stealthy install, the factory speaker pods of our 2008 Jeep JK were utilized to house the tweeter and midrange speakers, while custom speaker pods were fabricated and installed into the lower front kick panels for the woofer. Once the system was powered up a night and day difference was noticed over the stock speakers. If you want to hear your Jeep's audio system while driving down the road with the window open or the top down, then the three-way speakers are the way to go!

1

The factory front plastic speaker pods were removed from the dash and the front panels were removed to accommodate the future mounting plate for the three-way speaker system's tweeter and midrange speakers. A piece of MDF replaced the factory front and was secured via screws and black silicone to seal the edges. The pod was clamped together to ensure a solid bond between the two pieces.

2

Once sealed and dry, the edges of the MDF plate were lightly sanded to follow the contour of the pod.

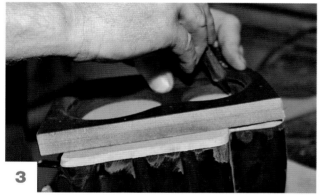

3

Since the tweeter and midrange speakers were being installed in the factory speaker pod, a template was used to trace their respective locations so that they could be cut out.

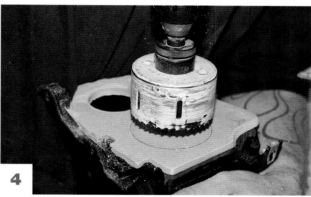

4

A hole saw was used to make the openings for the two speakers. It is important to remember that upon completion of drilling the holes, the silicone sealant must be checked for any breaches and that the interior of the pod must be cleaned thoroughly to allow optimum performance and durability to the speakers.

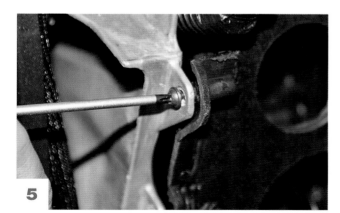

5

The speaker pod is reinstalled into the factory locations as if nothing was ever done to them, but we know and will soon hear different. Given their cavity size, the factory pods make a great enclosure, since they contain the same air space needed for the two-speaker setup.

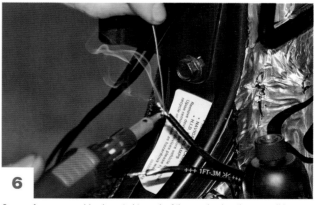

6

Oxygen-free copper wiring is routed to each of the speaker locations as solid unbroken pieces which provides for better sound quality and system performance. The wiring is connected to the crossover units, which have been installed inside the dashboard. Prior to their connection to the speakers, each of the stripped pieces of speaker wire is soldered for durability to minimize wire breaks at the speaker terminals.

7 Knowing that the Jeep would encounter numerous washboard-style roads and that there was a severe chance that connections could become dislodged or break off, rendering the speaker inoperable, the speaker connections were all soldered onto the speaker.

8 Often overlooked is the corrosion that the speaker connections experience, especially in a Jeep, given the amount of water and dust that they often drive through. As an added bit of protection, a piece of heat shrink tubing is sheathed over the speaker connections and heated in place to form a waterproof and dustproof cover that will not be degraded in time.

9 To accommodate the system's subwoofers, custom speaker enclosures were fabricated and installed in the lower front kick plates of the Jeep, and then wrapped in sound-damping material to absorb any vibrations or distortions.

10 In keeping with durability and longevity, the hardware used to install the kick plate–mounted subwoofers is stainless steel, since it is in such close proximity to the bottom of the door and a passenger's and the driver's feet.

11 Protecting the kick plate–mounted subwoofers was achieved by customizing the factory kick panels with steel and fiberglass reinforced grilles.

12 The final steps to the install are to mount the two front separates into the factory front speaker pods that required minor modifications.

13 Unfortunately, you are unable to hear these speakers in action, but take our word for it—never has music sounded so realistic. Who needs to go to a concert when you can listen to these Morels?

PROJECT 85
Install an Amplifier

 Time: 4 Hours

 Tools: Socket set, wire connector crimper, hand tools

 Talent:

Applicable Years: All

 Tab: $700

Parts Required: Amplifier, wiring, cable ties

 Tip: Prior to installation, determine the route of your power and ground cables. Knowing the route will make the component installation easier since you will be familiar with the compatibility of the connection points in relation to the wiring route.

 Performance Gain: Increases the power and volume of a stereo system

Complementary Project: Installation of an aftermarket head unit and speakers

Chances are that if you have ever put your window down or taken your hardtop or soft top off your Jeep while the radio was on, you instantly lost any ability to hear the music, due to the overpowering road and wind noise that you experienced. A simple answer to get back the lost acoustics when this occurs is to install an amplifier to your car audio system.

With literally hundreds of amplifiers on the market, choosing the correct unit that can be installed without taking up much space and that will have enough watts to overcome your noise issues and that will match with your type of speakers can be a daunting task.

When it comes to high-quality automotive audio amplification, the name usually at the top of the list is Zapco. Our choice due to their performance, adjustability, and sound

quality, the DCS Reference Series amplifiers are packed with loads of power and some of today's hottest technology. This is shown by the USB input on the unit, which allows it to be connected to a PC to set all of its functions. Best of all, the amplifier can be set as stereo pairs or as individual channels; the choice is yours. Another technological breakthrough on this series of amplifiers is the fact that traditional RCA cables have been replaced with an in-line SymbiLink transmitter, which improves noise rejection, lowers the inherent system noise floor, reduces distortion, and provides up to 16 volts of signal output.

For our installation, we utilized a four-channel, 1,000-watt DCS Reference Series 1000.4 amplifier to power our three-way component speakers that are attached to an Alpine head unit.

1 The Zapco DCS Reference Series amplifiers are some of the best in the industry, thanks to their digital circuitry and streamlined design. Don't let looks fool you though, they sound as good as it gets. Available in a variety of models priced to fit a wide range of budgets, the amplifiers are available in multiple channel configurations to fit virtually any audio system configuration.

2 We installed the Zapco amplifier inside the trunk area of our JK project vehicle. In this location, the amplifier can be kept out of sight and does not interfere or reduce cargo space.

3

Prior to installing the amplifier, it is a good idea to lay out the necessary cabling from the head unit to the amplifier. Doing so will verify the compatibility of the connection points in relation to the wiring route.

4

As with any electrical component, power and ground wires must be run to the battery to feed the amplifier the power it needs to operate properly. Typically, to avoid engine noise and unwanted feedback from the speaker wiring, the power cable and ground should be isolated and take another route.

5

Once all connections have been made, the next step is to secure the unit.

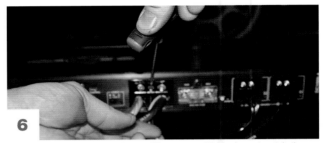

6

An accessory wire attached to the amplifier acts as a trickle charge to retain the amplifier settings when not powered on.

7

In order to fit in this location, a custom set of brackets was fabricated. The factory mounting locations on the amplifier were used for a solid point of attachment.

8

To provide additional protection and airflow to the amplifier, a false floor was fabricated from a combination of MDF, fiberglass, carpet, and perforated steel mesh to allow the driver the option to still place cargo in the area but not restrict the airflow to the amplifier.

9

The power cable is secured to the secondary battery.

10

Due to the high current the amplifier requires, an in-line fuse block combination was installed to the firewall of the Jeep. Keep in mind that the final step in the installation should be connecting the fuses. Saving this task for the very last not only protects the installer from injury, but the equipment as well from any possible surges, which could damage the amplifier.

11

The vehicle's voltage output can be found on the digital display beneath the two fuses of the in-line fuse block.

PROJECT 86
Install a CB Antenna Mount

 Time: 1 Hour

 Tools: Hand tools, drill, drill bit, socket set, tape measure

 Talent:

 Applicable Years: All

Tab: $75

 Parts Required: CB antenna, cable ties

 Tip: None

 Performance Gain: Provides a solid surface for the CB antenna

 Complementary Project: Installation of a CB radio

Mounting a CB antenna is never easy, given the complexity of trying to hide the coax cable, route it in a way that is impervious to water leaks, noise, and exhaust fumes, and in a secure location that will be protected from damage from rocks, tree limbs and other environmental foes. The Jeep Wrangler JK (two-door and four-door models) is no exception to this rule. While there are numerous generic CB mounts on the market, the majority of them are either not compatible with the JK or they just do not look right mounted on this particular model. Having experienced this issue firsthand, we chose to use Cool Tech LLC's new UltraMount Kit that has been made specifically for the JK models. Sold as a complete CB antenna kit, the best part of the kit is that it does not require any drilling of the body or sheet metal.

Everything needed for a trouble-free install has been included. Unlike traditional CB antenna mounts, the coax cable is routed through a factory 2-inch grommet into the vehicle's cab and then routed to the CB radio for connection. At the heart of the kit is a stainless steel bracket that has been designed to fit inside the stock JK license plate assembly and boost the conductivity of it. This is in contrast to other mounts that are simply pieces of metal that have been powder-coated, which reduces the conductivity. The included Firestick FL-44 4-foot fiberglass antenna is inserted into a small opening at the top of the license plate assembly and screwed into place, making the install appear as factory as possible.

1 The factory license plate assembly must be removed and disassembled to allow the stainless steel UltraMount to be installed.

2 The coax cable is routed into the vehicle's cab through a 2-inch factory grommet that has been cut to fit the cable. A small amount of RTV silicone is used to reseal the grommet.

3

Made from stainless steel, which is impervious to rust and also a better conductor for the CB signal than ordinary steel, the bracket is attached using the factory license plate assembly hardware.

4

When the bracket has been installed, a small hole must be made at the top of the license plate assembly to allow the antenna to pass through and be attached to the mount. This measurement is achieved by using a tape measure and making a small pilot hole from the underside of the bracket. The hole is then drilled at low speed to prevent the plastic from melting.

5

To aid in the routing of the coax cable, a mini-UHF connector, which has a diameter that is only slightly larger than the coax itself, has been used. To install the coax cable onto the CB radio, the supplied PL-259 connector must be attached to the coax and then onto the CB radio. Simply screw on the supplied PL-259 connector and you're done!

6

Once inside the cab, the coax cable is routed to the CB radio for connection.

7

With the excess coax slack taken up, and the bracket tightened, the license plate assembly is reassembled.

8

Prior to replacing the license plate backing plate, a small portion of it must be cut off to allow for clearance of the bracket. If not trimmed, the factory license backing plate could not be reinstalled, since the bracket is occupying the space.

9

The final step of the install is to screw the antenna onto the mount and tune, in accordance to the CB radio's specifications.

PROJECT 87
Install an Aftermarket Head Unit

 Time: 1 Hour

 Tools: Socket set, cordless drill

 Talent: 🔧🔧🔧

 Applicable Years: All

$ **Tab:** $300

 Parts Required: Trim ring kit, wire connectors, aftermarket head unit

 Tip: Special care should be taken when removing the dashboard trim pieces, as they are made from plastic and could crack.

(+) **Performance Gain:** Comfort

 Complementary Project: Install an amplifier

No trip in a Jeep is complete without a good set of tunes. Depending on your model and year of Jeep, there's a good chance that the factory head unit for the stereo is not performing as it once did. If it does, perhaps it is not compatible with many of today's electronic devices that we rely upon for communication and listening to music, such as Bluetooth cell phones and iPod/MP3 players. For our installation, we are replacing the stock head unit from a Cherokee Sport, which came from the factory with a CD player and radio unit, for one of Alpine Electronics' latest and greatest media receiver units, which supports the iPod.

The Alpine iDA-X200 digital media receiver features a Universal Serial Bus (USB) connection for all iPod devices and selected MP3 players that use Main Time Base (MTP) protocol and USB memory sticks. The connection between the devices is high-speed USB, which means that access to all of the songs, albums, and playlists on the media device are super fast. Plus, the all-digital connection means that the best, noise-free sound is received. Additional features include three sets of preouts for the future installation of an amplifier or three, a wireless remote control, and it is high definition (HD) and satellite radio ready. The unit is also Bluetooth ready, which means that your cell phone can be integrated into the audio system of the vehicle for true hands-free driving.

1 With the factory head unit removed, the new receiver must have a trim panel installed around it to allow it to be secured to the factory mounting locations.

2 On each side of the new receiver, small clips secure the single DIN receiver onto the trim piece.

3

An aftermarket wiring harness is connected to the leads on the receiver and plugs directly into the factory wiring harness, eliminating any need to cut into the factory harness.

4

Once the harness and wiring have been installed, the connection for the stock antenna is made.

5

Reinstalling the receiver into the dashboard should be performed with care to avoid loosening any of the antennae or harness connections. Also, the plastic around the radio may be brittle from age and could break, which will cause additional work to replace and considerable cost as well, since these types of pieces tend to be on the expensive side.

6

The receiver is secured to the dash with a cordless drill, using the stock hardware from the previous unit. Once again, the screws should not be tightened too tight, or the plastic tabs could break.

7

The remaining factory dashboard trim pieces are reinstalled.

8

The new receiver unit will provide countless hours of entertainment for all occupants. The iPod/MP3 player is connected via a small discreet cable that can be routed anywhere in the vehicle according to the owner's taste. For our install, we routed the cable in the glove compartment to keep the device away from prying eyes.

PROJECT 88
Install a Global Positioning System (GPS) Unit

 Time: 5 Hours

 Tools: Socket set, wire crimper, hand tools

 Talent:

 Applicable Years: All

Tab: $500

 Parts Required: Wire connectors, GPS unit

 Tip: The exact placement of the antenna should be away from any interference of metal surfaces.

 Performance Gain: Safety

 Complementary Project: Installation of an aftermarket head unit

Owning a Jeep is like having a license to go anywhere in the world, literally. During the numerous travels I have taken, I somehow always end up requiring assistance to get back onto my intended route. Not that it is necessarily a bad thing by any means, given some of the beautiful things that I have seen this way. Having a Global Positioning System (GPS) unit installed in a Jeep will assist with keeping you on course as well as serve as a ledger for where you have been, so that you may return there again. Other benefits to having one in your rig include the ability to provide rescuers with a firm set of coordinates for your position, if needed, as well as to share your location with other four wheelers.

Given the tight space constraints in a Jeep, it is somewhat challenging to have a GPS unit that is large enough to see, but small enough to be out of the way. Factor into the equation the need for the unit to be weatherproof and shockproof, and the list suddenly narrows down to a mere handful. Given their standing in the industry, as well as their high quality of craftsmanship, we chose a Lowrance GPS unit for our project vehicle.

The GlobalMap Baja 540c contains a 5-inch diagonal, 480x480-pixel LCD screen for excellent, glare-free viewing through a high-contrast Film Super Twist monochrome display with 16-level gray scale definition and advanced white LED backlighting. Capable of navigating motorists to their destination or tracking their course of travel, a 12-parallel channel GPS+WAAS receiver and a ruggedized external LGC-2000 Baja receiver/antenna for super fast satellite lock-ons and enhanced position accuracy to within 3 meters has been incorporated into the unit. The 540c is also memory card compatible with Lowrance's FreedomMap software and their MapCreate topographical software. Best of all it has been ruggedized and made shock-resistant to handle the off-road abuses encountered on the roads less traveled.

The Lowrance Baja 540c GPS unit is packed with features such as a 12-parallel channel GPS+WAAS receiver and a ruggedized external LGC-2000 Baja receiver/antenna for super-fast satellite lock-ons and enhanced position accuracy to within 3 meters has been incorporated into the unit. The unit also has a feature of selecting the display for day viewing or night viewing (pictured).

2

The GPS unit was mounted onto the center dashboard panel above the radio for easy access and the ability to plot our course when off-roading.

3

Side-mounted screws that secure the unit into the mount allow the user to adjust the angle of the screen for optimum viewing.

4

The wiring harness was routed through the dashboard and through a custom-made mounting plate.

5

The connections to the unit from the wiring harness are waterproof and feature twist lock connectors to ensure that the connections do not become loose when in rough conditions.

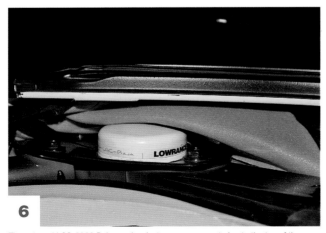

6

The external LGC-2000 Baja receiver/antenna was mounted onto the top of the Jeep's soundbar to keep it from prying eyes. When installing the antenna, it is important to remember to keep it within a direct line of sight to the sky, as it is a satellite antenna. Also, there should be no metal around the unit that could interfere with the signal. The antenna is able to transmit through the hardtop of our Jeep, because it is constructed of a composite material.

7

With the installation complete, the final order of business was to connect the wiring harness to a power source. For our application, we chose to connect it to a switchable power source with a fuse block for additional protection.

SECTION 9
WHEELS AND TIRES

Wheels and tires are an important part of a Jeep, given the wide variety of styles, sizes, and applications that are available for them. Depending on what combination you choose says a lot about your intended use for the vehicle as well as its intended style. This chapter will provide some assistance in selecting some of today's hottest wheels and tires; we also will address how to install a tire on a bead lock wheel, how to quickly and easily automatically adjust tire pressure, and how to handle a few other pertinent projects.

PROJECT 89
Mounting Tires onto Bead Lock Wheels

 Time: 45 Minutes per wheel

 Tools: Medium socket set, tire cage, torque wrench, air chuck, air compressor, tire gauge, tire lubricant

 Talent:

 Applicable Years: All

 Tab: $250–$400 for each wheel, depending on manufacturer

Parts Required: Use the new bolts, nuts, and washers that are included with each wheel, as the hardware is specifically sized for each wheel and manufacturer

 Tip: Apply a liberal amount of tire lubricant when installing the tire onto the wheel; also take extreme care when removing and reinstalling the OE tire pressure sensors (if vehicle is so equipped) as they can be easily damaged. On completion of the install, some vehicles may require that the OE tire pressure sensor monitoring system be reset to avoid the caution light from being displayed.

 Performance Gain: Ensures that the tire does not unseat itself from the rim when extremely low tire pressures are being used (6 psi and above), also provides additional strength and support laterally to the tire

 Complementary Project: Wheel locks and wheel balancing

It's one of those inevitable situations that every off-road enthusiast will be forced to endure at least once in their off-road travels; a tire becoming dismounted from the wheel. The tire can dismount because the tire's bead has become unseated as a result of the air pressure being too low or because the wheel has been damaged, causing the bead to break loose. These situations can be easily resolved and avoided by the use of wheels that are equipped with bead locks. Used mainly on race vehicles, bead locks have been around for quite some time and have been one of those items that everyone talks about, wants, or says they need, yet are unfamiliar with how they function.

Keeping in mind that not all bead locks are created equal, you have numerous elements to consider when choosing the appropriate style of bead lock for your intended application and usage. You need to consider such factors as whether the bead locks are cast into the wheel during production, or if they require weld-on installation, the size of the hardware, and the number of retaining bolts. Finally, consider whether the type of bead lock complements your vehicle in terms of the appropriate size, width, and intended use. Manufacturers such as American Expedition Vehicles offer wheels that are specifically cast during the manufacturing process to be

bead lock wheels. This type of forethought in design and construction can eliminate any leaks that may occur when a separate ring is welded onto a wheel. Also, single cast-designed wheels result in stronger, more reliable designs. For comparison purposes, a standard wheel with a weld-on bead lock may only be capable of withstanding 1,500 pounds per wheel without a reinforcing ring installed, versus a cast-designed unit, such as the American Expedition Vehicle's wheel, that may be rated at 3,800 pounds per wheel.

A bead lock wheel has two primary functions. The first function is to ensure that the tire does not unseat itself from the rim while having an extremely low air pressure (4 to 6 psi). The second function is to provide strength and support laterally to the tire while at full-speed during off-road conditions or rock crawling. The way in which both tasks are accomplished is by having the outer bead edge of the wheel removed or left off during the manufacturing process. A series of threaded inserts, placed into the front surface of the wheel, will serve as anchor points for the corresponding outer ring, which features a complementary pattern of holes through which the bolts are placed. Between both rings rests the tire's bead, which is clamped down by the sheer force of the retaining bolts. Once the tire is sandwiched between the two rings, a strong and safe seal is formed. The number and size of both the holes and the retaining bolts that fit inside of them vary, depending upon the diameter and size of the rim, the manufacturer and the intended application or conditions that the wheels will be used in—racing, rock crawling, or exploring. As a rule of thumb, the greater the number of bolts around the wheel, the greater the holding capability and greater ability the wheel has to seal itself. It is important to note that the hardware typically found on bead lock wheels is of Grade 8 quality or higher.

Typically, the majority of bead lock wheels are not Department of Transportation (DOT)–compliant for a variety of reasons. However, for manufacturers such as American Expedition Vehicles, their bead lock wheels are DOT-compliant, based upon the manufacturing processes of the wheels, the high quality of materials used, and the testing conditions that the wheels must undergo.

Now that you have made the decision to install a set of wheels equipped with bead locks, the only thing left to do is mount the tire onto the wheel. One of the added benefits associated with using bead locks is the fact that the tire can be changed anytime, anywhere, by anyone, as a tire-mounting machine is not needed. This is an especially helpful benefit when a tire has become damaged beyond repair and you are on a trail without the comforts of your local shop. Installation is fast, easy, and manageable.

1 Ready for anything in its path, this 17x8-inch American Expedition Vehicles Pintler bead lock wheel readily awaits a rough and open road, and a few rocks, of course. To begin, a 35x12.50x17 Toyo Open Country MT tire has been placed onto the AEV wheel.

2 With the absence of the outer tire bead, virtually any tire can be slipped onto the rim, eliminating the need for tire-mounting equipment. This is especially useful when replacing a tire on a trail or away from a tire shop. It is important to note that some bead lock wheels will only fit specific manufacturer's tires and sizes, due to the way the outer ring must fit into the bead of the tire, which typically varies between manufacturers. The American Expedition Vehicles Pintler bead lock wheels we are utilizing will accommodate any brand of tire.

3 Once the tire has been aligned evenly onto the wheel, the outer bead lock ring is aligned with the inner nut inserts. Once completed, the process of inserting the Grade 8 bolts and washers through the outer ring and into the inner ring should begin. It is important to perform this step by hand, making sure that none of the bolts become cross-threaded.

4 The outer bead lock ring contains 24 holes through which the $5/16$-inch Grade 8 bolts will pass to secure the tire to the wheel. As the bolts are installed, it is recommended that they be inserted according to the manufacturer's recommended tightening pattern (typically a star pattern) to become familiar with the pattern. When starting to insert the bolts, only make them finger tight until all have been installed. Also, be certain that the bolts do not become cross-threaded.

5

Once all of the bolts and washers have been started by hand, a socket may be used to finish tightening them. Don't forget to follow the manufacturer's recommended sequence for tightening the bolts.

6

After all of the bolts have been tightened, consult the manufacturer's instructions to verify the appropriate torque value and tightening sequence for the bolts. The torque value for these bolts is rated at 18 lbs-ft each.

7

With the retaining ring bolts torqued to the manufacturer's specifications, the only thing left to do is to add air, balance the wheel and tire combination, and enjoy. When airing the tires up, special care should be taken to place the tire inside a tire cage to minimize any injury that could occur in the event that the tire explodes. Also, the appropriate safety glasses, gloves, etc. should be worn while performing the installation.

8

The final step to the process is to install the tires onto the vehicle. Keep in mind that under no circumstances should the retaining ring bolts be retorqued while installed on the vehicle and under pressure. After the first 50 miles and once a month thereafter, the tires should be removed from the vehicle, aired down to 0 psi and the outer retaining bolts and washers retorqued to the manufacturer's specifications. This will ensure that the bolts are not compromised and can retain the tire onto the wheel with no issues.

PROJECT 90
Perform a Flat Repair

 Time: ½ Hour

 Tools: Tire plug kit

 Talent:

 Applicable Years: All models

Tab: $25 kit

 Parts Required: Tire plug

 Tip: Make sure all of the air is out of the tire prior to removing the foreign material; it will make working on the tire easier and safer than trying to fight the air escaping from the tire hole.

 Performance Gain: Maintenance

 Complementary Project: None

If it hasn't already happened to you, the laws of probability will make sure that it does. We're talking about a flat tire. While never really ready for something like this to happen, the best that one can do is be prepared for when it does. Available at your local off-road center or an auto parts store, tire plug kits are worth their weight in gold if you get a flat tire. While you may be thinking that's what a spare is for, keep in mind that there may be a time when you cannot remove the tire that has the issue due to tight working conditions, such a single or narrow lanes or the possibility that you are on a trail and it is not conducive to changing a tire given the conditions. For these reasons and for a piece of mind, every Jeep should have a tire kit on board.

The Safety Seal kit contains everything needed to repair a tire, as long as the puncture is located in the tread area of the tire. If the puncture is on the sidewall, the tire cannot be repaired for safety reasons.

Once the puncture is located, the air in the tire should be let out for safety. Once aired down, the object that caused the puncture should be removed with a pair of side cutters or pliers. The ream tool should be used to clean out the puncture prior to the insert tool and plug being used to fill the puncture hole. Once in the tire, the insert tool is twisted and removed, leaving the plug behind to be cut off even with the tread. When completed with the repair, air the tire back up, and you're on your way, safe and sound.

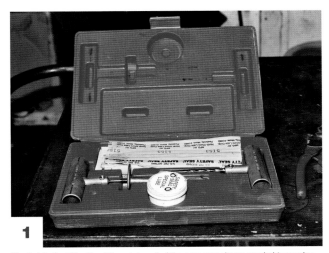

1 The Safety Seal Tire Plug kit contains all of the necessary items needed to repair a tire puncture, including a tire ream, insert tool, cutters, plug material, and lube.

2 A pair of side cutters is used to remove the object that caused the puncture.

3

With a small amount of lube applied to the tire, the ream tool is used to make the puncture clean, which will allow the plug to insert easily.

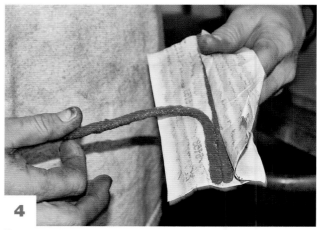

4

The plug material is soaked with a compound that seals the tire in a matter of seconds. The kit contains numerous plugs for those just-in-case situations.

5

The end of the insert tool contains an eyelet through which the tire plug is threaded. When finished being threaded, a generous amount of lubrication should be applied to the tip to make entry into the tire easier.

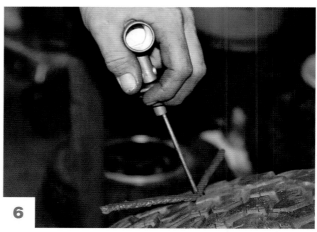

6

Inserting in a straight motion, the insert tool introduces the tire plug into the puncture. Once inserted in the tire, the insert tool is twisted and pulled out of the tire.

7

Any remnants of the remaining tire plug are cut off flush with the top of the tire tread.

8

Once the puncture has been filled, allow the plug to sit for a moment and air the tire back up to the proper psi. There you have it, ready to hit the road once again.

PROJECT 91
Replace Wheel Studs

 Time: 1½ Hours

 Tools: Socket set, impact gun, torque wrench

 Talent:

 Applicable Years: All models

Tab: $100 per axle

Parts Required: Wheel studs, grease

 Tip: Prior to the removal of the axles, the size, type, and style of wheel stud should be known to reduce additional downtime that the vehicle may be subjected to while locating a compatible stud.

 Performance Gain: Provides safety to the vehicle by ensuring the wheels are securely attached to the vehicle and will not come off

 Complementary Project: Installation of locking lug nuts.

Wheel studs are quite possibly some of the most important bolts on your Jeep. Their primary purpose is to keep the wheel and tire combination attached to the vehicle via the axle flange. From the factory, the strength of the wheel studs is acceptable; however, if you are an avid off-roader, you may want to upgrade the strength of them for added durability. While off-road driving, there are many instances where the threads of a wheel stud may become damaged by debris or rocks hitting a lug nut. A stud can be broken off due to a sudden impact to a wheel, or as a result of general wear and tear throughout the years. In some situations, such as ours, we were forced to replace the rear wheel studs on our project vehicle due to the fact that they were a ½-inch too short for our new wheel and tire. We wanted to upgrade their strength, as the new wheels were considerably thicker at the boltholes than our previous set and weighed considerably more. While the new wheel and tire combination could be installed onto our vehicle, the issue was that there was not enough surface area on the studs to safely install the lug nuts onto them. As a rule of thumb, a lug nut is considered to be safely secured onto a wheel stud after it has grabbed a minimum of 10 or 11 threads, but our lug nuts were grabbing only 3 to 4 threads.

In the event that you change your axles for units that are either stronger or contain additional splines, there is a good chance that the new studs will be threaded onto the flange, rather than pressed onto it as the stock units are. It is also important to note that depending upon the clearances for the stud in relation to brake calipers, etc., the front wheel studs may be different than the rear. The type of axle as well may dictate a difference between the front and rear.

As a general course of maintenance, wheel studs should be checked periodically to ensure that the integrity of their threads has not been compromised, that they are not loose from the flange and are able to spin freely, and that they are not bent or cracked. In the event that they are in any of these conditions, they should be replaced.

With the wheel and tire barely being held onto the axle, the lug nuts were removed in preparation of the wheel stud replacement.

Being that these studs were installed on the rear axle, they feature low shoulders, a condition that allows them to have enough clearance between the axle flange and other components, such as brake calipers. Another issue to note is that the studs feature full threads, as opposed to some that contain a shoulder.

3

Barely being daylighted through the rear rotor, the existing studs were a ½ inch too short for our application.

4

In order to remove the axles, the rear brake rotors and calipers must be removed and set aside. Using a thick piece of wire or a bent hanger to hold the caliper onto the frame will eliminate the need to completely remove the assembly from the vehicle.

5

In order to remove the axles, the four retaining bolts that secure the flange onto the axle tube must be removed.

6

Depending upon your specific type of axle, there is a possibility that your differential cover will have to be removed and a retention clip, which secures the axle to the differential, would have to be removed. For our application, this step was not required for the axles to be pulled.

7

Given that these axles are manufactured by Superior Axle & Gear, the wheel studs are threaded, which required the use of an impact gun to remove and reinstall the new units. It is important to note that while this step is occurring the axle should be placed in a position that will not cause damage to the shaft or its splines.

8

Once the studs have been replaced, a liberal amount of grease is applied to the splines to make things move as smoothly as possible upon reentry into the axle shaft and differential.

9

When reinserting the axle, special care should be taken to ensure that the splines do not drag or come into contact with the inner walls of the axle shaft, as the axle could become damaged.

10

With the axles safely reinstalled and the wheel studs providing additional surface area for the lug nuts, the last thing left to do was to torque the lug nuts.

PROJECT 92
Incorporate an Internal Bead Lock Insert into a Tire

 Time: 1½ Hours per wheel

 Tools: Drill, air chuck, compressed air

 Talent: ✶✶✶✶

 Applicable Years: All

Tab: $175 per wheel

 Parts Required: Internal bead lock insert

 Tip: None

 Performance Gain: Allows tire pressure to be reduced to single digits while retaining the tire on the rim

 Complementary Project: Install new tires

For some people, owning a conventional bead lock wheel is not an issue they concern themselves with; for others however, an internal bead lock is a much better alternative. The internal bead lock provides them with the same ability to run single-digit tire pressures without their worrying about their tire coming off the rim. They do not have to deal with the associated maintenance issues, not to mention that there is a lower risk of being injured when filling the tires up or airing the tires down. To put the method of an internal bead lock into context, a conventional bead lock mechanically clamps the outside tire bead onto the rim. The Staun Internal Bead Lock insert functions by locking both the inside and the outside beads of the tire to the rim.

Staun Internal Bead Locks are lightweight (about 5 pounds for 15 inchers) and the weight is evenly distributed from the inside to the outside of the rim. Further, since some of the weight is nearer the center of the rim, it minimizes imbalance effects. Another issue to consider is that with a conventional bead lock wheel, if it is aired down to near 0 psi, there is a good chance that either the rim or tire will become damaged. With the internal Staun unit, a portion of the tubeless cavity still contains air at high pressure and holds the rim above the ground, preventing the rim from pinching the tire on the ground.

One of the intricacies of the internal bead lock is that it inflates through its own valve stem and expands until it reaches the limits of the polyester reinforcing case assembly. The hefty polyester case top keeps the tube "down," dictating a very low profile. This, in turn, leaves the remainder of the tire (tire air chamber) to be inflated to your desired pressure. This space accommodates low-pressure flex as needed. The inserts are available in a range of sizes from 15 up to 17 inches. Aside from having to drill the outside lip of the wheel to accommodate the separate new filler valve, the only extra attention that should be used is when inserting the bead lock into the tire so that it does not become pinched or damaged.

1

The progression of the way an internal bead lock wheel operates is important to understand, since the minute the tire is placed back onto the wheel, the Staun unit disappears. *Photo courtesy of Staun Products*

227

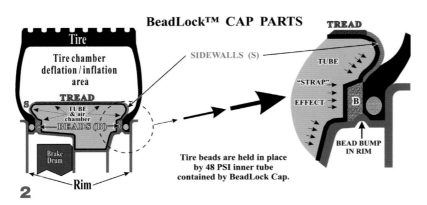

BeadLock™ CAP PARTS

Tire

Tire chamber
deflation / inflation
area

TREAD

TUBE
& air
chamber

BEADS (B)

Brake
Drum

Rim

SIDEWALLS (S)

TREAD

TUBE

"STRAP"

EFFECT

B

BEAD BUMP
IN RIM

Tire beads are held in place
by 48 PSI inner tube
contained by BeadLock Cap.

2

This illustration explains the general concept of how the bead lock insert functions when the tire is mounted. *Photo courtesy of Staun Products*

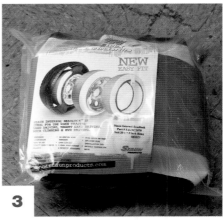

3

Rolled up in a bag, the Staun units are sold individually and are available for wheels between 15 and 17 inches. *Photo courtesy of Staun Products*

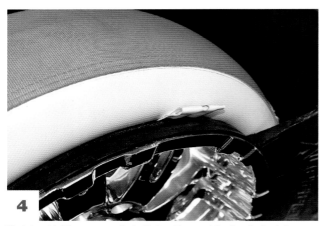

4

The internal holding power on the inside bead is enough to allow the tire to be run at near 0 psi, with no adverse affects to either the tire or wheel. *Photo courtesy of Staun Products*

5

As previously mentioned, a separate valve stem is required to keep the inflation of the insert adjusted accordingly. *Photo courtesy of Staun Products*

6

In this photo, both of the valve stems can be seen on the inner lip. The one at the top is the Staun unit. *Photo courtesy of Staun Products*

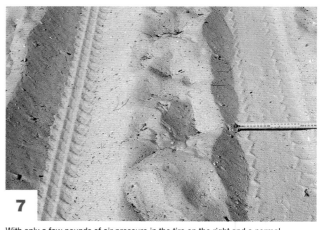

7

With only a few pounds of air pressure in the tire on the right and a normal operating psi for the tires on the left, it can be seen as to why airing down is important, given that the width of the tire has almost doubled. *Photo courtesy of Staun Products*

PROJECT 93
Select the Appropriate Tires

 Time: N/A

 Tools: N/A

 Talent:

Applicable Years: All models

Tab: Costs vary, depending on selected tires

 Parts Required: N/A

 Tip: Know what type of terrain you will be taking your vehicle into and where most of the driving you do will be—either street or off-road, as this could determine the tire you select.

 Performance Gain: Traction

 Complementary Project: N/A

Tires are one of the most important components on an off-road rig, especially a Jeep. Aside from their attributes to the Jeep that they are installed on, the proper set can mean all the difference between conquering the trail or having the trail conquer you. Designed for a wide variety of applications from sand to mud to the highways, the key to selecting a successful tire for your Jeep is choosing one that will complement your specific driving style and conditions. To help you choose the correct tire, some of today's more popular models are presented for your review and consideration.

Photo courtesy of BFGoodrich

Photo courtesy of Parnelli Jones

Photo courtesy of Interco Tire Corp.

BFGOODRICH KRAWLER T/A KX

BFGoodrich's Krawler T/A KX tire has been built for trail driving, given the unique tread pattern and rubber compound. In following with their tried and true durability, each tire consists of four-ply sidewalls and four-ply treads. The tire is available in load range C and is available in 35x13.50x15 and 37x12.50x17 sizes. They are also available partially designed for custom grooving patterns.

PARNELLI JONES DIRT GRIPZ

With a name like Parnelli Jones behind these tires, how can one go wrong? This 6- and 10-ply rated radial tire features two steel belts and two polyester radial plies, which incorporate 6- and 10-ply durability. Available in load ranges C, D, and E and sizes from 31x10.50x15 to 36x14.50x22, the large tread and sidewall lugs offer excellent off-road traction, while their computer-designed tread pattern provides a smooth ride with low noise while on the highway.

TRUXUS MUD-TERRAIN

The TruXus Mud-Terrain features large ground-biting lugs that provide excellent traction while driving through muddy trails or other similar conditions. Their siped tread blocks and tight tread pattern translates to a more comfortable and quiet highway drive. The 6- to 10-ply rating provides for tough and thick sidewalls while the rubber compound assists with chip- and cut-resistance. Available sizes range between 31x10.50x15 to 33x12.50x17.

Photo courtesy of Toyo

Photo courtesy of Interco Tire Corp

TOYO OPEN COUNTRY M/T

Toyo's Open Country M/T tire features aggressive off-road styling, thanks to the deep lug treads that have been designed to meet a variety of off-road conditions from deep sand to rock outcroppings. The specially formulated rubber compound has been engineered to provide maximum traction. Road noise is minimized, thanks to their computer-enhanced tread pattern, which also incorporated sidewall lugs for additional off-road performance when the tires are aired down. The six-ply tires are available in load ranges C, D, and E, with available sizes ranging between 35x13.50x15 to 37x13.50x24.

INTERCO TIRE IROK

Interco Tire's IROK tire features excellent traction in mud and snow and is a true performer while rock climbing, based upon its directional tread pattern and three-stage lug design. The IROKs are also available in either radial- or bias-ply configurations. Depending upon the tire size chosen, the sidewalls may be constructed of either four or six plys, while the treads are made up of either six- or eight-ply construction. The available load ranges of C, D, and E are also dependent upon the selected size. The tires are available in sizes ranging from 36x13.50x15 to 49x21.00x20.

Maxxis Creepy Crawler

Photo courtesy of Mickey Thompson Performance Tires & Wheels

MAXXIS CREEPY CRAWLER

Maxxi's Creepy Crawler is a trail favorite with an aggressive and durable tread pattern. The enormous horizontally siped and stepped lugs feature massive valleys for effective deep self-cleaning. Depending upon the size selected, which ranges between 35x12.50x15 to 40x13.50x17, either six- or eight-ply sidewalls and treads are available. The specially designed compound of this bias ply tire adds to its excellent traction in off-road conditions, as well as its puncture resistance and durability.

MICKEY THOMPSON BAJA MTZ RADIAL

Mickey Thompson's Baja MTZ radial has been designed with an aggressive tread that features massive lugs for optimum performance in the mud. The three-ply sidewall and six-ply tread will endure a great amount of debris before being compromised. Adding additional surface area to the tire when aired down are the Sidebiter sidewall treads. For optimum performance in wet conditions, the treads have been siped for added water evacuation. The available sizes range from 31x10.50R15LT up to 38x15.50R20LT, with load ranges of C, D, and E.

Photo courtesy of Nitto Tire USA

Photo courtesy of Pro Comp Tires

NITTO MUD GRAPPLER

Nitto's Mud Grappler has been designed to provide exceptional off-road traction, especially with their 15mm side lugs, which provide excellent sidewall traction and lend additional resistance to punctures and tears. Excellent rock-crawling and mud-traction characteristics are achieved through the computer-designed tread pattern, which features a high-void ratio for excellent self-cleaning of trail debris. Available in sizes ranging from 33x13.50x15 to 40x15.50x22, and load ranges C, D, and E, there is a tire designed to fit any application.

PRO COMP RADIAL XTERRAIN THREE-PLY

Pro Comp's aggressive radial X-terrain tire has been designed for any terrain anywhere. One of the tire's most distinguishing factors is the extreme traction compound that allows for the maximum puncture and tear resistance while maintaining the ultimate in flexibility and stability while aired down. The directional tread pattern is similar to that of a mud terrain which features aggressive, deep and wide tread lugs. Thick three-ply sidewalls and six-ply treads make them an instant hit for rocky trails. Available in load ranges C, D, and E, the tires are available in sizes ranging from 37x13.50x15 to 40x13.50x20.

Photo courtesy of General Tire

Photo courtesy of Goodyear

GENERAL TIRE GRABBER COMPETITION

General's Grabber Competition features a four-row tread pattern with multiple traction edges that provide traction in virtually any competitive condition, especially rock crawling. The extra deep treads allow the tire to mold itself around any obstacle for the ultimate in traction. The specially formulated rubber compound makes this tire extra sticky. Available in load range D, the three-ply unit is available in a 37x12.50x17 size.

GOODYEAR WRANGLER MT/R

Extra-aggressive tread and large lugs provide excellent traction in extreme mud, snow, rock, and sand conditions. The lugs extend down the sidewall to allow for better biting traction. The steel-belted radial design incorporates Durawall technology with silica compounding and three polyester plies for excellent resistance against cuts, tears, and punctures. Available in load range D, the three-ply tire is available in sizes ranging from 30x9.50R15 to 285/70R17.

PROJECT 94
Using and Adjusting Self-Deflating Valve Stems

  Time: 1/2 Hour

 Tools: None

 Talent: ⚙

🚙 **Applicable Years:** All

💲 **Tab:** $80 set of 4

 Parts Required: Valve stems

 Tip: Do not leave the valve stems on the wheel when they have completed airing the tire down.

 Performance Gain: Allows for faster and more accurate airing down of tires

 Complementary Project: None

Sometimes it is the little things in life that count. In this case, the little things are adjustable and self-deflating valve stems. One of the most innovative products ever brought to the off-road market, these valve stems minimize the amount of time it takes to air tires down to single digit numbers for those hard to conquer trails. What used to take a good 20 to 25 minutes to do now only takes half the time, and it is done with complete accuracy to all four tires. Back in the day, airing down tires meant having to stand there with the tip of a screwdriver or with the deflator tip found on the back of a tire pressure gauge and manually press the valve stem in to release the air. After numerous times of stopping, checking the tire pressure to see if enough had been let out and then continuing, it could be a long road ahead to get all four aired down and with some level of equality. That was until the creation of the Staun Tyre Deflators.

Each of the Staun Tyre Deflators has a predetermined psi set, so that all one must do is screw the deflator onto the tire's valve stem to start the process. A few minutes later the hissing of the escaping air is gone and your tires are ready to hit the trail. Constructed of solid brass, each deflator can be adjusted to whatever desired psi is required, between 6 and 30 psi, for either the trail or driver's taste. Adjusting the valves is easy, since there is an adjustment cap and a lock ring to hold the adjustment in place. With each 1/2 turn of the cap, the psi is decreased in 3-psi increments. The fastest way to adjust the caps, should the factory preset 18 psi not be enough, is to deflate a tire to the desired psi, install the deflator onto the wheel, and turn the adjustment cap until the air begins to

be released. Once at that setting, adjust the lock ring against the adjustment cap and you're done. Repeat this step three more times and you'll never have to wait around again.

1

The Staun Products Tyre Deflators are sold as a package of four brass deflators. Included with the set is a compact carrying case to protect them from becoming lost or riddled with debris.

Built of machined brass, the deflators are easily disassembled for cleaning and servicing. The center T-piston is the heart of the unit. Constructing the components from brass allows for tighter to acquired and better overall performance.

3

The factory valve covers must be removed for the Staun Tyre Deflator to be installed.

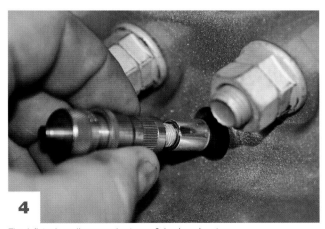

4

The deflator is easily screwed onto any Schrader valve stem.

5

To set the deflator to your desired psi, air a tire down to your desired psi, install it and begin turning the adjustment cap until air begins to escape. At that point, back off the adjustment cap until the escaping air stops.

6

With the adjustment cap set, turn the lock ring until it is resting below the adjustment cap. This lock ring will keep the adjustment cap from turning and becoming unset.

PROJECT 95
Install Wheel Spacers

 Time: 1 Hour

 Tools: Socket set, torque wrench

 Talent:

 Applicable Years: All

 Tab: $100 pair

 Parts Required: Lug nuts, wheel spacers

 Tip: Do not use an impact gun when installing the spacers.

 Performance Gain: Increases the track width of a vehicle and allows for various offset and backspaced wheels to be used

Complementary Project: New wheels and tires

Depending upon your suspension set up or desired wheel and tire combination on your Jeep, a set of wheel spacers may have your name on them. Designed to serve two functions for Jeep owners, wheel spacers are a quick and easy solution to what could be an expensive and frustrating situation. The first purpose that they serve is to provide an increase in clearance when larger than stock wheels and tires are used in conjunction with a larger suspension lift. Often, either the offset or backspacing on the new wheels is insufficient to allow it to operate properly. In this situation, a wheel spacer will extend the wheel and tire combination out further to allow for better clearance. The second function of wheel spacers is to allow for a wider variety of wheels and tires to be used, by allowing the bolt patterns to be changed from say a 5-on-4.5 to a 5-on-5.5 or vice versa.

Known for their high quality of construction and bulletproof hardware, Spidertrax has been providing the off-road market with high-quality wheel spacers since 1999. Manufactured for a wide variety of Jeeps, the Spidertrax wheel spacers are constructed from solid chunks of 6061 T6 aluminum and machined to exacting tolerances. For the ultimate in wear and durability, each wheel spacer is anodized in dark blue, using a double anodizing process for twice the corrosion resistance. In addition, each wheel spacer is wheel and hub centric for a perfect fit. Available for XJ, KJ, CJ, and YJ models, the spacers are available in 1¼-inch thickness. For the JK, WK, and Commander models the spacers are available from 1⅜-inch to 1½-inch thickness.

Each kit consists of two spacers, preinstalled wheel studs, lug nuts, and Loctite.

1 Spidertrax wheel spacers are made of 6061T6 anodized aluminum and machined to exacting tolerances. Available for XJ, KJ, CJ, and YJ models, the spacers are available in 1¼-inch thickness. For the JK, WK, and Commander models the spacers are available from 1⅜-inch to 1½-inch thickness. Each kit consists of two spacers, preinstalled wheel studs, lug nuts, and Loctite.

2 For added durability and wear, each wheel spacer is anodized in dark blue, using a double anodizing process for twice the corrosion resistance.

3 To begin the install process, the wheel and tire combination must be removed from the vehicle.

4 Each of the Spidertrax spacers is wheel and hub centric, which guarantees a perfect fit, while minimizing any excess play that may exist on either side of the spacer.

5 Once installed onto the hub, the included lug nuts should be threaded by hand onto the factory wheel studs. Prior to their installation, a small amount of Loctite should be placed on the threads of the wheel studs.

6 When all of the lug nut have been started by hand, a torque wrench is used to finish tightening them onto the hub to the manufacturer's specifications. It is important to note that an impact gun should not be used for this installation.

7 The wheel and tire combination is placed onto the wheel spacer.

8 As we mentioned previously, even the wheels and tires should be secured by a torque wrench and not an impact gun.

9 Upon completion of the install, the wheels and tires are extended 1½ inches further out from the vehicle, allowing for better clearance of the wheels and tires as well as more variety for different styles of wheels.

PROJECT 96
Select the Appropriate Wheels

 Time: N/A

 Tools: N/A

 Talent:

 Applicable Years: All models

Tab: Costs vary depending upon selected wheels

 Parts Required: N/A

 Tip: Know what type of terrain you will be taking your vehicle into and where most of your driving will be, street or off-road, as this could determine the type of wheels that you select.

 Performance Gain: Traction and appearance

 Complementary Project: N/A

A set of wheels says a lot about a vehicle; they are one of the most distinguishing items that can be placed on a Jeep to convey that vehicle's intended use and purpose. While some may appreciate a set of shiny chromed units, some may like the more subtle black finish, and yet some like a more functional wheel such as a bead lock-equipped unit. It really doesn't matter what type of wheels you run, as long as they are the correct size and backspacing for your intended application and they fit the bill when it comes to usability—either on or off the road.

To help you choose the correct tire, some of today's more popular models are presented for your review and consideration.

Photo courtesy of American Racing Equipment Inc.

Photo courtesy of KMC Wheels

Photo courtesy of KMC Wheels

AMERICAN RACING PUNISHER

American Racing's Punisher wheel significantly enhances resistance to brake dust, dirt, road film, and UV degradation, thanks to its Teflon finish. The high-luster machined face with simulated bead-lock flange treatment wheels will stand up to anything in its path as well (shown). Made of aluminum, these lightweight wheels are available in 16x8, 17x8, 18x9.5, and 20x10 configurations with a variety of Jeep bolt patterns and backspacing sizes.

RACELINE RENEGADE 6 WHEEL

Raceline's Renegade 6 wheel is the perfect wheel when you just want to blend in and yet be stylish at the same time. Built from durable, high-grade alloy material, the available finishes are chrome, black, and polished. The wheels are available in 16-, 17-, 18-, 19-, and 20-inch configurations, with Jeep specific backspacing and bolt patterns.

KMC WHEELS XD796 REVOLVER

KMC Wheels' XD 796 Revolver is a one-piece cast wheel with a six-spoke design that has jetted raised edge panels. The wheel is available in black, chrome, or polished finish and has a load rating of 3,100 pounds for each wheel. The wheels are available in 16-, 17-, 18-, 19-, and 20- inch configurations with Jeep model-specific backspacing and bolt patterns.

Photo courtesy of Walker Evans Racing

Photo Courtesy of Center Line

Photo courtesy of Hutchinson Inc.

WALKER EVANS BEAD-LOCKED WHEEL

These solid one-piece cast-aluminum beadlock wheels are as strong as the reputation of the man they are named after. With no welding used during their construction, the possibility of leaks is minimized. Each wheel is rated at 3,800 pounds and features Grade 8 hardware. The bolts thread into long steel inserts that are mounted securely into the wheel. The valve stems are moved back further into the wheel, eliminating the possibility of being damaged while out on the trail. The popular wheel is available in a 17x8.5-inch configuration. Backspacing is cut to order, and all standard Jeep bolt patterns are available.

CENTER LINE ICE WHEELS

Center Line's latest wheel is a DOT-approved wheel that utilizes an inner tire bead lock, requiring no additional bolts to hold the tire to the wheel, like many of the more conventional style bead lock wheels. The three-piece wheel contains a centering element that extends to the inner reaches of the tire's air chamber to create an internal bead lock, while allowing the use of conventional tires. Each wheel is manufactured from high-quality T-6061 billet aluminum and features a strong 3,200-pound load rating. The final finish is a triple-chrome-plated outer lip that may be replaced should it become damaged or scratched while off-roading. The wheel is available in a 17-inch diameter with five-lug configuration.

HUTCHINSON TWO-PIECE ROCK MONSTER BEAD LOCK WHEELS

Known for their extremely durable military spec, ISO 9001 quality bead lock wheels, the Hutchinson Rock Monster wheels have been designed to achieve maximum weight saving while not compromising the vehicle's load carrying capacities, all while allowing tire pressure to be reduced for the ultimate in off-road performance. Street legal and DOT-approved, the wheels contain a molded rubber sleeve that fits between the tire beads and the outer portions of the wheel that once installed locks both tire beads against the rim. Available for many of today's popular Jeep models and in sizes ranging from 15- to 17-inch.

Photo courtesy of Poison Spyder Customs

Photo courtesy of Mickey Thompson Performance Tires & Wheels

Photo courtesy of Allied Wheel Components

POISON SPYDER CUSTOMS LOCK WHEEL

Poison Spyder's latest creations are machined aluminum wheels that have been designed for the sole purpose of heavy-duty rock crawling, as evidenced by the outer bead lock trim ring and the durable construction. The wheel is available in a five-lug configuration and is available with various backspacing dimensions. The available sizes of the wheel are 15x9, 17x9, 18x9, and 20x10.

MICKEY THOMPSON M/T CLASSIC LOCK

Mickey Thompson's M/T Classic wheel combines all of the features of the Classic II wheel with the added styling of a simulated bead lock ring. Available in 15- to 18-inch diameters and a variety of widths, each wheel is backed by a lifetime guarantee.

ALLIED WHEEL COMPONENTS BLACK ROCK 8

Allied Wheel's Black Rock 8 wheel has been built and designed for hardcore off-road thrashing. Manufactured from heavy-duty steel alloy, the wheel contains a functional bead lock element that has been designed into the wheel to allow for even greater off-roading and rock crawling. The available sizes are 15x7, 15x8, 15x10, 16x8, 16x10, and 17x9 configurations with vehicle specific backspacing. Each wheel is finished with black paint and a chrome center cap.

Photo courtesy of Pro Comp Tires and Wheels

Photo Courtesy of American Expedition Vehicles

Photo Courtesy of Moto Metal

Photo courtesy of Granite Alloy

PRO COMP TIRE & WHEEL XTREME ALLOY

Pro Comp's Xtreme alloy wheel has been created with cast aluminum and built to endure the rigors of off-road abuse. Available in a variety of bolt patterns for some of today's more popular Jeeps, the wheel is available with either a matte black painted finish or polished finish. The available sizes include 16x8, 16x10, 17x9, 18x9, and 20x9.

AMERICAN EXPEDITION VEHICLES PINTLER BEAD LOCK WHEEL

AEV's Pintler bead lock wheel is one of the few DOT-approved bead lock wheels on the market that actually have the inserts for the bead lock ring cast into place and ready for an effortless installation of the tire. Each wheel is available in a 17x8.5-inch configuration and is finished in either argent or silver powder coat finish. The cast aluminum, five-lug wheel looks great on either a Jeep TJ or JK.

MOTO METAL MO957

Moto Metal's MO957 wheel is instantly distinguished from all other rims on the road or trail by their ominous black matte finish and tricked out spider web skeleton polished spoke outline. Available in 17x9, 18x9, and 20x9 configurations, this cast-aluminum wheel can be ordered in all bolt patterns to fit Jeeps.

GRANITE ALLOY GA8

Granite Alloy's GA8 wheel is an affordable and stylish wheel for some of today's more popular Jeeps. Finished in flat black with a matte clear coat, the wheel is available in 15- and 17-inch diameters in a variety of bolt patterns that are Jeep model specific.

Photo courtesy of Dick Cepek Tires & Wheels

Photo courtesy of Trail Ready Products

Photo courtesy of OMF Performance Products

DICK CEPEK DC-1 WHEEL

Dick Cepek's DC-1 wheel is the next generation off-road wheel. Featuring a highly polished finish, the wheel is available in 15- to 20-inch sizes with various backspace dimensions to match some of today's more popular Jeep models. The maximum amount of clearances for brake calipers and other steering and suspension components provides a better fit with newer suspension setups.

The DC-1 wheel is TPMS friendly and comes with stainless steel bolts on the outer lip that can be used to mount the optional simulated bead lock rings, which are sold separately.

TRAIL READY PRODUCTS STEEL BEAD LOCK WHEELS

Trail Ready Products identifies its steel bead lock wheel as the strongest steel wheel on the market. Fabricated from a solid ⅜-inch-thick 6061 T6 billet aluminum clamp ring, the wheels are available in a standard slim ring design or the legendary rock ring (shown). Each wheel comes with gold zinc-plated ⁵/₁₆-inch Grade 8 bolts for added durability when rubbed against rocks. Available finishes include anodized, powder-coated, or polished. The available sizes for the wheels range from 15 to 20 inches.

OMF PERFORMANCE BEAD LOCK WHEELS

OMF's bead locks are available to be added to a wide variety of wheels. Fabricated from high-quality 6061-T6 aluminum, the bead lock and inner reinforcing rings are considered to be some of the strongest and lightest on the market today. Installation by a qualified welder is recommended to ensure proper safety and performance of the bead locks. The bead locks are available in a variety of sizes from 15 to 20 inches and in a variety of colors and finishes.

SECTION 10
RECOVERY AND SAFETY ESSENTIALS

Ensuring that you have a safe trip off-road or even on your way to your destination is the role and responsibility of everyone on the trail and on the road. While like everything else in the world, some people are more prepared or dedicated to the cause than others, this chapter addresses some basic and common safety and recovery projects that will benefit you greatly.

PROJECT 97
Choose Trail Recovery Essentials

Time: N/A

Tools: N/A

Talent:

Applicable Years: All models

Tab: Costs vary depending upon item

Parts Required: N/A

Tip: Never leave home without these essential items; they could make the difference between getting home or being on the trails for some time.

Performance Gain: The ability to get unstuck and back on the trail

Complementary Project: N/A

As with anything we do in life, we must be prepared for life's unexpected emergencies. The same applies while off-roading. While you or members of your group may be prepared for whatever comes your way, sometimes others out on the trail are not.

In the event that either you or someone else requires extrication, winching, or recovery efforts, a few of these items featured may just be what the doctor ordered. Not only will they prove to be beneficial to the efforts, but having the right tool for the right situation will save time, require less manual labor, and will minimize the strain on your Jeep.

PICK-UP PRODUCTS VEHICLE SURVIVAL KIT

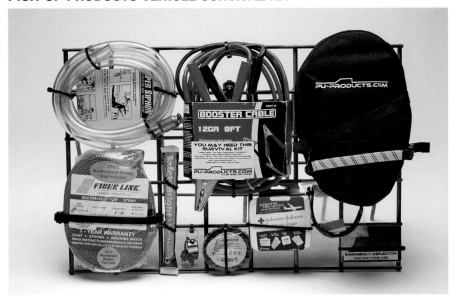

Photo courtesy of Pick-Up Products

Whether you are on the road or off the road, every Jeep should contain a survival kit such as this manufactured by Pick-Up Products, which contains 11 of the most important items needed for emergencies. Included in the kit are a pair of jumper cables, a super siphon, a recovery rope, a first aid kit, assorted zip ties, and a plethora of other survival items. All products contained in the kit fit inside the durable bag that comes with the kit. It's a definite must-have for any vehicle or situation.

PULL-PAL SELF RECOVERY ANCHOR

Photo courtesy of Pull-Pal

The Pull-Pal is recommended for all vehicles that travel off-road either solo or with a group; however, if you go on solo runs, don't leave home without one. Weighing in at only 36 pounds, the unit has been designed to work in most types of ground (including sand, hard-pan soil, and even snow), it can be used to both extract your vehicle without the use of another rig and can serve as an anchoring point from the rear when winching another vehicle out of harm's way.

When not in use, the Pull-Pal folds compactly to the size of an ordinary bumper jack for easy storage. Ruggedly constructed with a forged chrome-moly plow assembly, welded construction overall and assembled with Grade 8 bolts for strength and quality, this unit will get you unstuck in no time.

STAUN ADJUSTABLE TIRE DEFLATORS

Photo courtesy of Staun Products

Depending upon certain terrain or methods of getting unstuck, the need to reduce the air pressure in your tires from 30 to 6 psi may be necessary rather quickly. Each of the Staun deflator valves contains an adjustment range specific to the deflation level of your choice. Additionally, these high-quality units are extremely accurate to within 0.05 psi of the preset pressure they have been adjusted to. Weighing only 32 grams each, each valve is crafted from solid brass and comes backed by a five-year guarantee.

ARB OFF-ROAD RECOVERY KIT

Photo courtesy of Staun Products

ARB's off-road recovery kit features everything needed for virtually any extrication, any time, anywhere. Housed inside the large bag that has been tailored to fit the recovery kit is a 17,500-pound ARB snatch strap, a tree trunk protector strap, a winch extension strap, a snatch block, a recovery damper, a pair of D shackles, and a pair of gloves. Don't head for the trail without one.

ROVER'S NORTH SAND TRACKS

Photo courtesy of Rover's North Inc.

They're an item that has been seen on off-road race vehicles and on countless expedition trucks. Worth their weight in gold when you become stranded in sandy or loose terrain, Rover's North Sand Tracks definitely have their place while off-roading. Each track has been fabricated from lightweight aluminum that has been perforated to minimize their weight and to allow them to settle into the terrain for better grip. Using them is as simple as laying them in front of the vehicle and driving over them, and for this reason, multiple tracks are suggested. When not in use, they can be mounted atop a roof rack or placed somewhere inside your Jeep where access is easy and fast.

MAX AX MULTI-PURPOSE TOOL

Carrying every tool or piece of equipment on your Jeep for those "what if" scenarios, would require two things: a box van and a hefty budget. Thankfully, tools such as the Max Ax Multi-Purpose Tool have been created. What is essentially the equivalent of seven basic hand tools has been configured to only take up the space of one Hudson Bay-style ax.

Consisting of an unbreakable 36-inch composite poly-glass handle and a $3^{1}/_{2}$-pound ax head, an assortment of tool attachments can be installed to reconfigure the ax into a shovel, rake, pick, spade, etc. Each tool attachment is secured with custom pins that are easily secured into the ax head. When not in use, the ax is protected by a leather sheath, while the tool attachments are housed in a sturdy Cordura carry case.

The Max Ax Multi-Purpose Tool has been precisely engineered and manufactured to industry and military standards of strength and reliability, and every off-road vehicle should be equipped with one.

RAMSEY PATRIOT 9500 UT WINCH WITH SYNTHETIC ROPE

Photo courtesy of Ramsey

A winch is one of the most important pieces of equipment your Jeep can have installed on it. A prime example of a durable, and tried and true, winch is Ramsey's Patriot 9500 UT winch that delivers state-of-the-art winching technology with its new semiautomatic clutch design and semiautomatic shifting. In addition to the 138:1 gear ratio on the unit, a powerful high-torque 5.5-horsepower series wound motor has a no-load line speed of 35.4 feet per minute.

For the ultimate in durability, the drum is sealed along with the gear assembly. The 9500 UT comes prewound with 105 feet of 5/16-inch galvanized aircraft cable with replacement clevis hook and safety latch, which are controlled by Ramsey's wireless control system. Just what the doctor ordered for those when-in-need situations.

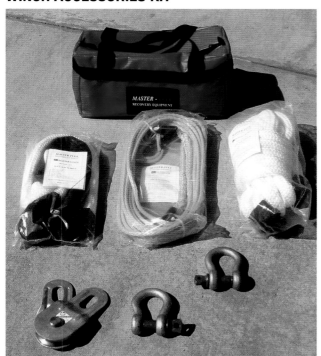

MASTER-PULL'S ULTIMATE RECOVERY GEAR WINCH ACCESSORIES KIT

A winch is only as good as the parts that support it; Master-Pull's ultimate recovery gear winch kit contains everything needed for virtually any extrication or recovery. Each kit contains a 5/16-inch x 50-foot 16,500-pound Superline winch extension cable with a heavy-duty sling hook, a swing block with built-in stainless steel ball bearing rollers, a 7/8-inch x 20-foot 28,500-pound yank strap, a 7/8-inch x 10-foot 28,500-pound tree saver strap, two 3/4-inch screw-pin shackles and a waterproof bag to keep everything in.

BROKEN AXLE TOOL

Photo courtesy of Staun Products

Think of this item as a splint for your trail vehicle's broken axle. In the same way that a splint keeps a limb immobilized and unable to move, the broken axle tool will do the same by keeping your wheel attached on the vehicle and unable to slip out of the axle shaft tubes as you drive down the trail to safety. Easily installed, once the tool is placed across the wheel that has the broken axle and is secured to the vehicle frame with cinch straps, the sealed roller bearings on the tool do the rest of the work until you are off the trail and can better address the situation and repair.

If space is a concern, the tool is also offered in a portable version as well. A definite must-have for any trail-capable Jeep.

PROJECT 98
Install a Wireless Winch Remote Control

 Time: 1 Hour

 Tools: Socket set, wire crimper, screwdriver, cable ties

 Talent:

Applicable Years: All

Tab: $183

 Parts Required: Wireless winch remote

 Tip: The factory direct plug-in controller should still be kept in the vehicle as a potential back-up to the remote control, should the remote's batteries become weak or if the controller is lost and cannot be found when the extrication is occurring.

Performance Gain: Safety and comfort

Complementary Project: Installation of a winch

Getting stuck in a situation that requires the use of a winch is never a welcome moment. Usually, there is some type of obstacle or condition on the trail that the driver is trying to avoid that got the vehicle in that situation in the first place. It might be rocks, mud, or inclement weather that the driver would just as soon avoid, instead of having to wallow in it to get to the front of the winch. Having to get out of the vehicle, plug in the winch controller, and then stand in harm's way as the winch is spooled back in while under load is not very safe or wise. The answer to keeping out of the muck and staying safe is to install a remote control winch unit that allows the winch to be operated wirelessly from up to 50 feet away.

Operating the system is as easy as turning the remote control unit on and pressing the "IN" or "OUT" buttons. The unit we chose to install is manufactured by Ramsey Winch. It can be operated on a wide variety of winches other than Ramsey's own brands. The transmitter is battery-powered and is equipped with a long-life battery and a power-saver circuit that automatically turns off in the event that the remote transmitter is left on. A visual indicator light on the transmitter is displayed when the unit is turned on. All of the items are weatherproof for durability and operation in any condition. Included with the transmitter and receiver is a magnetic mount antenna that can be placed in a discrete location. Once the system is operational, the transmitter can be kept on your key ring, in the vehicle, or anywhere else that is convenient until needed.

1 Once the wiring harness has been connected to a power source, the wiring harness is connected to the receiver box.

2

For safety purposes to the electronics, the receiver unit contains a dedicated ground that must be secured to the vehicle prior to its operating.

3

The cabling that goes between the antenna and the receiver box is routed through the engine compartment to the predetermined location for it. Since the antenna has a magnetic base, placement can be virtually anywhere on the vehicle.

4

The receiver box for our installation was mounted onto a custom bracket using nuts, bolts, and lock washers.

5

Keeping the receiver out of the way yet where it can be accessed, it was installed adjacent to the washer fluid reservoir.

6

The crossbrace attachment points at the core support were used as the mounting location for the receiver.

7

While it can be installed anywhere on the vehicle where there is metal, we opted to install the antenna behind the front grille of the Jeep. It rests on the crossbar of the radiator support and is protected from the elements better than if it were mounted in the open.

8

The wireless transmitter is battery operated and features an indicator light to let the user know when the unit is powered on or off. It can be operated from as far away as 50 feet from the winching vehicle.

9

The last item to be addressed in the install is the connection between the receiver and the winch, which is the same type of plug that the corded controllers use. In the event that the transmitter is lost or out of commission, simply pull the plug from the connector and insert the corded unit's plug.

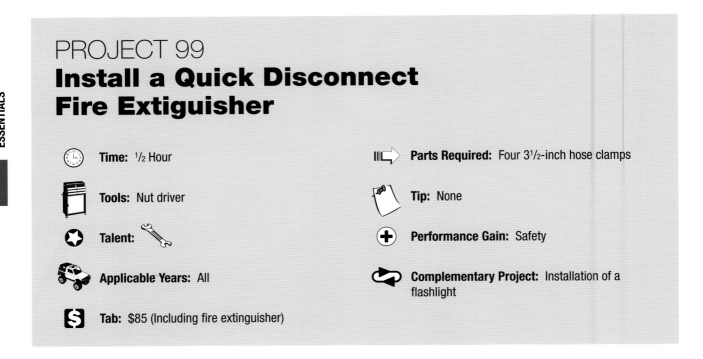

PROJECT 99
Install a Quick Disconnect Fire Extiguisher

Time: ½ Hour

Tools: Nut driver

Talent:

Applicable Years: All

Tab: $85 (Including fire extinguisher)

Parts Required: Four 3½-inch hose clamps

Tip: None

Performance Gain: Safety

Complementary Project: Installation of a flashlight

Driving is serious business. Given the opportunities for you or someone in the vehicle ahead, beside, or behind you to make a mistake, one should always be prepared. If you have ever participated in any driver's education course or been on an organized trail run, there are always standard safety items that the instructor or organizer suggests should be in every vehicle. A fire extinguisher is one of these items. In all likelihood, a fire extinguisher will never be used on the vehicle in which it's carried, but on someone else's. Given the limited amount of space in some Jeeps, the placement of a fire extinguisher can be a challenge, especially if you want to be able to access it quickly and without interference from cargo in and around the interior.

Race Prep Services, Inc., has fabricated a fire extinguisher bracket that not only keeps the unit out of the way of cargo, but that is also a quick-release mechanism that allows the extinguisher to be accessed in a matter of seconds. Constructed of high-quality ⅜-inch-thick steel plate, the two-piece mount can be easily mounted onto a variety of surfaces, both flat and round, with multiple fastening methods. To complete the package and keep the mount highly visible, fire engine red powder coating has been applied to it. Once a location for the mount has been established, one of three mounting options must be chosen. The mounting options consist of welding the mount onto a surface, using either screws or nuts and bolts, or using hose clamps. For our installation, we used hose clamps, given their ability to be moved quickly and without any trace of ever being in the previous location. Once mounted, the fire extinguisher is attached to the second half

of the mount via hose clamps as well. The two pieces of the mount are secured to each other by sliding the extinguisher side of the mount onto a bolt and then pushing it upward until the retainer pin holes are aligned. Once aligned, a spring-loaded retainer bolt is pushed into place and the extinguisher awaits duty when called upon. For our installation, we chose to install the extinguisher on the backside of our rear roll bar tube, which provides easy access.

1

The quick-release design of the RPS, Inc., fire extinguisher mount is built from solid steel plate and is powder-coated fire engine red for high visibility. A spring-loaded retaining pin keeps both halves of the mount together until pulled out.

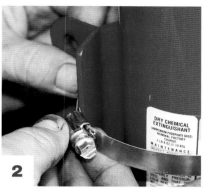

2

The first step of the install is to secure a new fire extinguisher that is fully charged and serviced onto the extinguisher half of the mount; this is done by using hose clamps.

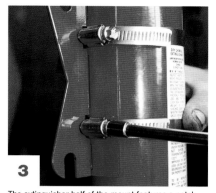

3

The extinguisher half of the mount features a notch in the bottom. This notch will slide onto a bolt that acts as both a pivot point for the mount and a stopper. The hole toward the upper portion of the mount is the location where the retainer pin slides in.

4

We selected the rear portion of the roll bar to mount the extinguisher and mount. This location was selected for its easy accessibility and ability to keep the extinguisher from being enveloped by cargo, which would make getting to it in an emergency impossible.

5

With the extinguisher mounted to the other half of the mount, the exact location was selected on the roll bar. When installing such an item, the ability to get to it quickly is paramount. This means that a restrictive area where the extinguisher may hit the hardtop or come into contact with any other obstacles would not be a safe choice.

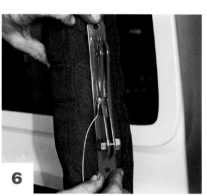

6

Some minor scraping and denting is a given when off-road driving. However, if the damage is severe enough to bend or compromise the integrity of crossbraces or suspension component mounts, they should be investigated and repaired.

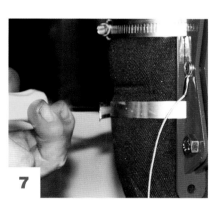

7

Once the final area was selected, two more hose clamps were threaded through the mount and tightened until they could not be moved.

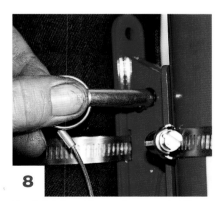

8

Once both halves of the mount are connected, the spring-loaded retaining pin was inserted.

9

The fire extinguisher is tested to ensure that its access is not compromised by any encumbrances. Given our location, the extinguisher released exactly as designed in a matter of seconds.

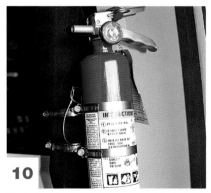

10

The final product reveals a necessary safety device awaiting the call of duty.

PROJECT 100
Install a Winch

Time: 3 Hours

Tools: Socket set, impact gun, torque wrench, hand tools

Talent:

Applicable Years: All models

Tab: $1,900 including basic winch mounting brackets

Parts Required: Winch, winch line

Tip: Prior to purchasing your winch, determine where on the vehicle it will be mounted, as well as what capacity you require to extricate your vehicle from a situation. All too often a winch is purchased by the owner, who learns too late that it does not fit its intended space or that it is undercapacity for the vehicle.

Performance Gain: Provides safety by providing a means of becoming extricated from a situation that has rendered the vehicle unmoveable

Complementary Project: Installation of a wireless winch remote.

In many cases, appearances are everything, and to some people, this is especially true when it comes to their rides. More often than not, the more equipment that is installed on a truck, the more points it receives for being classified as a true off-road rig. This is especially true when a winch is sighted on the front end of a truck. All too often, there really is no choice of where to install these lifesavers other than on a bumper or inside the cradle of a bumper that has a mounting system built especially for the winch. The latter of the two mounting options provides a cleaner overall front-end look as well as some additional protection from the elements for the winch and the winch line.

For our install we chose to install a Ramsey Patriot 9500 UT winch with a synthetic winch line into an American Expedition Vehicles front Jeep Wrangler JK bumper. The power of the Patriot 9500 UT is derived from a massive 5.5-horsepower, 12-volt DC series-wound electric reversible motor that is able to pull 9,500 pounds with ease. For those specialized applications, the winch is available in a 24-volt configuration. The power from the 5.5-horsepower motor is able to turn the winch drum and cable at a line speed of 35.4 feet per minute at the first layer with no load line speed via Ramsey's three-stage planetary gear system that creates a gear reduction ratio of 138:1. The 105 feet of $^3/_8$-inch Technora synthetic winch rope provides excellent heat resistance and increased durability and safety. A cam action clutch can be disengaged from the planetary gears for effortless free-spooling of the winch line. When the clutch is reengaged, an added level of safety and performance is introduced via an automatic load-retaining brake assembly, which assists in holding the tension on the line. An aluminum fairlead minimizes damage to the winch line and is easily maintainable.

Included with each Patriot 9500 UT is a set of 2-gauge battery cables and connectors that reach to 6 feet, with additional lengths available separately. The unit may be operated by two methods; the standard 12-foot wired pendant remote control unit or the optional wireless remote control unit that allows safe operation from as far away as 50 feet.

Between the numerous years of experience, the history of the company and the high-quality components used to manufacture the unit, there should be no doubt in anyone's mind that when the Patriot 9500 UT is on-scene, that the task at hand will be handled with speed and performance. The limited lifetime warranty and the fact that the unit is made in the United States also adds to the guarantee of years of hassle-free service.

We delivered our 2008 Jeep Wrangler JK to Mel Wade, owner of Off-Road Evolution in Fullerton, California, for the expert installation. Between his vast knowledge and customization abilities of any Jeep make and model, in conjunction with the fact that his installation staff are all avid off-roaders, we knew we our Jeep would be in more than capable hands.

1

The newest addition to the Patriot Series line of self-recovery winches is the 9,500-pound-capacity Profile 9500. Thanks to the stand-alone weather-resistant solenoid assembly, the main body of the winch is able to fit in a variety of locations. *Photo courtesy of Ramsey*

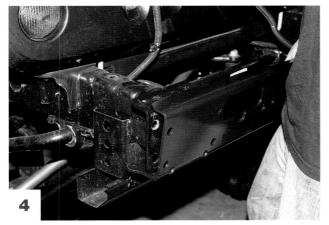

2

Ramsey's proven three-stage planetary gear system provides incredibly fast line speeds and a gear-reduction ratio of 138:1, which allows the full force of the 5.5-horsepower 12-volt DC series wound motor to be optimized. *Photo courtesy of Ramsey*

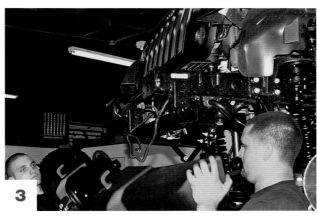

3

Before installing the Ramsey Patriot 9500 UT winch, the front American Expedition Vehicles bumper of the Jeep had to be removed. This included the front skid plate, factory fog lights, and tow hooks.

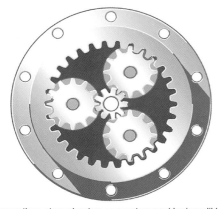

4

Once the front bumper has been removed and stored for safe keeping, the winch mounting kit is bolted into place and properly aligned, so the mounting plates are in proper alignment with the factory frame end plates.

5

Given the design of our winch, a small corner of the winch mounting plate had to be trimmed with a cut-off wheel.

The Ramsey winch is easily attached to the mounting plate using the supplied bolts in the kit. The winch attaches in the same manner as if it were being surface mounted onto a bumper.

As part of the preinstallation activities, all of the wires leading from the winch to the control box should be installed. Each wire is color coded to match up with each bolt on the winch.

The 2-gauge battery cables are routed in front of the radiator and to the battery, where they are terminated. The positive and ground cables should be run in parallel with each other and secured with cable ties for a clean appearance and ease of service.

An aluminum hawse fairlead, included with the kit, bolts directly to the winch mounting plate in the front. A hawse fairlead is typically used with synthetic line applications, since there are no pinch points that could damaged the line, unlike roller fairleads, which have four rollers and eight pinch points where the pliable line could become lodged.

The completed installation will provide years of service to its owner. As we mentioned earlier, notice how the AEV bumper protects the winch and the synthetic line from direct exposure to elements such as mud, dirt, and sand. In the final step, a removable winch hook was attached to the line and is attached to a shackle.

PROJECT 101
Replace a Winch Rope

🕐 **Time:** ½ Hour

🧰 **Tools:** Hand tools

⭐ **Talent:** 🔧

🚙 **Applicable Years:** All

💲 **Tab:** $500

➡️ **Parts Required:** Master-Pull Super Line XD Winch Line

📝 **Tip:** Perform the swap where the winch line can be stretched out in front of the vehicle.

➕ **Performance Gain:** Stronger and safer than conventional steel winch lines

🔄 **Complementary Project:** Installation of a hawse fairlead

Having a winch installed on your Jeep is one step in the right direction. However, when the time to use your winch to either extricate yourself or someone else on the trail comes, the condition and material of the winch line becomes just as important to the extrication, and even more important to bystander and driver safety. For years, steel cables have been wrapped around the drums of countless winches, causing extrications to be one of the most dangerous and nail-biting experiences one could ever encounter while off-road driving. Was the line going to snap and recoil, potentially injuring people? Was the operator going to become injured by a snag or fray in the cable? Was the cable tangled or stretched out beyond its useable life expectancy? While completely plausible and valid concerns, winching is an inherently dangerous operation, for just these reasons and numerous others.

To alleviate some of these concerns, we have chosen to upgrade our steel winch cable for a synthetic one manufactured by Master-Pull. The Superline XD synthetic winch rope is manufactured with the most advanced technology in synthetic rope manufacturing today. Beginning as a larger-diameter line, the rope is heated and stretched down to its final diameter, thereby giving the Superline XD an excellent breaking strength as it has the strength of a larger diameter line in a smaller diameter. This prestretching also provides better abrasion resistance to the rope than some other synthetic lines on the market. For even more abrasion resistance, the rope has a tightly braided cover along the entire length of it

and a chafe guard on the 10 feet closest to the drum. This cover gives the inner Superline XD core excellent protection against abrasion, especially that from dirt and sand. Other coverless winch ropes that do not contain the cover are susceptible to dirt and sand becoming lodged in between the strands of the rope, which can cause it to become frayed. In some cases, this leads to a 20 percent loss in the rope's breaking strength.

An additional benefit to using the Superline XD winch line is that it increases safety when being used, since the forces that exist when a winch line snaps and recoils is diminished considerably as the line has been prestretched. Also, the Superline XD will never get curls, kinks, or wire splinters again, thanks to the cover and material. The breaking strength of the line is far greater than that of other winch lines of the same diameter, in fact, 21,000 to 26,500 pounds versus 17,600 pounds for steel cable. Tasked with assisting us with the exchange on our Ramsey Patriot 9500 winch was Dave Wever, owner of Wever's Welding and Fabrication in San Marcos, California. Within a half hour of beginning the exchange, he had the original line removed from the drum and our new line installed ready to go. The exchange is rather simple in that the existing cable was spooled off the drum, the retention bolt was removed, and the new line was reinstalled with a new retention bolt onto the drum. The last things left to do were to thread the new line through the fairlead and spool it back onto the drum.

1

In its original configuration, our Ramsey Patriot 9500 winch contained steel cable as a winch line. While more than adequate to perform winching duties, a steel cable will require more maintenance and will not provide the same level of pulling power or safety as our Master-Pull Superline XD line. As shown in this photo, numerous strands of the wire cable were beginning to become frayed, and there were numerous kinks in it, which make spooling it in a much harder task for the operator and the winch itself.

2

The replacement Master-Pull Superline XD cable is capable of pulling 26,500 pounds without breaking. While this may seem high, keep in mind that when a snatch block is used and the cable is reattached to the winching vehicle that a 9,500-pound winch will really be applying 19,000 pounds on the rope.

3

The new Master-Pull Superline XD cable has numerous features over the wire cable. Some of them include a massive safety hook that has been attached to the crush-proof thimble at the end of the winch. The hook features a locking lever that either opens or closes the hook.

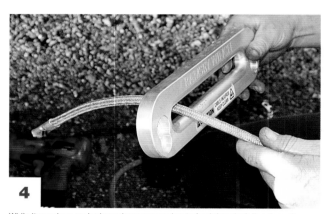

4

While it may be a no-brainer, always remember to feed the winch line through the fairlead before attaching it to the drum, otherwise the install will have to be performed twice.

5

With the new Master-Pull Superline XD resting comfortably on the winch, the safety features and increased ease of use, compared to its steel counterpart, make this a worthwhile effort.

6

When not in use, the safety hook should be secured to a shackle and tightened.

Resources

4x4 sPOD
John Angelastro
Precision Designs
661-755-8139
www.4x4s-pod.com

Adventure Innovations
P.O. Box 6673
Thousand Oaks, CA 91359
(805) 322-7001
info@adventure-innovations.com

All Four Wheel Drive
21765 Temescal Canyon Road
Corona, CA 92883
(951) 277-1037

Allied Wheel Components
(800) 529-4335
www.alliedwheel.com

Alpine Electronics of
America, Inc.
www.alpine-usa.com

American Expedition Vehicles
PO Box 621
Missoula, MT 59806
(406) 251-2100
www.aev-conversions.com

American Outfitters
3691 Via Mercado, Suite 7
La Mesa, CA 91941
(619) 670-4268
www.4x4hummer.com

American Racing
www.americanracing.com

ARB 4x4 Accessories, USA
(206) 264-1669
www.arbusa.com

ARB USA/Old Man Emu
Suspensions
(425) 264-1391
www.arbusa.com

BDS Suspension
(517) 279-2135
www.bds-suspension.com

BFGoodrich Tires
(864) 458-5000
www.bfgoodrichtires.com

Bilstein
14102 Stowe Drive
Poway, CA. 92064
(858) 386-5900
www.bilstein.com

Buggy Whip
George H. Porter Company
653 Hanson Lane
Ramona, CA 92065
(760) 789-3230

Camburg Engineering, Inc.
(714) 848-8880
www.camburg.com

Carson Manufacturing Company
5451 North Rural Street
P.O. Box 20464
Indianapolis, IN 46220-0464
(317) 257-3191
www.carson-mfg.com

Center Line Racing Wheels Inc.
(800) 345-8671
www.centerlinewheels.com

Clayton Off Road Manufacturing
(203) 757-0339
www.claytonoffroad.com

Cobra Electronics Corporation
6500 West Cortland Street
Chicago, IL 60707
(773) 889-8870
www.cobra.com

Cool-Tech, LLC
(661) 254-7948
www.cooltechllc.com

Currie Enterprises, Inc.
1480 North Tustin Avenue
Anaheim, CA 92807
714-528-6957
www.currieenterprises.com

Dan Hewitt Welding &
Fabrication
1545 Seminole Street
San Marcos, CA 92078
(760) 591-4662

David Clark Company
Incorporated
360 Franklin Street
P.O. Box 15054
Worcester, MA. 01615
(508) 751-5800
www.davidclark.com

Deaver Spring, Inc.
(714) 542-3703
www.deaverspring.com

Delta Tech Industries, LLC
807 Fee Ana Street
Placentia, CA 92870, USA
(714) 577-8028
www.deltatechindustries.com

Dick Cepek Performance Tires &

Wheels
(330) 928-9092
www.dickcepek.com

Dynamat
Dynamic Control of North
America, Inc.
3042 Symmes Road
Hamilton, Ohio 45015
(513) 860-5094
www.dynamat.com

Dynatrac Products, Inc.
7392 Count Circle
Huntington Beach, CA 92647
(714) 596-4461
www.dynatrac.com

Energy Suspension
1131 Via Callejon
San Clemente, CA 92673
(949) 361-3935
ww.energysuspension.com

Evolution Machining and
Fabrication
(403) 236-3545
www.evolutionmachine.com

Firestik Antenna Company
2614 E Adams Street
Phoenix, AZ 85034-1495
(602) 273-7151
www.firestik.com

Forrest Tool Company, Inc.
P.O. Box 768
Mendocino, CA 95460
Phone 707-937-2141
maxax@mcn.org

Fox Racing Shocks
(800) FOX-SHOX
www.foxracingshox.com

Full-Traction Suspensions
(800) 255-6464
www.fulltraction.com

Gale Banks Engineering
(800) 601-8072
www.bankspower.com

General Tire Company
(800) 847-3349
www.generaltire.com

Gen-Right Off Road
(805) 584-8635
www.genright.com

Goodyear Tire & Rubber
Company
(330) 796-2944
www.goodyear.com

Howell Engine Developments,
Inc.
6201 Industrial Way
Marine City, Michigan 48039
Phone: (810) 765-5100
www.howellefi.com

Hutchinson Industries, Inc.
www.rockmonsterwheels.com

Hypertech
3215 Appling Road
Bartlett, TN 38133
(901)382-8888
www.hypertech.com

Interco Tire Corp.
(318) 334-3814
www.intercotire.com

J.E. Reel Drive Line Specialists
448 S. Reservoir
Pomona, CA 91766
(909) 629-9002
www.reeldriveline.com

JKS Manufacturing
(308) 762-6949
www.jksmfg.com

K&N Engineering, Inc.
PO Box 1329
Riverside, California 92502
800-760-5319
www.knfilters.com

Kartek Off Road
(951) 737-2999
www.kartek.com

King Racing Shocks
12842 Joy Street
Garden Grove, CA 92840
(714) 530-8701
www.kingshocks.com

Lowrance Electronics
28156 Plymouth Road
Tulsa, OK 74128
(918) 437-6881
www.lowrance.com

Magnum Offroad
1235 Activity Drive, Suite A
Vista, CA 92081
(760) 599-4156
www.magnumoffroad.com

MasterCraft Race Products
11433 Woodside Avenue
Santee, CA 92071
(800) 565-4042
www.mastercraftseats.com

Master-Pull Recovery
Equipment, Inc.

4181 W. Maplewood Avenue
Bellingham, Washington 98226
(360) 714-1313
www.masterpull.com

Maxxis International
(770) 962-5932
www.maxxis.com

Mickey Thompson/Dick Cepek
    Performance Tires & Wheels
(330) 928-9092
www.mickeythompson tires.com

MOPAR Performance Products
www.mopar.om

Morel America
1301 Hempstead Turnpike
    Suite 1
Elmont, New York 11003
(877) 667-3511
www.morelhifi.com

Moto Metal Wheels
www.motometalwheels.com

Nitto Tire North America Inc.
(800) 648-8652
www.nittotire.com

Off Road Evolution
1829 West Commonwealth Ave.
Fullerton, CA 92833
(714) 870-5515

Off Road Trail Tools
(520) 579-2079
www.offroadtrailtools.com

Off Road Wharehouse
645 North Citracado Pkwy.
Escondido, CA 92025
(800) 341-7757
www.offroadwarehouse.com

OMF Performance Products
9860 Indiana Ave. Unit 17
Riverside, CA 92503
(909) 354-8272
www.omfperformance.com

OX
440 S. Pinellas Ave.
Tarpon Springs, FL 34689
(727) 230-7803
www.ox-usa.com

Parnelli Jones/Dirt Gripz Inc.
(330) 873-9582
www.dirtgriptires.com

Premier Power Welder
P.O. Box 639
Carbondale, CO 81623
(800) 541-1817
www.premierpowerwelder.com

Pro Comp Motorsports
(800) 776-0767
www.procompmotorsports.com

Poly Performance
(805) 783-2060
www.polyperformance.com

Power Steering Components
901 Finney Drive
Weatherford, Texas 76085- 2804
Phone: 817.270.0102
www.pscmotorsports.com

Pro Competition Tire &
    Wheel Co.
(866) 232-0665
www.procomptires.com

Pull-Pal, Inc.
(800) 541-1817
www.pullpal.com

PU-Products, LLC
(619) 334-1913
www.pu-products.com

PUREJEEP
(800) 255-6464
www.purejeep.com

PWR Performance Products
www.pwr-performance.com

QA1
(800) 721-7761
www.qa1.net

QS Components, Inc.
(888) 871-1210
www.racingrodends.com

Raceline Performance Wheels
(800) 52-WHEEL
www.racelinewheels.com
 Race Prep Services
1021 Calle Sombra, Suite A
San Clemente, CA 92673
(949) 361-4388

Ramsey Winch Company
1600 North Garnett Road
Tulsa, Oklahoma 74116
(918) 438-2760
www.ramseywinch.com

Rancho Suspensions
(734) 384-7804
www.gorancho.com

Robby Gordon Race Wheels
2980 E. Miraloma Ave.
Anaheim, CA 92806
(714) 632-0166
www.robbygordonoffroad.com

Rock Hard 4x4 Parts
1005 Twin Forks Lane
St. Paul, NE 68873
(308) 750-4690
www.rockhard4x4parts.com

Rovers North, Inc.
1319 Vermont Route 128

Westford, Vermont USA
    05494-9601
(802) 879-0032
www.roversnorth.com

Rubicon Express
(877) 367-7824
www.rubiconexpress.com

Safety Seal
North Shore Laboratories Corp.
40-44 Endicott Street
P.O. Box 568
Peabody, MA 01960
(800) 888-9021
www.safetyseal.com

Skyjacker Suspensions
(318) 388-0816
www.skyjacker.com

Snap-On Tools
(877) 762-7664
www.snapon.com

SoCal Custom
328 N El Camino Real
Encinitas, CA 92024
(760) 487-1234
www.socalcustom.info

Spidertrax Inc.
7510 Hygiene Road
Longmont, CO 80503
(800) 286-0898
www.spidertrax.com

Spyder Customs
(303) 777-4820
www.spydercustoms.com

Stinger Electronics
www.stingerelectronics.com

Staun USA Inc
P.O Box 12137
Costa Mesa, CA 92627
(949) 645 7733
harry@staunproducts.com

Superlift Suspension Systems
300 Huey Lenard Loop
West Monroe, LA 71292
(888) 299-4692
www.superlift.com

Superior Axle & Gear
9580 Commerce Center Drive
Rancho Cucamonga, CA 91730
(888) 522-AXLE
www.superioraxle.com

Tellico 4x4
(800) 566-3646
www.tellico4x4.com

Tera Manufacturing, Inc.
5251 South Commerce Dr.
Murray, Utah 84107
(801) 288-2585
www.teraflex.biz

Tire Rack
(800) 541-1777
www.tirerack.com

Toyo Tires
(800) 442-8696
www.toyo.com

Trail Ready Motorsports
1304 80th St. SW
Everette, WA
(425) 353-6776
www.trailready.com

Tuffy Security Products
25733 Road H
Cortez, CO 81321
(800) 348-8339
www.tuffyproducts.com

Valvoline
PO Box 14000
Lexington, KY 40512
(800) 327-8242
www.valvoline.com

Vision X Lighting USA
6501 E. Greenway
Suite 103-542
Scottsdale, AZ 85254
(800) 994-4460
www.visionxusa.com

Walker Evans Racing
2304 Fleetwood Dr.
Riverside, CA 92516
(909) 784-7223
www.walkerevansracing.com

Wever's Welding & Fabrication
1545 Seminole Street
San Marcos, CA 92078
(760) 954-WELD

Wheel Pros
(877) 943-3577
www.wheelpros.com

Wrangler NW Power Products
5061 N. Lagoon Ave
Portland, OR 97217-7634
(800) 962-2616
salesdept@wranglernw.com

Wurth USA Inc
93 Grant Street
Ramsey, NJ 07446
(201) 825 2710
www.wurthusa.com

Zapco
ARPA of America
11627 Palm Ave.
Manteca, CA 95337
(209) 599-2394
www.zapco.com

Index

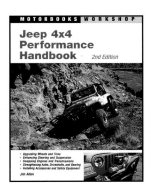

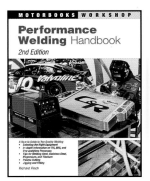
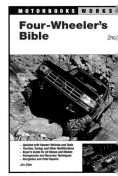